BILL GADSBY

NEW YORK RANGERS DEFENSE

ED SHACK

NEW YORK RANGERS WING

BERNIE GEOFFRION RIGHT WING
NEW YORK RANGERS

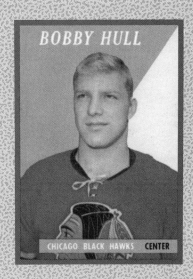

BOBBY HULL

CHICAGO BLACK HAWKS CENTER

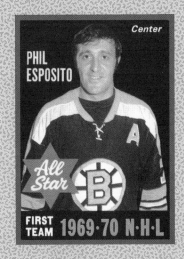

Center

PHIL ESPOSITO

All Star

FIRST TEAM 1969·70 N·H·L

To Pup,

Love From the Two of Us!

Christmas 1989.

David + Jo Ellen

After the Applause

After the Applause

Colleen and Gordie Howe

and Charles Wilkins

M&S

Endpaper art: Bill Hay hockey card supplied courtesy of the Hockey Hall of Fame and Museum. All other hockey cards are supplied courtesy of O-Pee-Chee Company Limited.

The photographs reproduced in the book appear courtesy of the players.

Canadian Cataloguing in Publication Data

Howe, Colleen.
  After the applause

ISBN 0-7710-4228-0

1. Hockey players – Canada – Retirement.   2. National Hockey League – Biography.   3. Hockey players – Canada – Biography.   I. Howe, Gordie, 1928-   . II. Wilkins, Charles.   III. Title.

GV848.5.A1H6 1989   796.96′2′0922   C89-095121-7

McClelland & Stewart Inc.
The Canadian Publishers
481 University Avenue
Toronto, Ontario
M5G 2E9

Printed and bound in the United States

Contents

Dedication

All of us who share our feelings with you through this book dedicate it to the fans, friends, family, and associates who have always shown us their "applause" through loyalty and understanding during the good and difficult times.

Introduction

My one true boyhood ambition, to play hockey for the Toronto Maple Leafs, was ruled out early by my remarkable wrist shot, which possessed all the potency of puffed wheat. And perhaps equally so by my skating, which if the wind was at my back was easily powerful enough to propel me across a sheet of clean ice at speeds of seven or eight miles an hour. Cruel realities notwithstanding, my fantasies of turning pro and singlehandedly delivering the Stanley Cup to the appreciative throngs of Hogtown – humbly accepting membership in the Hockey Hall of Fame, Order of Canada, Knights of Pythias, and so on – lingered well into my teenage years. Even casual skating on the outdoor rinks of Deep River or Cornwall, Ontario, where I grew up, was for me just a quick leap of the imagination from the heady world occupied by Bobby Hull, Gordie Howe, Bernie Geoffrion, and Rocket Richard.

If some astrologer had told me that twenty-five years hence I'd be asked (and paid) to travel the continent meeting and spending time with ten of the great hockey heroes of my youth, I'm sure I'd have happily abandoned my baseless dreams of a career in the big leagues and embraced a career in writing (as I eventually did anyway).

But that is what happened. One day in mid-December of last year I got a telephone call from Doug Gibson of

McClelland & Stewart in Toronto, a publisher with whom two years earlier I had collaborated on a book called *Paddle to the Amazon*. Doug wanted to know if I'd be interested in working with Colleen and Gordie Howe on a book of profiles of ten retired NHL and WHA greats and their wives. Colleen and Gordie had approached McClelland & Stewart with the idea during the summer.

As a matter of fact, yes, I would be interested.

A month later I set out from my home in Dundas, Ontario, on a 350-mile drive to meet Colleen and Gordie at their vacation hideaway near Traverse City, Michigan. There, during three enjoyable days, the three of us thrashed out an approach to the book. Foremost, we decided, it would look behind the lionizing mythology that so often surrounds, even traps, our hockey heroes and would reveal as intimately as possible the seldom-witnessed realities of their lives, and those of their families. It would take in active careers but would focus more substantially on life after retirement, which I was soon to find out has not been easy for some of the subjects. As Bill Gadsby commented to me, "Everything would be fine if the good Lord had given us the capability to play hockey until we were sixty-five. Then we wouldn't have to start life over at forty."

The profiles, we decided, would also encompass the players' wives, who for the most part are unknown to fans of the game but who perhaps possess a clearer perspective than anyone else on life behind the scenes and beyond the glory years.

The plan was this: Colleen and Gordie, who had already chosen ten couples to participate as subjects, would provide me with introductions to those couples, as well as any advice I might need in either my interviewing or writing. My job was to go to the subjects, record their stories, plus my own impressions of their lives, bring the material back, and shape it into a book.

Thus, on February 1, 1989, I set out on an eight-week odyssey that covered some 10,000 miles and took me to places as tiny as Demorestville, Ontario, as large as Chicago, Atlanta, and New York City; as far west as Calgary, Alberta, as far east as Mount Kisco, New York. Everywhere I went I was treated with generosity and openness. And from each stop along the way I carried off a host of images and recollections, most of which are recorded on the pages that follow.

I gathered other impressions as well. While not pertinent to the book at hand, they are nonetheless significantly imbedded in my personal memories of the eight weeks of travel: a 250-mile drive from Chicago to Detroit in the middle of the night in thirty-below weather, my wife Betty beside me, my ten-month-old son Matt in the back seat, the three of us heavily bundled in blankets to compensate for a broken heater that had allowed the car temperature to fall well below freezing; Betty tucking Matt into Jill and Stan Mikita's bed for his afternoon nap; Matt, again, fresh-faced and grinning, posing for a photo on the knee of Bill Gadsby, whose countenance bears the scars of some 700 surgical stitches; Gump Worsley slipping on his goalie mask and posing casually for a photo on the couch of his Beloeil home; Bobby Hull's nine-year-old daughter arriving home from school, standing politely in the kitchen and, at her dad's request, reciting a fine little speech she had prepared on her love of horses; Phil Esposito's freewheeling conversation during a late-night drive from Madison Square Garden to Upper Westchester County; a two-hour lunch with Marlene and Bernie Geoffrion at what must surely be the finest seafood restaurant in Atlanta; the gentle hospitality of Lucille and Maurice Richard; Ed Shack's hilarious recollections of his boyhood in Sudbury; Nancy and Bill Hay's kind provision of tickets for a Calgary Flames game and their guided tour of the impressive Calgary Saddledome.

For a few seconds one night in Michigan – for a very few seconds – I was transported beyond mere socializing and acquaintanceship with my boyhood heroes and actually became one of them. As I left a restaurant with Colleen and Gordie Howe, a bewildered young woman burst from the restaurant kitchen, approached the three of us, fixed her gaze on me, and said, "Are you Gordie Howe?"

"Yes, I am," I said, as Colleen and Gordie looked on, somewhat bemused.

"Would you mind signing an autograph for the guys in the kitchen?"

"Not at all," I told her, and she handed me a pen and a sheet of paper.

I began momentarily to write, paused for a second, then passed the honour along to Number Nine.

I trust you'll find as much pleasure in reading the profiles that follow as I found in researching and writing them.

Charles Wilkins
Dundas, Ontario
September, 1989

1

· · · · · · · · · · · · ·

A MILLION-TWO

Hey-hey, they're mighty good, they're mighty nice. They're good for YOU and baby TOO! CANDY APPLES! Get 'em right here!

Ed Shack
candy apple huckster
Sudbury, 1946

Bananas! Look at 'em! IGA 39 cents! Safeway 59! But we've got 'em for NINETEEN CENTS A POUND! Loblaws' No Frills!

Ed Shack
TV spokesman
Toronto, 1989

To understand Eddie Shack, it helps to know that he was a salesman long before he was a hockey player. And that he was a salesman *just* before he was a hockey player. And that he was a salesman *while* he was a hockey player. And that he was a salesman when he was no *longer* a hockey player.

He is *still* a salesman. He will *always* be a salesman.

In the forty-five years since Eddie made his first hundred dollars, he has hustled more goods than a back-street jobber: turkeys, chickens, hats, Christmas trees, clothing, Polish sausage, building supplies, sports equipment, cars, beer, candy apples. . . . He has done television endorsements for soft drinks, groceries, facial tissues, banking facilities, garbage bags ("I can't remember what kind") . . . more cars, more beer: *tastes-great-less-filling-BOY-I'm-gonna-keep-my-NOSE-outa-this-one!*

Unlike Eaton's of Canada, Eddie will happily be undersold. In fact, if he can force the price up auction-style, so much the better: "Last winter after an old-timers' game in Meaford I had a buncha fans around, and one of 'em wanted to buy my cowboy hat, then somebody else wanted it, so I started taking bids on it – got a hundred dollars for the thing! . . . Another time, I bought a golf bag for five bucks; it had a hole in the bottom. I patched it up with plywood and raffled it off at my golf course – a buck a ticket. The guy who won says, 'Look! It's got a hole in the bottom!' I told him, 'Ya only paid a buck for it! Whaddaya want?' "

If the price is right, you can buy Eddie Shack himself! Well, you can rent him anyway. For a thousand or fifteen hundred ("whatever I can get") Ed will gladly show up at a party or dinner and do what he did best during seventeen seasons as a professional hockey player – entertain. "I tell a few stories, shake a few hands, meet this guy, that guy, have some laughs, kibbitz a little – then I go home."

"Ed auctions off his old golf clubs every year," says his wife Norma. "He gets more for his old ones than he has to pay for new ones."

Norma, a near-ringer for Second City actress Catherine O'Hara, has also dabbled in buying and selling, although without Ed's flair. And sometimes without his success: "I've bought and sold stocks and turned $5,000 into $500 pretty fast," she winces. "Then again, Ed's gotten into some pretty bad business, too. One time, a pig farmer who I didn't trust at all took him for a lot of money."

One of Norma's jauntier and more successful ventures was buying Navajo Indian jewellery when Ed was playing for the Los Angeles Kings during the early 1970s and transporting it north to sell. "I had customers in half a dozen cities," she says. "My suitcase weighed a ton."

According to Ed, the couple has never had to worry about money. "We've never had to say to ourselves, 'Okay, here's $200, we've gotta live on it,' or 'Here's $500, we've gotta live on it.' Because I'm always hustling. If Norma thinks we need more money, she just says, 'Go get more money, Ed.' And out I go."

The nicest thing about Ed and Norma's "business-like" approach to the world is that it's all so remarkably good-natured. Ed rides his sales ability like a happy cowboy heading for the round-up. *"I just love selling stuff!"* he laughs. "Whaddaya wanta buy? Take a look! Make me an offer!"

"You've gotta watch him," says Norma. "He'll sell the chair right out from under you. I've seen him auction off his clothes."

"And she's worse than I am!" hoots Ed.

The question arises: Do Norma and Ed own anything that isn't for sale? Well, for starters there's their splendid new home on Oriole Parkway in Toronto. Definitely not up for grabs. Not after Norma spent months designing it, fine-tuning its architectural innovations, and commissioning stained glass and art. Not after she spent weeks choosing just the right ceramic floor tiles, kitchen cabinets, and furnishings, just the right carpets and lighting. And most certainly not after incorporating a sauna and Jacuzzi and two handsome fireplaces primarily to please Ed. Why, Ed himself spent four torrid weeks during the summer of 1988 ("We drank five barrels of draft") sweating with a construction crew to build a backyard garden and patio elegantly appropriate to the new digs. They wouldn't dream of parting with the place. In fact, when a real estate agent came knocking on their door last March explaining that he'd heard the house would be going on the market and that he'd be interested in buying it, Norma was left muttering about the condition of a world in which even a person's hearth and comfort were assumed to be available for mere lucre.

"You'd sell if the price was right," remarked Ed when the agent had been sent packing.

"I do not want to sell this house!" declared Norma.

"I said if the price was right."

"It'd have to be awfully right."

"I said if the price was right!"

Norma paused for a moment in her umbrage, and a mischievous smirk transformed her face. She looked at Ed and whispered, "A million-two." And the truth was out.

For as long as it remains in the family, the house is a glistening tribute to Norma's tastes and Ed's hockey career . . . and, to a lesser extent, to the career of their son Jim, a twenty-four-year-old graduate of the Ontario College of Art, now living and painting in New York City. Several of the more impressive paintings on the walls are Jim's creations, including a large Jackson Pollock-like acrylic and a more cryptic abstract watercolour in the family room downstairs. When Norma wanted an original for the dining room she commissioned her son, who produced a multiple photo-image (twenty repetitions) of a young Ed Shack sipping tea from a fine china cup. Norma refused to hang the piece. "That's all I need, another forty pictures of Eddie in the house!"

To be sure, Ed's likeness is already well seeded across the interior drywall: here in the uniform of the Pittsburgh Penguins; here with the Toronto Maple Leafs of the early sixties; here playing golf with Lee Trevino and Bobby Orr; over here exuding joy from beneath the brim of a magnificent straw hat.

On the downstairs mantel is a miniature replica of the Stanley Cup, a trophy on which Ed's name was engraved four times during the glory days of the modern Maple Leafs.

But of all parts of the house, the bunker-style garage out front is most essentially Ed's territory. Out here he keeps his golf gear, his hockey equipment, the cluttered trappings and memorabilia of fifty-one years on the planet. He also keeps his draft-beer dispenser, a much-loved convenience that until recently was stocked free by a beer company for whom he once filmed a television commercial. Four pairs of worn cowboy boots – Ed's sartorial trademark – sit on a shelf not six feet from the beer tap.

Eddie's mental activity is as varied and unpredictable as his career endeavours. Thoughts enter his head randomly, in such a way that decades rise and fall in seconds, the peoples of the world appear and disappear, planetary geography is reduced to the proportions of the backyard. His personal history surges forth in waves, one year crashing atop another, impossible to separate.

"Lemme tell ya what happened at school. I'm maybe six years old in grade one. I'm *good* in grade one. Then in grade two I get sick; I get my tonsils out, miss a few months. They put me to grade three anyway, and this time I get my appendix out, don't get my phonics in. They keep passing me. I go all the way to grade eight, but by this time my main thing is making money. See, I had my driver's licence when I was thirteen – lied to get it. If you got caught lying for your licence it cost you a hundred, but I could afford that; I'd been working at the Sudbury farmers' market since I was eight, cleaning up and stuff. When I was ten or eleven I got my own counter, selling turkeys and chickens and 'kobassy' – no refrigeration or anything, just get the flies outa there. I got my meat from Dan Rain's meat market, next door to my parents' place, downtown Sudbury. I was making eight, ten bucks a day. And of course I was doin' other stuff, too. Like selling candy apples in the circus when it came to town. I was such a good salesman that one year the manager wanted me to join up, go on the road. My mother went crazy – I had to promise not to go. But, boy, did I love it – making all that money, coming home at eleven at night."

To pad his burgeoning income at age twelve, Ed began moonlighting as a car and truck washer at a local Ford dealership. "Schooling was a total disaster by this time," he says nonchalantly. "I went into an opportunity class – that's for your slow learners – and this teacher was a real . . . well, it was totally with the fists, right? One day, I said to him, 'You hit me and I'm gonna drop you right here and now.' Every day he'd send me out in the hall, and I'd say, 'That's enough of this,' and I'd walk out of the school and go straight to the market to work. I'd get the strap the next day, twenty-five times on each hand, but I'd just bounce right outa there smiling. I was a big strong kid because I worked all the time. No push-ups, nothin' like that – I just carried quarters of beef around the butcher shop, that stuff."

For a boy who would eventually play more than a thousand games in the National Hockey League, Ed's pre-teen interest in hockey was curiously minimal. "I just didn't care about it," he shrugs. "I mean, we had a backyard rink, and I used to fool around on it with Tim Horton and Bryan Campbell; they lived near me. But it was just shinny. The only reason I played Bantam when I was thirteen was that my dad said I had to get out and play with the kids. I didn't care about kids, and my parents were pretty concerned about me – especially my education, 'cause every time I got my report card it was zero, zero, zero, zero, zero. I'd cheat on my tests but it wouldn't do any good. The school didn't like me, and I didn't like the school – didn't like the way it was run. Too bossy. If we were playing ball, I'd try to hit the ball through the school windows. I was bad. I had a lot of fights. Finally, my parents' attitude was 'Whatever Eddie wants.' "

Norma says, "I think what really happened with Ed in school was that his stubbornness simply took over. He's always had a *very* strong stubborn streak. If he likes something he puts heart and soul into it. If he doesn't like something, forget it."

At the age of fourteen, Eddie abandoned the rigours of formal education and went to play Junior hockey in Guelph,

Ontario. The Sudbury-area scout who sent him to Guelph had never seen him play. But he knew Ed was strong, and he knew he could skate. He also knew he needed direction and that he wasn't going to get it in Sudbury. To this day, Ed believes that had he not gotten a tryout in Junior hockey, he'd still be living in his home town – "And I'd be an absolute rotten loser. Oh, I wanted out, and Junior hockey did it for me."

Ever the hustler, Ed was barely settled in Guelph when he landed a job at Hale's meat market. "I went to the owner and said, 'I can't read or write but I can work.' I could read the scales and kill the beef and stuff. I used a sledgehammer. It wasn't easy for me to work so hard and play hockey, too. But I had to work. See, when I left Sudbury I was making forty-nine bucks a week at Dominion Stores. At Guelph I was only making forty from hockey. You've gotta understand that I've always tried to raise my income every year. That's why I never signed a two-year contract in hockey – if I had I would have gotten the same pay two years in a row. I always felt I was a better player than I'd shown, and they'd see this and would pay me more the second year. . . . Anyway, when I was in Guelph I used to buy hats from the Biltmore hat factory – they sponsored the team – and I'd carry them around in my car. At that time I had a convertible – I'd have hats in the back seat, hats in the trunk, hats in the convertible well – maybe fifty hats in all. I'd come up to a guy and say, 'A man is not properly dressed without a hat.' I wore one all the time. I'd pull into a car dealership; I'd always sell a few. Bought 'em for three bucks, sold 'em for ten. I'd sell to my teammates, too. I'd say, 'Boy, I've got some great deals, boom, let's have 'er, guys!' And I'd get cash. When I went home to Sudbury I'd always take a load. . . . Even when I played for the Maple Leafs, I'd head out to Guelph and get a load of hats when the other guys were going to the bar.

"I was very disciplined my last year in Guelph. It was the same as my last year in Sudbury. I got serious – I wanted to make the NHL, the New York Rangers, and I did."

Eddie's first coach with the Rangers, Phil Watson, was at the time the closest thing in the National Hockey League to an out-and-out despot. Ex-Rangers still recall vividly how after an exhausting game in Madison Square Garden during the late 1950s he sent his team back out on the ice for an hour of stiff skating drills. In spite of his methods, he had as much trouble containing the bellicose newcomer, Ed Shack, as Ed's teachers had had in Sudbury: "He hated me, and I hated him," says Ed, his loathing of the man still manifest in his voice. "Once we were in Montreal – we'd lost seven games in a row or something – and after practice Phil gets us in the dressing room, and he says, 'Okay, let's have an open meeting. Nothing you say will be held against you. Nothing!' Andy Bathgate and Harry Howell and Dean Prentice and Larry Popein all had their say, and it came to me, and I said, 'Phil, all you've said to me, everything you've ever told me as a coach, has gone in this ear and out this one.' Well, that cancelled the whole meeting right there. He starts yelling and screaming something awful. So I go back to the Mount Royal Hotel, and the trainer, Frank Paice, comes up to me and says, 'Eddie?' And I says, 'Whadda *you* want, ya little runt?' And he says, 'Here's your ticket to Springfield.' 'Springfield!' I yelled, 'cause nothin' was supposed to be held against ya, right? I think that was the lowest moment in my whole career. I had to phone home and tell Mom they were sending me down. I felt jabbed by these guys after they promised nothing would be held against ya.

"But I had a great time in Springfield – with Eddie Shore, right? He cracked your back, but I had fun with him. Then the Rangers called – they needed me in New York, but I told 'em, 'Nope, I'm not comin' back – go stick it.' And they said, 'Well, er . . . you could help our club.' And I told 'em, '*Nobody* could help your club!'

"In the end I went, but I still couldn't stand Watson. And I hated New York – it's an animal city. I was living on Long Island. Irv Spencer and I had this little shack. It was so small you had to turn sideways to walk around in it. I had cabin fever something fierce."

Ed's liberation came during the winter of 1960 in the form of a trade to the Toronto Maple Leafs. "One day Red Sullivan comes over and tells me I've been shipped out, and I says, 'You're full of it.' But he says, 'No, you're going to the Leafs!' And I says, 'If I am, I'm gonna start walkin' right now!'

"But it was true – I was lucky. If I'd stayed in New York, this Watson would have ruined my whole career."

Phil Watson was not alone in his inability to master the towheaded butcher from northern Ontario. League thumpers, too, had their hands full with Ed. "When I broke in," he explains, "everybody had to challenge you – that's if you were a fighter type. If you got the crap kicked outa ya, ya'd get it kicked outa ya all over the league. But if you stood up for yourself, you were all right.

"Once when I was in training with the Rangers at Niagara Falls, Larry Zeidel speared me – he was a stick man; he was playing for some farm team, Rochester maybe – and I said to him, 'Larry, you do that one more time, and I'll break this stick right over your head.' I'm twenty years old, eh? So he speared me again, and I let him have it. If you did that today you'd go to jail. Matter of fact we *did* go to jail. We got kicked out of the game, and we were sitting in the stands, and he comes after me, and I hit him, and he goes down. I could have given it to him good while he was on the floor, but I was a gentleman, I held back. So off we go to jail; he's in one cell, I'm in the other, and I say to him through the bars, 'What's the matter with you, Larry, has the plate in your head shifted?' A few minutes later the Rangers bailed me out – wheeled me right outa town.

"Larry hit me with his stick again when he played for Philadelphia; I was with Boston then. And I let him have it again; it was messy – a lotta blood. He hit me *three times* before I hit him back.... That was the toughest part of

hockey, the fighting. It wore you down. At one point I enjoyed fighting, but as I got older I got away from it."

One thing Ed never got away from was his ineluctable
desire to entertain, to bring a sense of theatre and humour to
the rink. He was hockey's version of a (barely) guided missile
– reckless speed, fiery enthusiasm, explosion on contact.
When he was with the Boston Bruins in 1969 (he played for
six teams in all: New York, Toronto, Boston, Los Angeles,
Buffalo, Pittsburgh, then back to Toronto), he developed a
dervish-like manoeuvre he called "the twirl," to be used on
special occasions such as his arrival in an arena or his post-
game appearance as one of the three stars of a game. On such
occasions, he would race forty or fifty feet across the ice,
throw on the brakes, and go into a snowy, semi-airborne
twist, more a dance than a leap, one and a half turns, legs and
elbows flying, eyes wild. "Sometimes I fell down, but that
was okay – they loved it all the more.

"I always brought in crowds, got things jumpin'," enthuses Ed. "When I played my last two years in Toronto in the
seventies, I wasn't doin' much with the Leafs, so I said, 'Send
me to Oklahoma City.' And I went down there and we had
some fun. Tiger Williams was there, Pat Boutette, a buncha
guys. The night I played my first game was a big deal; they
were selling beer for a nickel a glass; they filled the place. I did
the twirl right away, had 'em going right off the bat."

It was Ed's power to attract fans that had inspired Punch
Imlach, general manager of the Buffalo Sabres, to acquire the
right winger's contract from the Los Angeles Kings a few
years earlier. "They weren't getting any crowds down there,"
recalls Ed. "I got there and, boom, they filled the joint. So
Punch is happy and I'm happy. But then Punch got sick, and
John . . . John . . . John . . . John somebody took over the club,
and I told him to go stick it. Who was *he*? – just the guy who
made the hotel and plane reservations! Suddenly he's the
boss! I couldn't stand him. And he wasn't too keen either. So I
checked out of Buffalo, went over to Pittsburgh and got 'em

fired up over there. I gave 'em a coupla twirls, and right away the crowds started pouring in.

"The time I *really* wanted to do the twirl was after the Leafs traded me to Boston in 1969. At that point I hated the Maple Leafs for trading me. I wanted to stick 'em – Keon, Ellis, anybody. I remember when we were warming up for our first game in Toronto that year, I skated by [Leaf goalie] Johnny Bower, and I said, 'Last night I dreamed I hit ya right in the head with the puck, John.' I get along great with these guys now, but that was my thinking then. . . . After that first game, I wanted to be the number-one star, so I could be out on the ice by myself – the twirl, right? But that Foster Hewitt, he wouldn't pick me; he didn't like me."

"No, Foster didn't like Ed," corroborates Norma. "I once listened to a tape of a broadcast from the last game of 1963 when Ed scored the goal that gave the Leafs the Cup. He screamed, 'And Kent Douglas scores!' Then his voice suddenly got very flat, and he said, 'Oh . . . no . . . it was Shack.' "

"I was glad to get out of hockey after my last couple of years," says Ed. "It was '73, '74 when I came back to Toronto, and it wasn't the same as it was in our Stanley Cup years. Back then, guys would come to your rescue if you were in trouble. But later, with guys like Salming and Hammerstrom 'n' stuff, they wouldn't back you up, wouldn't come to your rescue if you were getting your head kicked in. . . . I didn't like Salming. He couldn't give a pass; he couldn't snap it so it stayed flat. So I'd pass it right back to him the way he gave it to me. And he'd dress in these old clothes. In our day, you had to look good. I was always a clean dresser."

"That wasn't really your problem with Salming," challenges Norma. "Jim McKenny dressed in old clothes, and you hit it off with him just fine. Your own son dresses that way!"

"That's okay for him; he's not in the public eye."

"You just didn't hit it off with Salming."

"Half the time he looked like a street bum."

Ed reflects for a moment and says, "I didn't miss hockey at all when I left it. It's a ruthless business. I said thank you, 'bye."

Barely a minute later he declares, "I have hockey to thank for making me what I am right now. I'd never have gotten away with the things I've done if I hadn't been Ed Shack the hockey player. If I was Ed Blow from Sudbury, they'd have said, 'Are you nuts in the head? Get lost!' Being a hockey player has always helped me b.s. my way around."

Hockey aside, it is apparent that Norma, too, has contributed substantially to making Ed what he is today, to tempering his personality and presence. A stonemason's daughter from the tiny town of Keene, Ontario, Norma met Ed on a golf course in Peterborough in September of 1961, the year that Ed and the Maple Leafs won their first of four Stanley Cups in the 1960s. She says, "My father was a big hockey fan, so I'd heard of Frank Mahovlich, Red Kelly, and so on, but I'd never heard of Ed Shack. I wasn't too sure I liked Ed at first. He was loud. But when I heard him talking about life in New York City during his days with the Rangers, he seemed more interesting."

Two months later, Norma moved to Toronto with a girlfriend and got a job in an insurance office. "I'd talked to Eddie a couple of times by phone in the meantime, and I told him I'd call when I got there. So I did, and he asked me to go to a hockey game. It was the first one I'd ever seen. . . . We dated through the winter and spring and were married that August. We had two children, Cathy and Jim, almost right away."

Norma counts her and Ed's first few years in Toronto as their finest in hockey. "I remember going to Stafford Smythe's home for a party after the Leafs won the Stanley Cup for the first time. There were so many people in the house you couldn't move. I was nineteen years old. I thought, 'Oh, this is wonderful, this hockey life.' And of course the

Leafs won the Cup three years in a row, so I probably imagined it would always be that good."

Although he won four Stanley Cups in Toronto and never won another after leaving in 1969, Ed himself does not put a premium on his years with the Maple Leafs. He says, "You've gotta think money when you think of your best years, and I wasn't making much money back then. I mean, what is a Stanley Cup? Phfffffft! I was happy enough, but I'm gonna be happy anyway; I'm that type – doesn't matter if I'm sitting on the can. I'd be a happy plumber! A happy butcher! I might go a little nuts once in a while, but I'd by happy. No, when you talk about happy, my best years were when Norma and I were moving around to these various cities where I played, buying and selling houses for a profit. We bought and sold all sorts of places. I always liked to put my money where it counted. I never blew money; I was very close; I pinched my pennies. Mind you, our earliest places in Toronto were just rentals. First one was an upstairs joint at Royal York Road and the Lakeshore – couldn't stand the place, $125 a month. Then the horse farmer M.J. Boylen names a horse after me. His farm was in Malton, at Dixie and Derry Road, so I go out there to see the horse, and there's a farmhouse on the property. I don't see nothin' in it. And Boylen says, 'No, we're not doing nothin' with it.' So I says, 'Well, if my horse, my namesake, is going to be right here, how would you like me right here, too, living in that house? What about it? Let's talk about it!' It was a two-bedroom house. We moved in – $100 a month. I was making about ten, eleven thousand with the Leafs – most I ever made was eighty. Then we moved again. We were just in the *middle* of moving – packing stuff and loading it – when I met Johnny Johnson, the car dealer. He was having a rose parade, one of these things where they throw a few roses around, and he wanted me to come and sit in a convertible in his parade. So I tell Norma, 'I gotta go; this sounds like it might be good; I might make some money.' So I went in his parade – I was sick of moving anyway, got outa lifting furniture 'n' stuff. And then Johnny Johnson says, 'Do you wanta come and work for me?' I says, 'Sure!' and I start goin' down there regularly, sittin' on the cars in the showroom, signing autographs and stuff. And he's using my name in his ads. So I drove his cars for years, then I switched to another dealership, and I was getting *a hundred bucks a week* plus a free car! I still do that – I'm workin' for George Stockfish Motors in North Bay, a Ford dealership. I do their commercials. Ya know somethin'? I've *never owned a car*! . . . Well, I've owned a few, I guess. Quite a few, really. I've had an awful lot free, though."

But complimentary cars are a mere side dish compared to the more lucrative endeavours in which the Shacks have been involved over the years. "Real estate is really where we've made our money," says Norma. "We were among the first hockey people to buy a house in the city where the team was located. See, back in the sixties, all the players used to go home for the summer. They just rented. . . . We bought our first house in Toronto for $32,000, and an established player like Andy Bathgate wouldn't pay more than $19,000. And here Ed was on the border of being traded *all the time.* A lot of the guys just didn't see a house as an investment. And we furnished that house, too. Didn't leave anything out. When Ed was traded to Boston the next year, we sold the place for a $5,000 profit."

"If you're not willing to gamble, you'll never make the profits," declares Ed. "When I came back to Toronto in '73, I had no cash; it was all tied up. We needed a house. But instead of buying a house at $40,000, I go lookin' for one that's $125,000. Where am I gonna get the money? Easy. I go to one bank and get $25,000, then I go to another bank and get another $20,000. My lawyer says, 'Are you cracked, Ed? You can't do that!' And I says, 'Would you shut up!' See, I knew I could pay for it. I had my salary, and I also knew that Frank Mahovlich and Johnny Bower and these guys didn't want to speak at any banquets – they were all friends of mine from the old Maple Leaf days – so I'd take all their banquets,

$300 a night. . . . When it came time to sell that house I asked the real estate agent how much it was worth. He told me 205 to 230. I called him a liar – sold it myself for 250 the next week. We paid 190 for our next house at Bayview and Steeles. We dumped it for 400."

In 1970, the Shacks made their wisest and most profitable investment by far, taking an $80,000 windfall from the sale of their house in Los Angeles and sinking it into an unserviced tract of farmland on the Humber River near the intersections of Highway 7 and 27, northwest of Toronto. The plan was to build a golf course.

By June of 1972, the place was astir with the swish of clubs, shouts of 'Fore!', and with the somewhat less decorous shouts of Ed Shack, tootling around in his dune buggy hawking refreshments. "I went into this thing with three other guys. Two of them were lawyers, who didn't know anything about golf (now, there are just the two lawyers and me), so a lot of the work of making this land into a golf course fell to me. And lemme tell ya, I *worked*. After we got the place built, I'd be out there all day every day, taking care of it, cleaning up, talkin' to people, selling beer, raffling stuff off, whatever I had to do to make it go. . . . I hear the place is worth about forty million now. And of course it brings in a good profit every year, too. See, I went into this so I'd have something after hockey. You hafta do *something* if you're a hockey player; we've got the worst pension on earth. I talked to Bert Olmstead in Calgary a while back, and he told me that $23 million of our fund has just, well, you know, *putified*, or whatever you call it . . . with the computer and all that. I mean, if you work at a regular job you know how much is in your pension, how much you're gonna get, right? With us it's just totally – well, you don't know. I played seventeen years and I get nine thousand a year. Our pension fund was earning 3 per cent interest when some were earning 20 per cent. I'll tell ya, everything that's been done with that pension goes against my thinking. Pensions are a business. They've gotta be run properly. My business philosophy is, keep everything simple, clean, and neat. Look after the nickels and dimes; go for value; buy right, sell right. They haven't done that.

"What I think is that way back in the old six-team days, us players should have got together, pooled our money, and invested in property the way I did with these guys at my golf course. We could have raised enough money to buy some valuable real estate. We could have developed it, kept on developing, kept on buying. We could have bought houses, farms, offices, whatever you like. See, some of the guys haven't done that well since they quit. They didn't manage their money right, and they didn't learn to do anything other than play hockey for an income. These guys could have managed this thing for us, gotten jobs out of it. For the rest of us it wouldn't have been a job so much as an investment. But we'd all have been in it together making money.

"All you have to do is look around, and you see that most NHL owners couldn't care less what happens to us when we're through. Take a guy like Ballard – it's me me me me me me with that guy. You're not gonna get any help from him. . . . One time, McDonald's Restaurants brought in some big shots from Japan or someplace and they were going to have lunch at centre ice at the Gardens while the Toronto and Chicago old-timers played a game of hockey around them. McDonald's was going to pay us to play, and Ballard told them, 'If Shack's making any money outa this, you can't do it.' He won't give his old hockey players the sweat out of his armpit. No, he probably *would* give ya that – it wouldn't cost him anything. He won't even set up an old-timers' room at the Gardens! He's the only guy in the league who hasn't done it. If it wasn't for hockey players, he'd have squat. And what's he giving back to us? . . . Right!"

Norma says, "Fortunately for us, Ed hasn't needed the help like some of the guys have. He's very capable, very intuitive. I've learned a lot about business from him."

For the most part, Norma and Ed work together on their business endeavours. But not always. "We'll go along for months consulting one another on every little thing we do," she says. "Everything's great. Then suddenly Ed will decide he doesn't need my advice on something. And sometimes what he gets into is truly successful. Sometimes it's not. The important thing is that I recognize this need of his just to get out there and do things on his own once in a while. I accept it. Sometimes I go *my* own way. For instance, I played the commodities market for a year. I thought I knew all about it after reading a couple of books on it, but I didn't, and it got pretty hairy. I've never been so nervous or preoccupied in my life. Ed kept telling me I was going to have a nervous break-down. I had to get out. . . . That's not to say it bothers me to act on my own. Not at all. I mean, with Ed away so much during his hockey days, I *had* to act on my own. In fact, during those years I became a totally independent person – raising children, doing business, whatever. I can do every-thing myself, buy a house, decorate a house, sell a house, move across a continent. If it hadn't been for hockey I wouldn't have had nearly the opportunities I've had."

Norma volunteers that other things about her marriage to Ed have not been as rewarding as the measure of independ-ence she has achieved: "We've had some major disagree-ments over the years, mostly because of our different inter-ests. We've even thought about parting ways. Ed says I won't go anywhere with him, but I don't like a lot of the functions he goes to. Too many people. And as far as some of these people are concerned, I'm not even a human being. We'll be at a function, and somebody'll come up to Ed and be falling all over him, and Ed'll introduce me, and the person will say hello, but then the next time we see that person they won't even know who I am, let alone my name. You can start to feel as if you don't exist. . . . I like small groups of people who I know and care about. I like going to visit our old friends from other teams – that's fun. I just don't go to many of Ed's social things.

"By the same token, I haven't been able to include Ed in a lot of things I like. I take him to movies, and he snores through them. That's his idea of relaxing, snoring through a movie. I'm artistic; I love the theatre and ballet. I've never been pigeonholed to hockey. A lot of the girls were and are. In fact, near the end of Ed's career, I didn't even go to many games. Some people might say we're incompatible. Maybe we are. I mean, in some ways it's been a tough marriage. And as years go by, it's tougher than it was at first. You don't have the children at home to focus you. But in other ways it's been a great marriage, and still is. I've had all this freedom. I'm lucky in that I like my own company. When I'm on my own, I'll go to movies, plays, art galleries – or I'll often just stay home and read – I love curling up with a good book."

Unlike Norma, Ed has never known the pleasures of a good book. Extraordinary though it seems in the late twentieth century – especially for a man whose shrewdness in business has earned him millions of dollars – Ed cannot read or write. "I was aware of this almost as soon as I met him," reveals Norma. "He was talking about riding the subway in New York, and he mentioned how hard it was to get the stops right, and I wondered. Then when I told my dad I'd met Ed Shack, he said, 'Did you know he can't read or write?' "

Ed says, "I *should* learn to read and write." He throws open his hands in a gesture of apparent helplessness. "I do need it; it'd be nice. I've never even been able to read about myself! But I've *been* to school. I went in Guelph when I played Junior. I had a private tutor – he couldn't teach me. Then I went in New York; the Rangers tried to get me to learn, but I couldn't. I've been in Toronto, too. I've put the effort in, but it won't come. I'm not one of these people who sees things backwards either. Learning to read just frustrates me. So I say forget it. But because I'm weak in areas like education and reading, I've compensated in other areas like business and hockey. It's like if one of your arms shrivels up or something, your other one grows strong. It's nature."

Ed's latest attempt to learn to read came in 1988 in Toronto when he enrolled with a private tutor, a retired school teacher. "He didn't tell me," says Norma. "But I noticed he was getting up earlier, and one day I asked him what was going on. He said, 'I'm learning to read,' and off he went. His study book would have, say, a little picture of a cat and the letters c-a-t beside it."

"I quit when my teacher made me go up to the attic to study," smiles Ed. "It was one of these tiny wee storage attics – you had to pull down a little set of stairs to get up to it. I crawled up, and I was sittin' there, and I said, 'That's enough of this.' "

Understandably, even the simplest chores and procedures necessary to functioning in the modern world – procedures generally taken entirely for granted – can be complex challenges to a man without the benefits of literacy. Asked how he would find, say, Kilbourne Street in Toronto if he needed to get to it, Ed responds that he'd look for the 'kuh' sound on the sign, and hope he had the right 'kuh.' He admits that on occasion he has shown up at a wrong address. "You learn little tricks," he says. "When I go into a restaurant, for example, I can't read the menu, so I always say, 'What's the special?' Or if I'm with people who have eaten in that restaurant before, I'll say to them, 'What do you suggest?' Or I'll ask the waitress what she suggests. There's this restaurant in Buffalo owned by a guy named Louie. When I was playing with the Sabres I'd take the guys on the team in there. I knew some of the dishes, so I'd say, 'Louie, give me the titiloni or whatever you call it.' The next day I'd say, 'Louie, gimme the chicken livers.' The guys all thought I knew what I was doin'. . . . I know which restaurants are good at certain dishes, so if I get a feeling for, say, Italian sausages I'll go to such-and-such a place, prime rib someplace else. I might even study the menu a little bit before I order – make it look good. . . . What's embarrassing is when you're on a train, and they throw you this menu and a pencil and you have to tick off what you want. If I'm by myself, I just tell 'em I don't have my glasses, could they read it to me?"

Eddie has developed an equally effective ruse for checking into hotels. "A long time ago I learned how to write my old address in Sudbury, 629 Horobin Street H-O-R-O-B-I-N, Sudbury S-U-D-B-U-R-Y. Whenever I go into a hotel, I put that down, that's it. If the clerk knows who I am or where I live, he just thinks I must have a summer place there or something."

Even the relatively simple task of signing an autograph can present difficulties for Ed. "I can write my name, no problem," he says. "I learned that a long time ago. But the kids always want it made out to Calvin or Jeremy or something. I know the easy ones like John, J-O-H-N. When they give me the hard ones, I just ignore them and write 'Best Wishes' – I learned that one."

When secretarial skills are needed, Ed gets willing help from Norma, who writes (and reads) all letters pertaining to family business and sets up Ed's public engagements. "I give about thirty speeches a year," he says. "Some for pay, some for charity. Sometimes they say, 'What are you gonna talk about?' And I say, 'Leave that to me.' I never plan what I'm gonna say. I can't write anything down anyway. I just tell the people what's on my mind – like it or lump it."

Norma says, "I like to answer the phone when somebody calls asking him to appear somewhere. He's not as good a negotiator as I am. I get him the fees he deserves – he attracts a lot of people to these functions. He'll say to me, 'Oh, they only want me to appear in Toronto; I'll go for a little less.' *I* tell them, 'Here's the price. Take it or leave it.' "

"I like to go for the jugular, too," protests Ed. "But sometimes you can't get it. I'd rather have half a loaf than no loaf at all."

One of Eddie's tastier loaves these days is the Christmas tree business, which begins for him in late November each year and ends abruptly at six p.m. on Christmas Eve. He entered the field several years ago after meeting a Christmas tree entrepreneur on the golf course. The following December, he worked with him selling trees on the corner of Leslie and Sheppard. "Now I sell on my own at Bathurst and St. Clair. I buy the trees from farmers and truck 'em into town. I get right out there myself – rain, sleet, whatever. I hoot and holler. *'C'mon, get your Christmas tree – Christmas comes but once a year; get your Christmas tree right here!'* People see me, and they say, 'Hey! Eddie Shack!' Sometimes, they say, 'You're not Eddie Shack!' And I say, 'I sure feel like him!' I get as much as I can for a tree. And I give a few to St. Mike's Church there on the corner. . . . One time I even sold Christmas trees to old Ballard. I took them down to the Gardens, a whole buncha them; he put them up all over the building, even out along Carlton Street on top of the sign. And ya know what he wanted to pay me for them? Nothin'! He wanted to give me a plug on the scoreboard: Eddie Shack's Christmas Trees. I said, 'Forget about putting the name on the board, Harold – just gimme the $400 you owe me.'. . . To this day, he's never paid me."

Four hundred dollars notwithstanding, Norma speculates that Ed's devotion to the tree business is not entirely monetary. "Take away his costs," she says, "and I'm not sure his profits even amount to that much. Really, the tree lot is a stage for him! It appeals to his love of an audience. He loves performing, loves the attention of the people passing. In some ways it's a kind of replacement for the applause of the hockey crowds. Except that on the tree lot, he's the complete show. I'm not taking anything away from him, either. He's very good at it. He has fun at it."

If Norma could encourage *more* fun in Ed's life, it would be in the area of intercontinental travel. "He doesn't want to travel at all," she says. "When we went to Vienna a couple of years ago, we'd been there three days in this beautiful hotel, and he said, 'Let's go home; I miss the dog.' So he came home to Twiggy by himself. I stayed and went on to Greece. But I'd *really* like to see Asia. When I saw *The Jewel in the Crown* I wanted to see India and Pakistan so badly. My friends said, 'India! Why would you want to go there? It's so poor!' I just told them I wanted to go there. I still do. I like to see how other people live."

"I like travelling with the old-timers," grins Ed. "We go right across Canada – Vancouver, Calgary, Moncton. Sometimes we go to the States. We take my big eight-seater van."

Ed acknowledges that if he *were* to go abroad he'd prefer Africa to most destinations.

"We'll have to go soon," brightens Norma, "or we're not going to see too many animals. Apparently, there aren't many left in some places."

"They're all playin' in the NHL!" hoots Ed. "– But seriously, I don't feel I *have* to travel. I've got everything right here – a fireplace, a backyard, a sauna. I've got a *golf course*. What more could anybody want?"

2

Gump and Doreen Worsley

· · · · · · · · · · · ·

THE LIFE WE LIVE

Beneath the unused bar, in the unused rec room, in a dark and unused corner of the basement of Gump and Doreen Worsley's home (a lightbulb had to be fetched for the room's empty light socket, so that a visitor could see the surroundings), there are a few pieces of tattered goaltender's equipment. If asked for an assessment of them, you'd probably guess that they'd belonged to some kid during the thirties or forties and had been discarded to rot long before the kid came of age. The arm protectors are cobbled together in a hundred places with bits of string and thread. There is nothing in them more substantial than wool quilting – *thin* wool quilting – and they look as if they'd barely protect against a piece of flying chewing gum or the lash of a twig, let alone a puck sailing in at a hundred miles an hour.

The belly protector is equally ineffectual-looking – an amoebic-shaped pallet of quarter-inch foam rubber, covered in stained green cotton and bearing six small soft-leather patches. The aggregate area of the leather is approximately that of a dinner plate and might cover three or four of the vital abdominal organs of a very small man (that's "cover," but by no means properly protect).

For a laugh, Gump slips the belly pad on over his navy polo shirt. In conforming to the contours of his stomach, the pad takes on the shape and appearance of a turtle shell. Gump looks comfortable in the feckless old thing. As well he might. He first wore it more than forty years ago as an eighteen-year-old Junior in Verdun, Quebec. He was still wearing it ten years after that as a New York Ranger, and six years after that when he won his first Stanley Cup as a member of the Montreal Canadiens. He was wearing it ten years after *that* when he played his last game as a Minnesota North Star, and ten years after *that* when he joined a dozen of his contemporaries for an old-timers' game in New York City.

The truth is that since leaving Montreal as a teenager, Gump has never owned another set of goaltending equipment. His allegiance to the old gear is partly superstition, partly comfort, partly that he has never seen the need for anything more substantial in the way of protection.

Shortly after being traded from New York to Montreal in 1963, Gump entered the Canadiens' dressing room and emptied his equipment bag. Canadiens' coach Toe Blake happened by, glanced at Gump's gear, and asked where the rest of it was.

"That's all there is," responded the goaltender.

Blake looked at him in disbelief, looked back at the equipment, and said, "You're nuts, Gump. You're really nuts."

● ● ●

What makes a goalie? Reflexes? Courage? Flexibility? Timing? All of the above? One certainty is that it has little to do with body type. One of the greatest of the modern goalies, Ken Dryden, is tall and lanky. So is Ron Hextall of the Philadelphia Flyers. Allan Bester of the Toronto Maple Leafs and Darren Pang of the Chicago Blackhawks are short and thin. Gump is short and . . . well, he could hardly be called thin. In fact, if you didn't know better, you would not suspect that he was ever an athlete at all, let alone a Hall of Fame pro at one of the most difficult, dangerous, and acrobatic positions known to sport. Doreen pulls no punches in stating that Gump "has always had a big belly." Her grandmother once said to her that although Gump was a nice boy, she was sure he had "a growth of some sort under his shirt."

Gump accepts with a shrug most but not all comments on his shape. When New York Ranger coach Phil Watson accused him of being a "beer belly," he reacted angrily, making it clear that he drank not beer but the more civilized Seagram's V.O. whisky.

Gump claims to have been asked a thousand times what makes a good goaltender. "I always tell them the same thing. It helps to be crazy. Not all goalies are crazy, of course. Only about 90 per cent of them."

•   •   •

When Lorne Worsley was a kid in the Point St. Charles section of central Montreal, it occurred to his friend George Ferguson that he resembled the comic strip character Andy Gump, whose blonde hair flew from his head at all angles. "That was before I went to the brush-cut and got things under control," says Gump. George dubbed his friend accordingly, and the name stuck. And stuck.

Back then, Gump was a forward – not a very big one. By the age of fourteen he stood four feet, eleven inches and weighed eighty-five pounds. One day his coach in Point St. Charles took him aside and gave him the best bit of advice he has ever had: "If you want to continue in the game, get over there and put those goalie pads on. You're too little to play anywhere else."

"Not many kids envision themselves as goalies," says Gump. "Too hard, not enough glory." Nevertheless, he strapped on the pads, and within four years was perhaps the finest young goaltender in the province of Quebec. He played Junior hockey for the Verdun Cyclones and moonlighted with a CNR team in a senior commercial league.

One day before a game in Verdun, an acquaintance appeared at the rink and said, "Gump, I have a girl with me in the stands, and she'd like to have your autograph."

The girl turned out to be a pretty, green-eyed teenager named Doreen Chapman, who lived within a mile or so of the rink. Gump was smitten. "He always said I was a rink rat," laughs Doreen. "But I wasn't. I just liked hockey. . . . We started dating and soon found out that our parents had known one another since before we were born."

The romance blossomed, and Doreen could hardly be blamed for her dejection when, the following year, Lorne left Montreal to play for the New York Rovers, a Senior team that shared Madison Square Garden with the parent Rangers. "But at New Year's of that first year, he invited me down to see him play," she says. "I went, and while I was there we got engaged."

The following year Gump turned pro with the St. Paul Saints of the old U.S. Hockey League. The courtship that six months earlier had been so effulgent began to fade. Gump says, "When I came home after the season, we decided we should either call it off or get married, because I was away seven or eight months of the year."

On June 30, 1951, the two exchanged vows. Gump was twenty-one, Doreen eighteen.

"We were pretty green," Doreen admits. "But you can't say it didn't last."

In September of 1952, Gump made his first stop in the NHL, with the New York Rangers. He backstopped the team for eleven years, returning to Montreal with his family during the summers. For the most part the Rangers were losers, seldom making the playoffs, being eliminated pronto when they did. Asked during the mid-fifties which team gave him the most trouble, Gump uttered his most famous *bon mot*: "The Rangers."

In reality, his biggest trouble was coach Phil Watson, who ruled the team with an erratic, dictatorial hand from 1955 to 1960. Gump once claimed that he was Watson's "whipping boy," which wasn't far from the truth. One day while Doreen was pregnant with her second child, Dean – "really big," as she puts it – she received a phone call from Watson, who wanted to see her; would she come to practice with Gump the next day? "I went down," she says, "and he took me into his office and gave me a big lecture about how terrible the team was doing, and how it was all Lorne's fault because he was getting too much sex. So I stood up, and I went right up to him and touched him with my stomach and said, 'That's how close I get to Lorne these days! Understand?' The wives were real second-class citizens back then. Strictly window-dressing. If the Rangers had had their way, we wouldn't even have *been* with our husbands in New York; we'd have been back home in Canada."

• • •

It is practically a given of hockey that teams do not win championships without superior goaltending. Consider the Cup winners of the past forty years, and you invariably find them staffed with the leading goalies of the day: Jacques Plante, Glenn Hall, Johnny Bower, Terry Sawchuk, Bernie Parent, Ken Dryden, Billy Smith, Gump Worsley.

But champions or not, goaltenders own a special status, a peculiar level of admiration, among hockey players. For it is they, more than any others, who represent the primitive mystique of the game. They are the poets, the restless spirits, the eccentrics of hockey. Their equipment alone speaks volumes about the uniqueness of their work – layer upon layer of leather, cotton wadding, and plastic; leg pads three inches thick and nearly a foot wide; gauntlets that are all but bulletproof.

And yet it is apparent even to those who know little about hockey that the goaltender is in mortal danger every time a forward or defenceman winds up for a shot. To watch game films from the 1950s and 1960s and to see a Terry Sawchuk, a Glenn Hall, a Gump Worsley squatting in his crease, thrusting out his unprotected face to better see the puck screaming toward him through a maze of players – to see him there apparently heedless of the risk to his life – is enough to make the contemporary viewer cringe.

"People used to ask me, 'Do you worry about getting hurt?' " says Gump. "And I always told them, 'It's the one thing a goalie can *not* worry about.' If you get scared, you're gonna tighten, you're gonna pull up, then you're through, you've gotta get out. That's why in the old days, we used to go right back in the net when we got hurt. You can't sit around thinking, Hey, I could have lost an eye."

On numerous occasions, Gump very nearly *did* lose an eye. "Once Bernie Geoffrion hit me with a slapshot in the face," he recalls. "Fortunately I saw it coming and turned my face a bit. It hit me flat and bounced twenty-five rows up into the seats. It cut me, but a goalie would rather have a good clean cut than a bruise. A cut releases the pressure; a bruise just keeps on hurting."

On another occasion Bobby Hull took a shot that nearly ended Gump's career, if not his life. "It hit him on the ear and he dropped like a stone," says Doreen. "It could have been worse, but when Bob realized the shot was rising, he yelled, 'Look out, Gumpy!' and Lorne was able to turn his head just in time."

Gump contends that the greats of the game – the "superstars" – have always been more considerate of goaltenders than the abundant thumpers and journeymen. "Once when we were playing Detroit, Gordie Howe was going for his 500th or 600th goal, and I was down, and the puck was about a foot from my face. Gordie had his stick on it. If he'd shot it, both the puck and stick would have hit me in the face. Instead of shooting, Gordie just slid the puck underneath me. He said, 'I'll get my goal later.' A lotta guys would have drilled it into my kisser."

It was not until Gump had played twenty-two seasons of professional hockey, more than 900 games, that he put on a mask for the last six games of his career. "I never thought about Lorne losing an eye or anything like that until that final year in Minnesota," says Doreen. "Then it started to get to me, and I made him get a mask."

A few years earlier, for a game at the Montreal Forum, Gump had got Doreen a seat beside the goal judge directly behind his net. "I didn't think I'd be playing much longer, and, just for once, I wanted her to get a look at things from a goalie's perspective," he says. As it turned out, Doreen was so intimidated by approaching pucks that, at one point, she leapt up, knocking the goal judge right off his seat. "It scared the *heck* out of me!" she says. "I thought, Lorne must be out of his *mind* to have stood there so long! The puck comes so fast you can't even see it! I'll tell you, it's wild – is it ever crazy!"

• • •

The inherent dangers and pressures of the goaltender's art are borne better by some than others. Throughout his career, Terry Sawchuk suffered from intense nervous disorders, at one time retiring prematurely (he returned to hockey the next season), claiming that his nerves were "completely shot." After the Maple Leafs won the Stanley Cup in 1967, Sawchuk, who had played brilliantly in the deciding game, was physically and psychologically tortured to the point that he was incapable of celebrating with his teammates in the dressing room. Instead, he sat impassively in the corner, sucking mechanically on a cigarette, unable even to smile.

Perhaps the most renowned case of goaltender's nerves belonged to Glenn Hall, an eleven-time all-star with Detroit, Chicago, and St. Louis during the fifties and sixties. Hall's affliction was such that before every game, and often between periods, he would retire to the dressing-room toilet for a vomiting session. If a spell of nerves caught up with him during play he would bang on the ice with his stick. Attuned and sympathetic to his problem, referees would temporarily halt a game while he visited the dressing room.

Asked once for his assessment of a goaltender's lot, Jacques Plante replied, "Imagine yourself sitting in your office quietly doing your job. You make one little mistake, and suddenly a red light goes on over your head, and 15,000 people stand up and start screaming at you."

As even-tempered as he was, Gump, too, suffered the slings and arrows of the goaltender's outrageous fortune. He once claimed that goaltending had driven him close to alcoholism. The stresses were intense in New York, where he played for a chronically weak team, but were even worse in Montreal, where he played for a juggernaut that won four Stanley Cups within five years of his being traded to the team in 1963.

Gump says, "In Montreal, you're *expected* to win – by the fans, by the media, by team management. We'd lose a couple, and people on the street would say to me, 'You lousy so-and-so.' Then we'd win a few, and I'd be a hero. I always wanted to walk up to these fair-weather types and punch them square in the mouth. Even the kids got hassled at school. One of the boys' French teachers once said to him, "If you want to pass French, get your father to get me two tickets for a playoff game."

So acute were the stresses in Montreal that in November of 1968, Gump suffered a nervous breakdown. "One day in the middle of a storm, we caught an Air France flight out of Montreal on our way to Los Angeles," he says in describing the events that triggered his collapse. "I hated flying – it scared me to death, always had, ever since my very first flight back in 1950 when I was with the New York Rovers. On that flight, an engine caught fire and the pilot shut it down, and of course the prop stopped. I saw this out the window, and I didn't know a plane could fly with only three engines – back then, nobody knew anything about flying. I thought we were going down."

On the Air France flight in 1968, the turbulence was so extreme that, throughout, passengers and flight crew were forced to stay strapped in their seats, the crew unable even to serve food. When the flight put down in Chicago, Gump announced to team captain Jean Beliveau that he was through with hockey, he was fed up, he was quitting, he was taking the train home. He asked Beliveau if he would mind notifying the coach. "Jean tried to talk me out of it," says Gump, "but as far as I was concerned I was done."

By Doreen's assessment, Gump was a "nervous wreck" by the time he got back to Montreal. "He was no sooner in the door than he wanted to go to a bar. The phone was ringing off the hook, but he didn't want to talk to anybody. So we went to a place in Beloeil and had a few drinks."

Over the next few days, Gump descended into what he calls "a horrible stupor. . . . I didn't want to see any of our friends or family, or to talk to them. My father kept telling me, 'Get back and play; get back and play.' So I stopped talking to him."

"I've never seen *anyone* so *depressed*," says Doreen. "And it came out in the oddest ways. He really got worried about snow, for instance. He'd get up during the night and say, 'I wonder if we're going to get snowed in.' He was so concerned about snow, which had never before bothered him in the least. I'd say, 'Lorne, who cares? You don't have to go anywhere!'. . . In the daytime, he just sat around brooding. Didn't want to talk about hockey, didn't watch it on TV, didn't want anything to do with it. All he wanted to do was go to the bars and drink."

The turning point came when Gump visited a Montreal psychiatrist at the suggestion of Canadiens' general manager Sam Pollock. "Sam was very good about it," confides Gump. "He said, 'Don't worry about playing; just get yourself straightened out.' I went to the shrink a few times, and he just let me ramble on, trying to get to the root of my problem. I can't really say what it was about the visits that helped me, but I gradually started feeling better about myself."

Doreen explains that the breakdown had not been caused primarily by flying, as they had suspected. "I'm not saying flying wasn't *involved*. In fact, every time Lorne came home from a road trip, he had a story about the airplane. But this was as much a symptom of what was going on as anything else. The psychiatrist figured the real problem was the pressure of playing in Montreal. You *have to win* in Montreal; there's no way you *can't* win."

"The coach was a factor, too," says Gump. "I never liked practising, and Claude Ruel was big on practice. Push, push, push, all the time."

In January of 1969, Gump returned to the Canadiens' net and played well through the remainder of the season, helping the team capture the Stanley Cup in May of that year. But by December of the following season, his gremlins had again shown their faces. "I was nearly forty by this time," he says, "and I went and told Sam Pollock that I was through. Sam said, 'You can't quit the Montreal Canadiens, nobody quits the Canadiens!' And I said, 'Well, I just did!' I left his office, phoned Doreen, and told her I'd quit. 'That's good,' she said. 'C'mon home.' "

● ● ●

One of Gump's few successes during his years with the Rangers had been winning the Calder Trophy as Rookie of the Year in 1952. The thousand dollars that went with the trophy became the down payment on a house in Beloeil, Quebec, a half-hour's drive southeast of Montreal. Asked about the pronunciation of the town's name, Doreen explains that it is "Bell-ile" in English, "Bell-oy" in French. She also explains that it means "good eye," a fitting name indeed for the domicile of a man who for more than two decades relied on his eyesight to apprehend four-ounce chunks of black rubber being propelled toward him at speeds of over 100 miles per hour.

"The house was to be a starter," says Gump, "a stepping stone to something bigger." Nearly forty years later, however, the Worsleys are still in the unpretentious three-bedroom bungalow. "We just never felt the need of anything bigger or fancier," says Gump. "At one point I said to Doreen that I'd get the basement done up swank, and she said, 'I don't want to live in a dungeon.' So we added a room on the ground floor instead." Today, that room is the most comfortable and lived-in part of the house. On one of its walls is a sturdy brick fireplace, on another, the true hearth of the twentieth century, the television. A number of Gump's trophies are on display on the mantel and shelves, although many more are stowed away forgotten. "He keeps telling me to put them all away," says Doreen, "but I like to leave a few of them out."

In all, there is something singularly uncompetitive about the Worsley home – materialism in its most tolerable key. The furnishings are modest, the architecture simple, the yard unremarkable. The street is Everyman's street. One of the finer features of the place – apart from the good will that emanates from within – is the view from the back window. It includes, at perhaps a mile's distance, a 500-foot-high mass of rock and foliage known as Mount St. Hilaire. The mountain and several others like it to the south rise like primal mysteries out of the surrounding plain of the Eastern Townships, as if a great fist had punched them up from beneath the crust of the earth.

Gump and Doreen's only concession to extravagance – and a minor one at that – is a modest above-ground swimming pool in the backyard. "We put it in in 1969, the year I went to Minnesota," says Gump. "We couldn't have an in-ground pool because Doreen was afraid the frogs would jump into it."

The frogs?

"Oh yeah," says Gump, "she's scared to death of frogs. They jump in, and they turn pure white from the chlorine."

So far, the above-ground defence is working. Not one chlorinated amphibian has appeared in the pool since its installation twenty years ago.

• • •

While driving from Beloeil to the Forum on game nights

during Gump's years with the Canadiens, Gump and Doreen frequently had advance notice as to whether or not the team was going to win the night's contest. "We used to pass a corner where you could put fifty cents into a machine and buy stove oil," says Gump. "If somebody was there getting oil when we passed, we never lost."

To sweeten the team's luck, Doreen always carried a talisman to the games – a small smooth stone, given to her by goaltender Charlie Hodge's wife. To further the metaphysical cause, she invariably left her gloves on until the opposition scored, at which point she promptly removed them. During playoffs, she often lit a church candle in aid of Gump's team – always in the colour of his uniform.

Gump says, "Some players are so superstitious that if you move a piece of their equipment while they're getting dressed, they'll take everything off, hang it all back up and start over."

An hour before the start of the seventh game of the 1964 Stanley Cup Final between the Canadiens and the Chicago Black Hawks, Gump and Doreen were sitting in the Forum lounge having a cup of coffee. Gump was recovering from an injury and was not scheduled to play. Suddenly, the Canadiens' trainer, Larry Aubut, appeared and told Gump to go and get his uniform on – he would be playing after all. "As soon as he left, I got the jitters," Doreen says. "I put my coffee down and ordered a gin and tonic. Then a funny thing happened. A little old man came up to me and said, 'Here's an extra hand to help your husband.'" The man slipped her a tiny brown plastic doll's hand, which she held in her palm throughout the game. Gump earned a shutout that night, and the Canadiens won the Stanley Cup.

Gump himself might well have been considered something of an omen. A bad one. Every team he played for before he joined the NHL – the Verdun Cyclones, the New York Rovers, the St. Paul Saints, and the Saskatoon Quakers – went out of business shortly after he left them.

• • •

Two months after he walked out on the Canadiens, Gump was contacted by Wren Blair, general manager of the Minnesota North Stars. The Stars had not won in twenty-one games and were desperate for goaltending. Making the playoffs was a lost cause, but respectability was not. Would Gump join the team?

"At that point, Gump hated hockey," says Doreen, "and I thought it was bad for him to go out on a sour note. So when he asked me what I thought, I said I felt he should go and finish the year in Minnesota."

Gump signed immediately, played inspired hockey, and the North Stars made the playoffs on the final weekend of the season. Back at the ranch, the Canadiens missed the playoffs for the first time in twenty-two years.

The next day, Doreen told a radio interviewer that the Canadiens' fate served them right. "They peddled my husband like an old shoe, and now he's in the playoffs and they're not."

In all, Gump played five seasons with the North Stars, but he and Doreen never took out American citizenship, largely because American troops were still in Vietnam and they did not want their sons drafted into the U.S. Army. "If they'd gotten their legs blown off in an American war, we'd have been to blame," says Gump. "If Canada's in a war, and they have to go, that's another matter. It's not our responsibility."

• • •

During his playing days with the North Stars, Gump was the team's player representative and, as such, fielded numerous complaints and queries from his younger teammates. "One time," he says, "a guy we called Cement Head broke his jaw, and his wife phoned up and said, 'What am I going to do? He can't eat.' I said, 'First, you'll have to buy a blender so you can blend all his food into liquid. Then you get a drinking straw so he can drink it.'

"She goes out and buys him a *crazy straw* – you know, one of those straws with about six feet of twists and turns. You have to suck out half a quart of air before you get anything! The guy was so weak he didn't have enough suction to get to the food!"

• • •

After his fourth year in Minnesota, Gump was set to retire. He was weary, he was sore, he was fed up after twenty-one years of professional hockey. But he was told by the team's general manager that if he were to play one more year he would be given a five-year contract – one to play, four to scout.

He signed the contract and ten months later played his last NHL game. "The transition into scouting was easy," he shrugs. "I'd certainly had enough playing. And unlike some of the guys, I didn't miss the attention of the fans, because it never stopped for me. Even now, fifteen years later, I still get asked for autographs all the time – coast to coast! That's what playing twenty-two years without a mask did for me. Everybody recognizes me. When I was scouting, Lou Nanne, my GM, would sometimes say to me, 'Do you know *everybody* in this world?' I can walk into a place with guys who played twenty years in the NHL, and people don't know who they are. But they know me, because I was a stationary figure and I played sixty minutes a game. People saw a lot of me on TV."

Gump believes that he was spared the resentments that haunt many players after retirement because he was not forced out of the game as players so often are. "No team ever said to me, 'We don't want you to play anymore.' I quit because I couldn't stand it any longer. I kept *trying* to quit, and they kept asking me back. Even at the end, they *still* wanted me to go another year, promised me all sorts of bonuses, big salary, whatever. The truth is that, when I retired in 1975, I was forty-five years old and could have collected my pension right then."

For the next fourteen years, Gump spent his winters searching out talent in the drafty small-town arenas where the big-leaguers of the future invariably begin their ascent. It is not the sort of work that would appeal to every Hall-of-Famer; it can mean second-rate motels, cheeseburgers on the fly, car travel over icy roads. But Gump has never had even the smallest pretensions or the faintest delusions of grandeur. And he enjoyed the work immensely.

Doreen was less enthused by it. "That first year, I went through hell," she winces. "I just went nuts! I love hockey, and *I really missed going to the games twice a week*! I'd sit around here doing needlepoint. I kept saying to Lorne, 'Let's go to a hockey game, let's go to a game.' But you see, as a scout, he was seeing four or five games a week. So by Saturday night, when I was itching to go, he'd had his fill of hockey. In spite of this, of course, I was glad to see him so contented. I've always felt thankful that he didn't leave the game with resentments. Nothing gnawing away at him inside."

"I won the Stanley Cup!" exclaims Gump. "I fulfilled a dream! I have nothing to complain about."

• • •

One day, in discussing Gump's numerous athletic achievements and trophies, Doreen stops in mid-sentence, jumps up, and declares, "I'll show you one of his *real* trophies." She leaves the room, returning momentarily with the empty claw of a thirty-pound lobster caught and given to Gump several years ago in Nova Scotia. In describing the gustatory olympics that were waged around the lobster's consumption, Gump and Doreen give the impression that, as a memento, the claw means as much to them as the scaled-down Stanley Cup and Vezina Trophy that sit atop their mantel: "Oh, I tell you this was some beast," says Gump. "It took me two hands just to lift the thing. People tell you big lobsters aren't any good to eat, but don't believe it. The guy who gave it to us cooked it and made a delicious chowder with *big* chunks of lobster in it – it was great, very tender, very succulent. Oh, it was super. It was delicious. It was just super."

Gump enjoys baking bread, cookies, and cakes, and has a fine touch with homemade soups. He is also an energetic barbecue chef and has been known to shovel a path through the snow to the family barbecue so that he can use it in the middle of winter. His long-standing romance with food is confirmed in his 1975 autobiography, *They Call Me Gump*. There, the puckish chronicler sets down a formidable recipe – 1 cup butter, 1½ cups sugar, 1 cup coconut, etc. – for his favourite confection, pineapple squares, or pineapple Gumpies as Doreen calls them. (Elsewhere in the book, Gump lists his favourite bar in each NHL city.)

"Getting into the kitchen is one way I have of relaxing," he says. "And of course I love the food. I take the stuff I make to Doreen for sampling, and she says, 'It's great, Gump. Now get back in there and get to work on the pans.'

"And I do. It's part of the deal."

• • •

In the spring of 1988, the Minnesota North Stars hired a new general manager, Jack Ferraro. A short while later, most of the club's coaches and scouts received Dear John letters from dear Jack, informing them that their relationship with the Stars was over – it was time to look for new jobs. At first, Gump did not receive a letter and was uncertain about his future.

The uncertainty ended on June 21 when Ferraro phoned him to say that his services were no longer needed.

"Would you mind telling me why?" asked Gump.

"I'm putting some of my own people in," Ferraro told him.

"Thank you very much," said Gump, and an eighteen-year relationship with the team, during which time Gump had contributed extensively to the Stars' well-being, was no more.

"It was a mean thing, and Lorne was hurt by it," says Doreen. "Especially the way it was done. It would have been nice if they'd been a little more considerate. Even if he'd gotten a letter like everybody else."

"What it came down to," says Gump, "was that nobody had the guts to come to me personally and say 'Okay, next year we're gonna clean house and start over. We're sorry.' They had the new guy phone with the bad news."

The only good thing about the firing was the timing, inasmuch as Doreen had been after Gump to quit anyway. "He was on the road a lot, and I was getting fed up with living alone after all these years," she says. "I've still got our daughter Lianne here, but she works downtown, so she's not around that much. When Lorne was going out west scouting, he'd be gone maybe two weeks, then he'd be home for a while, then he'd be gone to Ontario for a week. It was getting to the point where when things went wrong he never seemed to be here."

And things had started to go wrong. Gump says, "My brother died of cancer; my mother died; Doreen's mother and father have been ill. When I wasn't here, Doreen would have to go see my mother in the hospital. Then I got ulcers. I was planning to quit anyway when I hit sixty in 1990. So when I got the axe, I just didn't bother looking for another job."

Which is not to say that other jobs have not come looking for Gump. During the past year, he has had offers to do public relations work for his former general manager Wren Blair's tourist resort in Haliburton, to coach the Concordia University hockey team, and to host a morning sports show on radio station CFCF in Montreal.

His rationale in turning down the offers is indisputable: "I don't need the money, and I don't need the hassle."

• • •

One reason Gump doesn't need the money is that Doreen has

been an assiduous banker and investor over the years. "She's put it away so that every month now we have a cheque coming due," he says. "At first, of course, there wasn't much to put away. But things really got going for us when I went from the Rangers to the Canadiens. We had our mortgage paid off by then, and we only had the one house to keep (before that we'd had our own house and a rented place in New York). Plus, I was earning more in Montreal and had more playoff money. I guess it was in the back of our minds that at some point I might get badly injured and wouldn't be able to play anymore, and that we'd better take care of the future. Unfortunately, a lot of NHL players assume they're going to make the big money for the rest of their lives, and most of them aren't."

Doreen says, "The only thing we always hoped was that we'd be able to live the same way after hockey as we did while Lorne was playing. And it hasn't been hard at all, mainly because we've never lived high off the hog or hung around with millionaires. The lower income has barely affected us." Doreen observes that she and Gump would probably have achieved their current financial stability a little sooner if Gump hadn't bought three Cadillacs along the way.

"When you come from Point St. Charles," says Gump, "your ambition is to own a Cadillac. But I didn't have enough money to buy one until we got to Minnesota. I guess I made eighty-odd thousand my best year there. Wren Blair, the general manager, was good to me. Every summer we still go up to his resort in Haliburton, Ontario, and he always says that if it hadn't been for me he'd have had five fewer years in the NHL. As far as he was concerned I saved his job. In fact, some NHL owners have told me I saved that franchise – it was dying, and things gradually turned around."

"He paid cash for that first Cadillac," says Doreen. "It was a custom order. Silver blue."

"Then I bought a couple more," says Gump. "I guess you could say I'm better at spending than I am at saving. I like buying. Especially gifts. Doreen won't buy herself anything! I buy her clothes!"

"He buys me *good* clothes," she says, as if after twenty-nine years of marriage she is still impressed, even surprised, by the fact. "He's bought me furs and stoles. Three years ago, he bought me a long mink coat."

"I told her that her old one looked awful," deadpans Gump.

"I didn't believe him," she says, "but I went to the fur store with him, anyway, and picked one out. When he saw it, he said, 'You don't want that one. Here's the right one over here.' It was a much more expensive coat."

"We brought it home," says Gump, "and we put it beside the old one, and she said, 'You mean, I was wearing that!' It was twenty years old. . . . I know Doreen's size in everything, and I know the kids' sizes. When I go on the road, I buy clothes for everybody, and they always fit."

Doreen says, "He can't remember the kids' ages, but he knows what size clothes to buy them."

"And I don't care about the price," says Gump. "I go into a store, and I say, 'That's what I want. How much is it?' I don't buy crap."

That, explains Doreen, is why she manages the money. "I've got it all," she laughs. "He doesn't have a cent. I guess that's why he stays with me."

● ● ●

After forty-two years of organized shinny, Gump's most persistent daily concern is still the game that made him. He reads about it in the newspapers, follows it on radio and television sportscasts, and, every night throughout the winter, does his best to find a game on television.

When the game is over, he watches the news and goes to bed. In the morning he rises early. Always has. But nowadays instead of rushing off to the rink or the airport at seven a.m., or to an arena at the other end of the province, he takes a leisurely shave, eats a leisurely breakfast, and embarks on a leisurely drive to the local shopping centre. There, he picks up the newspaper and usually stops for coffee with his old buddies from Beloeil. "That's his job!" proclaims Doreen.

When he isn't on the job, Gump does any number of things around the house, including relaxing by the pool in summer, cooking or barbecuing, or playing the electric organ by numbers. (As a goaltender in Minnesota, he often played the organ for two hours at a time as a means of calming himself.)

On Friday, he cleans house – vacuuming, dusting, sweeping – but he is not so fully liberated as to tackle toilets or windows. And daily, at noon hour, he and Doreen settle by the tube for their sustaining fix of *The Guiding Light* and *As the World Turns.*

"It's not what you'd call an exciting life," says Doreen, "but it's the life we live, and it does have its moments." As if on cue, Gump launches into a story about an event in New York not long ago, where he and Doreen met the actor Michael Tylo from *The Guiding Light.* "Oh, I was thrilled," he says. "Tylo didn't believe I watched the soaps, until I told him exactly who he was in the show. I said, 'You're Henry Chamberlain's son!' And that hadn't even been revealed to the audience yet. It was supposed to be a mystery. I'd figured it out. . . . Afterwards, we went to Studio 54, and he said, 'We'll never get in! Look at the line-up.' But as soon as the doorman saw me, he said, 'Hey! Gumpy! Good to see ya! C'mon in!'

"And in we went. Doreen and I love to dance. We jitterbug. We have a routine."

On the dance floor, as well as in Beloeil.

"All in all, we have a very good marriage," says Doreen. "Gump has always been extremely considerate of me. When he'd get home from a scouting trip, for instance, he'd always call from the airport and say, 'Pick me up! Let's go out for dinner!' "

Gump says, "A lot of the guys used to say, 'How can you go to another restaurant when you've been eating in restaurants for two weeks?' I'd say, '*I* have been; Doreen hasn't.' You've gotta be fair. Some of the guys don't see it that way, because they're the stars, so to speak. I don't play up the star business – at home or anywhere else."

His claim notwithstanding, Gump has been known to use his reputation as a hockey player to gain the occasional (minor) favour. Doreen says, "I remember one night I phoned for reservations at a restaurant and couldn't get them. We were supposed to be going out with friends. Lorne came home, said, 'Did you get the reservations?' I said, 'The place is booked up.' He said, 'Did you give my name?' I said, 'Of course not.' So he phoned and said, 'This is Gump Worsley. Have you got room for six tonight?' They said, 'What time can we expect you?' "

Although amused by the story, Doreen makes her view of such practices clear: "It's unfair to the next guy. I like to see everyone treated fairly."

"But some restaurants *like* to have us there," objects Gump. "A lot of them stick us right in the middle of the restaurant where people will see us. It's good publicity. If we're waiting in line, the maitre d' will see us and say, 'Oh, Mr. Worsley, we have your table now.' We haven't even made reservations! . . . The fact is, an NHL hockey player can't avoid a certain amount of preferential treatment in a hockey city like Montreal. So I might as well enjoy it. At the same time, I never forget that I'm nobody special. I'm not one of these guys who won't make an appearance unless I'm paid so many thousand dollars. Who are we as hockey players to think we can demand five, ten grand? Maybe some guys, but not me. I'll go make a speech for a couple of hundred dollars, sometimes less if it's for a good cause. It's just not in my personality to demand a lot of money. If I'm going to a charity function, I don't want to do it on my own dollar. But if they pay my expenses, and maybe a little extra if they've got it, I'll go. I go to New York every year for the Boys' Club of New York fund-raiser. They make more than $150,000 in one night. I don't get paid for it. Neither do any of the other athletes who go. Except expenses. Stan Mikita goes. Bobby Orr goes. We'll give our time for a good cause. You've gotta give if you're going to receive. And as hockey players we've already received a lot. I'm just happy to be able to give something back."

3

Bill and Nancy Hay

• • • • • • • • • • • • •

OPTIMISTS

Nancy Hay is a woman of spirit and dignity, and when she tells the story it is not for sympathy or for the story's own rather dramatic sake. "We've lived with it and accepted it," she says softly, "and I don't mind talking about it, particularly if it will help other people with handicapped children. At this point, I can perhaps *be* of help; I've had a lot of experience in the field."

That experience began on February 26, 1962, at Berwyn Memorial Hospital in Chicago. Nancy was twenty-four years old. "The baby was born at seven o'clock at night," she says, "and they didn't bring him to me until four o'clock the next afternoon. So I was beginning to worry. Fortunately Bill was there, not on a road trip. In those days, even if a baby was due, the players went off with the team.

"Before they brought the baby in, the doctors came to Bill and me and told us about his problems, explained his illness, Sturge Webber Syndrome. He had a birthmark on one side of his face, which was an outer sign of difficulties with the brain, but the birthmark was the first thing you'd notice. You'd think, My, the baby has this awful cosmetic problem. And there was an eye problem, glaucoma, which made one eye slightly larger than the other. Even though the real problems were deeper, these were the things we'd be noticing first, so these were the things they explained first. At this stage, of course, I didn't even know what questions to ask about what they were telling us. Back then, there was very little information available on advances in medicine – at least I wasn't aware of any.

"So the doctors gave us this story, and there were four press photographers waiting outside the room, because here was a hockey player and his wife who'd had a baby, a boy no less, and they wanted to get pictures of us. They'd been waiting two hours – they'd been stalled by the hospital. I can remember it all as vividly as if it were happening right now. The hardest thing for me to do when the photographers came in the room – this was right after the doctor had brought the baby in; there was Bill and me, and I had Donald in my arms – was to keep from crying, was just to *get those pictures over with* before the tears came. I mean, we were stunned. We'd just heard our child had a severe disability, and suddenly there were flashbulbs going off. I've still got the pictures somewhere. There are occurrences in your past that you can't bring to mind no matter how hard you try to dredge up the memories, but this particular moment stands out with total clarity for me."

Nancy submits that their son's birth was the most traumatic experience that she and Bill have ever endured. "It threw us completely, changed our lives. We might have thought we knew how to handle it, but we were young, and we really didn't. In fact, I think that in the beginning, our naiveté about the seriousness of it all protected us. If we'd known how very profound the disabilities were going to become, heaven knows how we would have reacted. And of course at that time, there weren't the support systems there are now for parents of handicapped children, or for the children themselves."

When Nancy left the hospital, she had no nearby family to which she could turn for comfort and, frequently, no husband, as Bill was away for up to four days a week on road trips. In addition to Donald, she also had two tiny daughters, Penny and Pam, to take care of. "But that was probably a blessing," she smiles. "I was so busy. And of course the girls gave me another emotional outlet. It all would have been far more traumatic if Donald had been a first child. I've often thought about that. I'm not sure we would have had any more.

"I'd say that, through it all, we experienced the same grief process that you go through with a death in the family. First, there was the denial – we just felt, This can't be happening to us, this only happens to other people. Then there was anger – why me? – and then gradually acceptance. It happens slowly, but it does happen."

Bill and Nancy had arrived in Chicago in 1959, as green as broccoli. Bill had just completed a year of semi-pro hockey in Calgary and was one of several young stars destined to spring the Black Hawks from a ten-year lease on the NHL basement. "I'd never even *seen* an NHL game when I got there," laughs Bill. "Oh, I was green, all right. I remember during the first game I played, our coach, Rudy Pilous, came into the dressing room between periods and compared the guys who weren't skating to the Zamboni – 'The Zamboni's moving faster than you are,' sort of thing. And this came up several times again. So during the second game, I leaned over to Bobby Hull and said, 'Who's this guy Zamboni that Rudy keeps talking about?' And he told me it was the ice-cleaning machine."

While not denying that Bill was somewhat wet behind the ears during the early days in Chicago, Nancy contends that through hockey he at least had focus and a sense of belonging. "As for me," she says, "here was this little naive girl from Winnipeg, twenty years old, with a baby – we had Pam at that point – plunked in an old apartment on Diversey Avenue, a few blocks from the site of the St. Valentine's Day Massacre. Cement floors. A single lightbulb in the kitchen.

Enamel sinks. The old-style cage elevators. And I was alone much of the time, because Bill was on the road. For me, this was all a big, *big* transition. A friend of my parents came down to visit me, phoned my mother when he got back, and said, 'You'd better get to Chicago and get your daughter out of there.' My mother and dad had never been too thrilled about my being down there, anyway, or even about my being married to a hockey player. Their idea was that, we had a child, Bill had finished school, he should be looking for a proper job, finding a home, so on. I mean, they weren't entirely off base; hockey *was* a pretty rough-and-tumble existence back then, at least when you were starting out. Nobody owned a home in the city where they played – salaries weren't high enough. You took what you could get, and for us it usually wasn't much. Through Bill's first year, we didn't even own a car.''

The latter insufficiency was met in the autumn of 1960, when Bill laid out $300 (Nancy says $200) for a geriatric two-door Ford. "At that time," says Bill, "my teammates Ted Lindsay, Glen Skov, and Eric Nesterenko lived in an apartment building across the street from us. And they'd ride to the rink in my car; Ted's and Glen's cars were with their families back in Detroit, and Eric was a bachelor at the time and didn't have a car. Anyway, we were on the way to the rink one day – we were a little late – and I said to Lindsay, 'Here, you drive.' As it turned out, he got stopped by a cop going through a red light or something, and the cop wanted to take him to the station. Ted had been a big star in Detroit for sixteen years, and he said, 'I'm Ted Lindsay, and I'm on my way to the Stadium to play a hockey game, and we're late.' And the cop stepped back and said, 'You're not Ted Lindsay; if you were you wouldn't be driving an old wreck like this.' At this point, I stood up from the back seat and said, 'Listen, officer, you can do whatever you want with Ted Lindsay – take him away, for all I care – but don't cut up my car!' ''

Success as a player came quickly and deservedly to Bill. At the end of his first NHL season, he was awarded the Calder Trophy as the NHL's top rookie, outdistancing teammate Stan Mikita and Detroit's Murray Oliver for the award. The following year, he and the Black Hawks brought the Stanley Cup to Chicago for the first (and last) time since 1937. But for all the effect the trophies had on Bill's ego, he might as well have won a kilo or two of Chicago smoked brisket. Certainly, few players have ever been as unselfish on the ice, or as self-effacing off it. While known for both his savvy and his stylish puck skills – not to mention his size and aggressive play – Bill seemingly took as much pleasure out of setting up a goal or helping prevent one with a piece of energetic backchecking as he did out of scoring one. He says, "I always felt that I could help the team more by bringing out the best in players like Bobby Hull than I could by concentrating on myself." (Bill, it is worth noting, was Hull's centreman during three of the leftwinger's fifty-goal-plus seasons.)

Out of uniform, Bill was equally unassuming. "Some of the players and their families wore the hockey on their sleeves a little bit; they thought they were special. And you can ride that road, but then when it's over, it's over, and there's a very abrupt change. And it can be difficult for players and their families to adjust. We never travelled that road, never really sought or enjoyed the limelight. When I was at the rink, I always had as much fun with the rink rats as with the people who sat in the expensive boxes – in fact, more fun. Nancy observed all this, and always went her own route, too. If people wanted to talk hockey, we were polite about it – always have been. But for the most part we had other things to do. That's how our daughters got to be so well balanced and respected. The hockey doesn't mean anything to them."

Lest it be thought that Bill's low-key attitude was the result of a bashful or diffident personality, consider the following story, told by Stan Mikita's wife Jill: "On the way home from the Stanley Cup party in 1961, several of us were heading out the Eisenhower Expressway, going about sixty miles an hour, when Bill suddenly opened the car door, stuck his foot out, and started dragging his shoe on the pavement, yelling at the driver – I can't remember who it was; Glenn Hall maybe – to *please* slow down. That same day, we stopped at a railway crossing. The gate was down, and Bill jumped out and started fooling with it – I guess he was trying to lift it; the train had gone by. When it started rising, he hung on to it! There he was hanging way up above the train tracks with his legs kicking; it's a wonder the guy didn't get killed."

As a further sample of Bill's eccentricities, Jill describes, in a somewhat chastened voice, how one day when she addressed him by his nickname, "Red," he growled, "Don't you ever call me that again, Jill. The name is W.C. Hay, thank you."

"And he meant it," says Jill.

Asked about his severe injunction years later, Bill explodes with laughter. "What I told her was that my name was W.C., as in Water Closet. Jill never could tell when I was fooling around. I never cared what she called me."

At the age of fifty-three (and now an oil company executive), William C. may have outgrown his nickname, but he has far from outgrown his sense of humour. At a recent tribute to hockey greats from the past, he was called upon to "roast" Bobby Hull, who, among other Hall-of-Famers, was present at the tribute. Uninhibited by either the black-tie atmosphere of the event or the stature of his prey, Bill marched on stage wearing a tawdry blonde wig and launched a series of devilish jokes about Hull's toupee and somewhat extravagant past.

"It's easy to take yourself too seriously when you're involved in pro hockey," says Nancy. "A lot of the guys did, and of course it's encouraged by the teams – it's all deadly serious. But we've always been able to laugh. And over the years it's helped us survive not only hockey but our other difficulties as well."

But it was more than just the laughs or the refusal to take the game seriously – or the resolute self-effacement – that gave Bill his distinction in big-league hockey. Although it does not show up in the record books, he is well remembered as the man who shattered pro hockey's long-standing education barrier. By sticking with the Black Hawks in 1959, he became the first university graduate to play regularly in the NHL.

Bill didn't exactly show up in Chicago wearing a mortar-board and expounding Plato, but he was nonetheless treated as something of a curiosity by his teammates during his first few months on the job. "Most of the NHL players at that time had started to play hockey full-time in high school," says Nancy, "and here was a guy who'd been hanging around university campuses for four or five years. There were questions about whether he was tough enough, talented enough, to make it. Why wasn't he doing something else if he had a degree? The common thinking back then was that a player was too *old* to start an NHL career if he'd been through university. In a purely scholastic sense, I think some of the players were a little in awe of him. But his making it paved the way for a lot of kids to go to college and still make the NHL."

Nancy and Bill were already married when, two years earlier, Bill had entered his senior year in geology at Colorado College, Colorado Springs. The previous April (1957) he had led his college hockey team, the Colorado College Tigers, to an NCAA championship, and he was hoping (in vain) to repeat the accomplishment before he graduated. If it had been up to Bill alone, he might already have been in the NHL by that time, via the more traditional route of Junior hockey. But his father, Charles Hay, a university grad who owned a small oil company in Saskatchewan and who would one day be president of Gulf Canada, had different ideas. Charles had first impressed those ideas upon his son in 1953 when Bill was a seventeen-year-old whiz with the Regina Pats of the Western Canada Junior League. "At the time," says Bill, "my professional rights were owned by the Montreal Canadiens, who wanted me to go down east and play in their system. In fact, their general manager, Sam Pollock, decided that he was going to come out west to talk to me. I was to meet him at the York Hotel. But before the meeting, my dad said he thought he'd just come along and listen to what Sam had to say, but not say anything *himself*, of course – he wasn't going to butt in. As it turned out, the two of them did most of the jawing, had quite a discussion, my dad arguing the education route, Sam arguing the hockey route. I listened to them for a while, then at twelve noon I got up and left, and they became the best of pals."

Bill's dad was a man not just of principles but a man shrewdly capable of putting his principles to work. "When the scouts would come to try to sign Bill," says Nancy, "they'd offer him maybe a thousand dollars to turn pro, but for everything they'd offer, Bill's dad would say, 'Well, I can give him that.' So the scouts had no bargaining power, except that Bill wanted to play hockey. I know he wanted a degree, too, but deep in his heart his ambition was to play in the NHL. In the end, I guess Bill's dad won – or maybe they both won – in that Bill was able to go to school *and* play hockey."

It is a fateful detail of history that if the Canadian oil boom had begun a year or two earlier, Bill might never have shown his face in the NHL. Upon graduation, he had been invited to try out with the Canadiens. But after two weeks in camp, he was told to report to the club's minor-league team in Quebec City. "That wasn't for me," he says. "I told them, 'I'm sorry, fellas, but I'm married and my wife's pregnant. We're going back to Calgary; I'll go to work as a geologist.' So I walked the streets of Calgary as a geologist, looking for a job in the oil business. But the boom was still around the corner, and there were no jobs available."

"If there *had* been," says Nancy, "I'd have been quite happy to stay right in Calgary. I'm not so sure about Bill, but I think he might have been happy enough, too."

Under the circumstances, he called the coach of the semi-pro Calgary Stampeders and, in his own words, "begged him for a tryout."

Bill had a productive year in Calgary and the following season his rights were purchased from Montreal by the Chicago Black Hawks for the then mighty sum of $25,000. "We made quite an effort to get him," says Tommy Ivan, the seventy-seven-year-old vice-president of the Black Hawks. "And he was worth it. I first saw him in school, and I liked him both as a player and as a man."

Bill's retirement from hockey eight years later, at thirty-two, was no more typical than his arrival had been in 1959. For one thing, he quit at an age when most front-line players of his era were looking optimistically at four or five more years under the Big Top. After all, the NHL had just doubled in size from six teams to twelve, so that even journeyman players could expect to cruise on – or dodder on, as the case might be – well into their thirties, without serious competition for their jobs. "I could have kept going pretty well as long as I'd wanted to," says Bill. "My playing rights had been taken by the St. Louis Blues in the expansion draft. And the Blues' owner, Sid Solomon III, called me several times, urging me to come and play. In fact, I went to St. Louis to visit with him one weekend. Not that I was tempted to come out of retirement; it's just that he was offering so much money – $200,000 a season; five times what I'd made the previous year in Chicago – that I felt I owed it to him to go and see him personally, to explain my situation. See, I felt that if I played I'd be playing strictly for the money. Many professional athletes *do* play for the money – they get used to the lifestyle – but that wasn't for me. They made me an offer I couldn't refuse, and I refused it. I didn't want to be in the game anymore."

For Nancy, Bill's retirement meant a chance to unpack wedding gifts that had been sitting in boxes for eight years.

"It just felt great," she says. "All the time Bill played, we never really had any roots, no sense of permanence or community. Always on the move: Calgary in the summers, Chicago in the winters. As I got older I felt increasingly frustrated by this, almost entirely unable to get anything of my own going in the community. I mean, Bill's career was just *everything*. Not that I ever resented the hockey itself. It was our living, and it was a good one. It's given us a lot. But all winter, every winter, we lived our lives around these *games* and whether the Black Hawks won or lost.

"I remember really feeling it was time to get out during the 1965 finals between the Black Hawks and the Canadiens. The lease was up on the place we were renting, and we'd had to move out into a motel – three kids and me. I'd made the move myself, because the players always stayed out at Rockford during the playoffs and weren't allowed to come home. The idea was that their families would distract them. If I wanted to see Bill, all I could do was take the kids to the Stadium and we'd wave at daddy as he left on the bus.

"When they lost the Cup in the seventh game, I really thought, Do we want to keep doing this? But we did carry on for a couple more seasons. If I hadn't enjoyed the hockey itself, I'd have been sunk, because it was really almost all we had."

Bill, too, was weary of the hockey life – reason enough to leave it behind. But beyond that weariness, he also harboured a deep-rooted dream to work full-time – not to mention that he had the promise of a job – in the oil industry. "I was different than a lot of players in that I had this definite career to go to," he says. "I don't mean to imply that success in the oil business was by any means guaranteed me. Some people might think that because I was Bill Hay the hockey player, everything just fell into my lap. And I won't deny that my reputation from hockey was advantageous, so long as I handled it properly. But I had to work hard like anybody else in the field if I was going to deliver the goods. Bow Valley Industries hired me as a geologist, not as a p.r. man."

Bill suggests that if he *did* have an ace up his sleeve when he entered the oil field, it was that for the past eight years he had always returned to Calgary during the off-season and worked for Esso Resources. "The day I got back would be the day I started work," he says. "And I wasn't just picking up technical or field knowledge either; I was meeting people and gaining all sorts of experience fitting into the community. It all helped when it came time to shut down in Chicago and get on with our lives.

"I'm not saying for a minute that I didn't miss hockey. The transition is tough no matter how well prepared you are for it. But I've seen enough guys come off the ice and fall flat on their faces to know that when you have to give it up, it helps to have something planned for the future."

When you meet Bill Hay, the first thing that strikes you about him is his size – big shoulders, big face, big handshake. Big presence, all around. His authority and self-confidence and good humour seem to fill up a room in the same inescapable way that a cinematic close-up fills a screen, or a vapour extends to the limits of its enclosure. His voice, too, is big – not so much in volume as in resonance and depth. It is all but impossible to imagine him uttering anything like a scream. His hollering, if it were to erupt, would be far closer to a diesel engine at 6,000 rpms than to a siren. His red hair is grey at the temples, and his girth is somewhat matured, but his hairline is strong, and his ice-blue eyes are cheerfully youthful. In both spirit and physique, he is ideally suited to the oil industry – a big industry with a bold presence and substantial mien.

The only thing that has remained small about Bill over the years is his ego; he is as unpretentious and unassuming as ever, seemingly as unimpressed by his own considerable accomplishments as he was in his Stanley Cup days. His curriculum vitae (which he confines to a single page) lists a mere five items under "Career." The first is his term with the

Chicago Black Hawks (1958-67), the last his current position as senior vice-president of Bow Valley Resource Services in Calgary.

Although he is in charge of Bow Valley's oil-drilling operations, which gross $60 million a year, Bill's office on the sixteenth floor of the Cadillac Fairview Building might easily be mistaken for that of a mid-level civil servant. It is plainly furnished and unadorned by artifice. Its only luxury is its spectacular view across the western reaches of Calgary to the Rocky Mountains some fifty miles away. On a clear day in February, the snow-topped mountains – the "rock pile," as Bill calls them – make an unearthly line of rickrack along the horizon: 11,000-foot peaks rendered amiable and harmless by distance.

Unlike the work habitats of many former hockey stars, Bill's office bears no evidence of past athletic glory. "My playing days never even come to mind anymore," he says, with a conclusive shake of the head. "I can go for months on end and not give the Stanley Cup or the Calder Trophy or any of those things a thought." Suddenly Bill is laughing: "I have a problem remembering what I did yesterday, let alone twenty-five years ago. Some people still remember me as a hockey player and seem to enjoy doing that. But it's what's going on today and tomorrow that excites me. The scrapbook means zip."

Above his own protestations, Bill concedes that his days with the Black Hawks have given him "a good solid footing" for his extensive volunteer work in amateur hockey. Among other things, he is the current chairman of the Olympic Saddledome Foundation, a community-based group that operates the Calgary Saddledome; a director of Hockey Canada, responsible for the country's national hockey program; a member of the selection committee of the Hockey Hall of Fame; and a director of the Canada Special Olympics.

Beyond his volunteer work – his "fun," as Bill calls it – he regularly puts in a ten-hour day in the oil patch, where he commands the largest collection of shallow-drilling rigs in the country. "We also have deep-drilling rigs," he notes, "but those are contracted out to the Shells, the Gulfs, the Mobils, anybody who wants to drill for oil or natural gas."

During the early 1980s, Bill spent more time on the road than he had ever spent as a hockey player: two weeks out of four. But with the crumbling of the oil market in 1986 came a curtailment of Bow Valley's international operations and a corresponding curtailment of Bill's trips to exotic outposts such as Algeria, Pakistan, China, Thailand, and Indonesia. "Here at home, I had to lay off nearly 80 per cent of our people," he says regretfully. "It was hard; I didn't like doing it. I've always been on the side of the underdog. But considering that our deep-drilling rigs were profiting a million dollars a month at one point and are now lucky to make a million a year, we didn't have many options."

Boom or bust, Bill is vigorous in his affection for the oil industry. "Really, I just love it," he enthuses. "I like the people. Good people. Couldn't do better. I love it just as much as I ever loved hockey."

As Donald Hay emerged from infancy during the mid-1960s, the extent of his handicaps began to reveal themselves. "One of his arms was quite crippled," says Nancy, "and one leg was slightly shorter than the other. His co-ordination was poor, and his learning capabilities were severely affected, although he could walk and talk. But his biggest problem was that he had seizures. By the time he reached five or six he was having up to twenty or thirty of these seizures a day. I took him to doctors here in Calgary, and I always got the same story; there was very little they could do for him."

Nancy Hay is an elegant, pretty woman, with short dark hair and an engaging smile. She is open and hard-working and apparently unintimidated by the truth, in whatever form it takes.

As Bill's career developed in the oil business, her career, too, was taking shape. Slowly. And not without a great deal of deeply personal sacrifice. For the first fifteen years of her son Donald's life, she devoted every available hour to his well-being and care. At the same time, she fretted that her daughters, Pam and Penny, were being deprived of their fair share of parental attention and emotion. "Donald's life has affected everything we've done since he was born," she says without a trace of resentment, "– our community life, our family life, and certainly our emotional life. In emotional terms I know that it was as hard on Bill as it was on me through the early years. But in the day-to-day workings of our lives, it probably had more effect on me, because I had to give the care, and I had to talk to the care workers and the doctors. The onus was on me a lot of the time."

In 1968, when Donald was six, Nancy happened upon a magazine article about a child with Sturge Webber Syndrome who had undergone radical but beneficial brain surgery. "So I phoned our doctor, who followed up on the information I gave her, and we ended up taking Donald down to the Hospital for Sick Children in Toronto. And he had what is called a hemispherectomy, which removes the diseased half of the brain. This was supposed to eliminate the seizures, and it was expected that the other half of the brain would take over. If the operation is done early in a child's life, he can live perfectly normally and can have an average IQ. But because Donald was six, there were risks involved, one of which was paralysis. It was terribly serious surgery."

The initial results of Donald's operation were positive, and when he emerged at length from the hospital in Toronto, his seizures were under control. "It wasn't until three years later," says Nancy, "that he began to show signs of a problem – he'd fall down, lose his balance. There was blood in the spinal column. We'd known before the surgery that this could occur, but we'd had the choice of problems like this or of him ending up a vegetable – the seizures were literally destroying him. So this was certainly the lesser of the evils, and he did have two or three good years.

"When his skull cavity started filling up with fluid, the doctors installed shunts to drain it off. But in the meantime, he was losing weight; he was just wasting away."

Bill says, "Then we got him eating better. Every Saturday I'd take him out to McDonald's – first a nibble, then a bite, then a burger. But in trying to get him to eat, I was eating so much myself that I went from 190 up to 250 pounds. But I was having fun all the way. Eventually, we got him eating pretty well, but then the shunts that drained the skull cavity started plugging up, and it affected his legs so that he couldn't walk."

Throughout the mid-1970s, Donald's condition deteriorated. "The doctors told me that if we wanted to we could put him into a permanent-care institution," says Nancy. "But we wanted to have him at home for as long as we could. Then one day out at the cottage in B.C., his condition got so bad that I was afraid we were going to lose him, so I brought him into Calgary and had him admitted to hospital."

Within days, Donald, who was now twelve years old, lapsed into a semi-coma and remained that way for nearly a year, being fed intravenously. "There was really nothing the doctors could do," says Nancy. "It was just a matter of biding our time, hoping that he'd get better, even in the face of an absolutely dreadful prognosis."

"I'd go and sit with him every day," says Bill. "I'd hold his hand, and I'd talk to him. We were still looking on the bright side. Then one day, as I was sitting there holding his hand, I felt him give my finger a little squeeze, just a little pressure, and even though he was still only partially conscious, I knew that he was going to come round, that he'd be all right."

Nancy says, "This was when our daughters were in their early teenage years, which I'm afraid are a bit of a blur for me, because we were focusing so much on Donald. That was always difficult – to spread the attention to all the kids, not to pay *too* much attention to Donald, who really needed full-time care. But really our girls went through their teenage years on their own. I was at the hospital every day, and Bill's career was going crazy – he was working extremely long hours. The wonderful thing about the girls was the way they were able to flow with our difficulties – they always handled themselves so well with their handicapped brother. As far as they were concerned he was going to be treated like anybody else. They were never ashamed of him, and never tried to hide the fact that they had a brother with a problem. They included him in everything. And they were always so optimistic! And so was *Donald* – he was such an up kind of kid. He's always had a very good sense of humour. I've learned an awful lot from all of them. They turned me into an eternal optimist. It's been the key to my survival."

By a happy combination of medical treatment and providence – and against heavy odds – Donald eventually rallied, as Bill had predicted, and was able to leave hospital in a wheelchair. After several months, however, Nancy and Bill were faced with an agonizing decision: whether or not to keep Donald at home, which would have meant constant care, or place him in an appropriate institution. "I found myself being overly protective to begin with," says Nancy. "You can't help it with a child like that. But then we decided that he might be all right in another environment, and we tried him in an extended-care facility, then another one, neither of which were very satisfactory. So in 1980 we tried him in a group home, where he's lived ever since. There are six people in the home, although right now we're trying to get the number reduced to four so that he has more of a family atmosphere. I'd have to say that, all in all, he's made the adjustment to the new situation better than we have. Because for us, no matter how hard we fight it, there's a guilt feeling that he should have the same quality of life that we have. Finally, we've just had to accept that it can't happen, although certainly there were times when we felt we should simply devote our whole lives to him. It affected Bill's and *my* relationship for a while. I guess I was slightly resentful that Bill was able to carry on his career, while I was providing constant care at home and at the hospital. Not that he wasn't terribly supportive – he was. It's just that I had trouble dealing with our respective roles in all this. And it was a long time before I realized that the way to deal with my problems wasn't to stew about them but to make changes. I had to come to terms with the fact that I could *not* devote my whole life to Donald, that I had a husband and two daughters and of course *myself* to attend to."

In September of 1982, at the age of forty-four, Nancy returned to school full-time, enrolling in the social work program at Mount Royal College in Calgary. "I hadn't been there long," she says, "when I came to the realization that what most of the beneficiaries of our social programs needed was *money* to get them out of the ruts they're in. I'm talking about all the people with difficulties, the thousands on welfare, for instance, who'd like to pull up their socks but can't because all their resources and energy are going into merely surviving from one day to the next. They have nothing left when it comes to improving their circumstances. And the workers themselves need more money for their programs if they're going to accomplish anything. I began to think that maybe I should get into the fund-raising field, that maybe that was where I could do the most good."

One day, toward the end of her second year at school, Nancy received a phone call from a friend who explained that she was trying to get a few people together to start a Calgary Ronald McDonald House (a residence for out-of-town families whose children are hospitalized in the city). "Having taken a child to a hospital out of town, and having hung around for six weeks, I thought this was wonderful," says Nancy. "I went to a meeting, and it was the beginning of a transition into a year and a half of full-time fund-raising for me. We opened the house three years ago, and I was thrilled.

"Since then I've been involved in a number of community fund-raisers, and I've felt productive, although I never went back to finish my degree. At the moment, I'm on the board of Ronald McDonald House and the board of Calgary Residential Services, the agency that runs Donald's group home. Right now, we're trying to get government funding to build some new homes." Nancy is also involved in raising funds for the Cerebral Palsy Association and recently started fundraising for the Canadian Cancer Society. "There's a lot to do out there if you want to do it," she says.

Today, at twenty-seven, Donald attends a sheltered workshop during the week and comes home to Nancy and Bill on weekends. He weighs 120 pounds and is permanently confined to a wheelchair. "His physical difficulties outweigh his mental difficulties," says Nancy. "But he never complains about his condition. In fact, he never says much at all about it, except for the odd time when I've heard him say, 'Gee, I wish I could walk.' But by and large, he's a happy, well-adjusted person."

"We have lots of fun with him," says Bill, who has become Donald's major care-giver now that Nancy can no longer lift him. "We get something going every weekend – in town, out of town, always something." A favourite weekend destination is the family's cedar log cabin at Lake Windermere between Fairmont Hotsprings and Radium Hotsprings in the mountains of British Columbia. It is a place that Nancy and Bill began building in 1958, after Bill's first season with the Black Hawks. "We bought the lot for I think $500," says Nancy (Bill says $1,000), "and every year we'd spend Bill's playoff bonuses pouring another slab on the foundation and adding another room. Any extra money always went out to the lake. It's kind of a special place – the kids have always spent their summers there. The girls worked out there as teenagers – in restaurants, as lifeguards, whatever."

"We were out there last weekend," says Bill. "We picked Donald up at the group home at five o'clock Friday in the van, bought some junk food, and away we went. Donald likes country music, so I have some tapes that I put on. Nancy sits in the back, and we chat, listen to the tapes, eat the garbage. Sometimes we stop at Banff, sometimes not. It's an easy three-hour drive through the mountains. We look at the

A young Eddie Shack, in an official
Toronto Maple Leafs photograph.

Ed and his daughter, Cathy, at the
Toronto Maple Leaf Christmas
party, 1964.

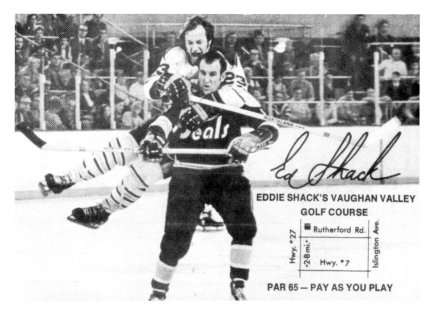

EDDIE SHACK'S VAUGHAN VALLEY
GOLF COURSE

Rutherford Rd.

Hwy. #27

·2·8 mi.·

Hwy. #7

Islington Ave.

PAR 65 — PAY AS YOU PLAY

Eddie greets an old friend.

Ed and Norma Shack, 1978.

Gump as a second year pro with
the Saskatoon Quakers, 1951.

Doreen and Gump, 1984.

Gump finished his career with the
Minnesota North Stars.

Bill Hay joined the Chicago Black Hawks in 1959.

Nancy and Bill, 1989.

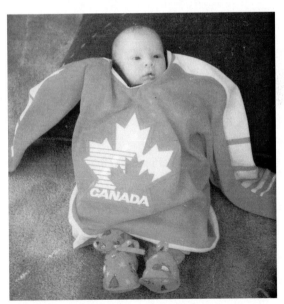

The Hays' first grandson, Billy D. Brown, sporting
a national team sweater and booties.

Phil, Gordie, and Bobby prior to a "masters" game, 1983.

Cherise, Donna, and Phil Esposito.

The Boomer (right), with teammates Dickie Moore and
Jean Beliveau, during his fifty-goal season of 1960.

Marlene was about to launch a professional skating career when she met Bernie. This picture was taken the day before their wedding.

Boom and Marlene, happy to be in Atlanta.

animals – elk, deer, the odd bear in the summertime; sometimes mountain sheep. We just winterized out there, so we can use the place year-round. Saturday morning, we go into the town of Windermere, look around. It's surprising the number of people Donald knows who Nancy and I don't know. They come up and say, 'Hi, Donald!' And he's laughing all the time, has a very good attitude. We'll buy donuts and so on, then return to the cabin about noon and put a movie on. Last Saturday was such a nice day that I put my skates on and went for an hour's skate around the lake. In the evening we'll often watch TV – Donald likes action, but he doesn't like hockey, although he's aware of my career a bit, because he knows he was born in Chicago and because, when we're together, people often come up to me and talk hockey. We were out at Windermere over Christmas, our first Christmas there, and that was a terrific holiday. We had the ice in front for skating – we'd park the van on the ice for a change shack, and Donald would be in it, blowing the whistle, and the girls and their husbands and Pam's kids would be in and out getting warm. It was beautiful."

On weekends when they don't go to the lake, Bill often takes Donald to an indoor shopping mall on Saturday morning. "We'll move around, have a slurpee, laugh all the time," says Bill. "The funny thing I notice is that people walking around us are always nervous to look at Donald because of his handicap, in case they seem to be staring. They don't know what he's laughing at – he's laughing because of what I'm saying to him. But every one of those people starts to chuckle as they walk by. One thing I'll say about Donald: he's never cried, even through the hardest operations. We cried some along the way. It was just so difficult sometimes not to be able to do anything for him."

Bill and Nancy's responsibilities are significantly lightened these days by the faithful support of their daughters and son-in-laws. "They're all wonderfully attentive," says Nancy. "Penny and Grant live near the group home and drop in on Donald all the time. And if we're out of town, Pam and Dan will have Donald over for dinner, for an evening, whatever. They just call up Handi-bus, and he's on his way. It's been interesting to watch Pam's three-year-old relating to Donald in the wheelchair. At first he was afraid of the chair, but then he figured out that it had wheels like a toy. The person in it was still not quite comprehensible to him, but then gradually he began to relate to Donald, too. Now their relationship is very relaxed."

Bill points to the family's closeness, and to the way Pam and Penny have turned out, as evidence that Nancy's one-time doubts about the quality of mothering she was able to give the girls were unfounded. "They're both remarkably close to their mother," he says. "In fact, they're probably *better* people for having gone through what they did."

The girls' closeness to Nancy took an amusing twist last summer when the three entered a team triathlon event near Windermere. "I did the biking, they did the swimming and running," says Nancy. "I got to the little spot where all the bikers were waiting in their rubber pants and their special shoes and with their fancy bikes, and I had my little five-speed with my purse on the back – Bill loves to describe the scene; he couldn't believe it. A fellow turned to me and said, 'Lady, you can't park your bike here; this is a race.' I said, 'Well, I'm in it.' Fortunately for me, Pam is a pretty good swimmer. She got out of the water I think ninth in a field of 100, so I had the satisfaction of taking off in front of all these hotshots. I came third from last, but I did finish. Thirty miles."

Among the family's myriad group activities, one of the most cherished is an annual event that goes back to 1976 when Bill was president of the Calgary Cowboys of the World Hockey Association. "The team folded that year," says Bill, "and I went down to say good-bye to the general manager, Joe Crozier, and there was a fellow with a station wagon by the arena, the old Corral, and he was loading all the leftover scarves and toques and trinkets and so on that the team had had for sale at the concession stands. I said to Joe,

'What's that guy doing?' And he said, 'He bought all that stuff for fifty cents on the dollar.' And I said, 'Well, I'd like to buy that stuff; I've got a better use for it than he has.' So the following Christmas I dressed up in a Santa Claus costume, and Donald and I went around to the various medical-care homes and facilities where he'd lived after he returned from his first big operation in Toronto, and we gave away these toques and scarves and so on to the kids. And that developed into quite a Christmas event. In subsequent years Pam and Penny and their friends would go with us when we loaded up the van. I had five years' worth of Cowboy stuff. Then as we started running out, I'd buy stuff, and we'd get some from Team Canada and the Flames. We go every year – with the grandchildren now – and we make our rounds. Christmas Eve at five o'clock. Last year, we started off going to the homes of Pam's and Penny's friends, to see their kids, then we went to the Foothills Hospital, then on to McDonald's, where we had little street kids right upside down in the bag, looking over the prizes."

Bill pauses momentarily, smiles, and says, "Some people might think that our lives have been restricted because of Donald, and I won't say they haven't at times – it's never been easy. But overall our lives have been far *broader* because of him. He's opened our eyes to things we never would have seen otherwise. We've learned a lot. And we've had fun, too. It all depends on how you view the world."

4

• • • • • • • • • • • •

IN THE CAPITAL OF
THE WORLD

It was a mild afternoon in mid-March, nearly seventy days before the fall of the axe – before the New York *Daily News* would run the unforgiving headline: ESPO'S A GONER. Yet even then, ten weeks before the fact, Phil Esposito had an uncanny suspicion that his marriage to the Rangers was unlikely to last. And he didn't hesitate to say so as I sat with him in his office on the fourth floor of Madison Square Garden.

At one point, as he delivered a particularly dark assessment of the nature of his work, he stopped mid-sentence and said, "When's this book coming out?"

"In October," I told him.

"Good," he said, "I'll probably be out of here by then – I'm almost sure I will." A journalist's dream: the liberated subject who can, and will, say what he wants with impunity.

The only thing Phil didn't foresee that day was the harsh means of his departure after three years as general manager of the New York Rangers. "I imagine when it happens I'll just walk away from it," he said, "– pack up and leave."

But not all aspects of Phil's perspective were entirely in sync that afternoon. Within ten minutes of his revelations about quitting, he declared that he would one day lead the

Rangers to the Stanley Cup. It was no idle boast. He was as certain of it as if it had been revealed to him from above. "That's the goal," he said. "That's what I'm building toward."

When I arrived at Phil's office that day, he was in the middle of a dramatic long-distance telephone conversation, objecting passionately to a Toronto *Globe and Mail* article that had depicted him as "a typical New Yorker – loud, cocky and insensitive." As his objections gained momentum so did the volume of his voice, until he was all but shouting into the phone that New Yorkers were *not* the insensitive animals they were assumed to be; *that New Yorkers were not to be mistaken for the armies of rude New York taxi drivers, most of whom came from elsewhere anyway; that New Yorkers, contrary to their press image, are as sensitive and decent and humane as anybody anywhere, and that the next time such-and-such a writer badmouths New Yorkers and Phil Esposito he'd better be prepared to do it to Phil's face and not gutlessly behind his back, and* . . . well . . . yes . . . Phil was upset.

But having vented his anger, he set down the phone, becalmed, hospitable, and, indeed, quite unlike a rude New York taxi driver, who probably came from somewhere else anyway.

Phil himself came from somewhere else: Sault Ste. Marie, Ontario, a smallish northern city on the far eastern spur of Lake Superior, a place light years from the bustle and grime of Manhattan. And although he has not lived in the Soo for more than thirty years, he has far from outgrown the small-town viewpoint and habits with which he grew up. "It was funny when I started going to the theatre in New York," he smiled. "I'm so big I'd always be worrying about whether or not the guy behind me could see. Here was this forty-year-old kid from the Soo slouched way down in his seat so as not to block the view. I'd come out of the theatre all hunched over. My wife is a Bostonian; she'd say, 'Sit up, Phil! Don't worry about it! They'll see around you!' But I could never shake this uncomfortable feeling that I was spoiling it for somebody else. That's my small-town background. . . . And I hate standing in line. In the Soo, ten people was a big line-up; if I saw that big a crowd, I'd walk away, do something else. My father used to pack a lunch if he was going for a twenty-minute drive! Now, I drive two hours a day just to get to work and back. My father's rolling in his grave watching me.''

On this particular afternoon, Phil looked very New York-ish in fine Italian cap-toed shoes, black-and-white striped shirt with plain white collar, flowered silk tie, and an elegant black suit, double-breasted and impeccably tailored of wool and silk. His office, too, was a study in New Yorkish good taste: immense Sheraton desk; plush carpet; built-in bar and television; chesterfield; easy chairs; subtly recessed lighting. On a side table sat a small lamp, the base of which was a scaled-down replica of the Stanley Cup and with a shade bearing the logo of the New York Rangers.

The comfortable trappings notwithstanding, it was apparent that all was not well at 33rd and 7th Avenue. Phil was upset – deeply disturbed. The job was getting to him; the coach was getting to him; the players were getting to him; his bosses were getting to him. In fact, if one facet of his office, more than any other, hinted at his life within the Ranger organization in those latter days – a life slowly closing around him – it was (almost too obviously) that the place had no windows. "I have absolutely no outlets for my stress on this job," he admitted quietly at one point. "As a player I was able to release the pressures through the hockey itself. Here, all I do is absorb, absorb, absorb. Sometimes I don't know how I survive it. I should be getting some recreation, but I haven't got time. It should help me to get out to our home in the country, but as soon as I get there the phone starts ringing! I know one thing: I've got to find a vent. I keep thinking that if I get through this year I'll be all right. Then I figure I'll never make it through this year, that I'd just as soon pack it in. I mean hockey is such a *precarious* business, and I feel a hundred times more vulnerable as a GM than I ever did as a player. Every time we lose, I start to get doubts. Right now I'm thinking, Holy cripes, we've lost six out of our last seven games, we've been terrible, we're in a prolonged slump, our power play is horrendous, and I start imagining that I can *help* this power play. But I'm frustrated because I don't really know how to go about it – to help my coach, Michel Bergeron, without interfering, without sounding as if I'm trying to do his job for him. I mean, I respect him too much as a coach to force myself on him. And it's frustrating me. It's eating my guts out. The only way to get in there would be to *fire* Michel, and I don't want to do that. As a GM, you're supposed to be able to separate yourself from your coach, but for me that's impossible. I'm a second guesser by nature."

Phil was particularly bothered that afternoon by the way in which the pressures of his work were beginning to impinge on his life at home. He said, "The other day for the first time in a very long time, I allowed my frustrations to affect my relationship with my wife. And that's not fair – getting impatient with her over what's going on here. I was sorry about it. I sent her flowers. I even get impatient with my three-year-old daughter. The other night I called home, and when she answered the phone and wanted to talk, I said, 'Get Mommy!' And she said, 'Why?' I said, 'Just get her.' Then, of course, I felt guilty. I should have had time to talk to her. I feel guilty about what I do at work sometimes, too. In spite of my reputation for trading – and I'll admit I've made a lot of trades; what did the paper say, forty-two? – I don't *like* trading guys; it upsets their lives something awful. I feel badly about it. But if I say that, I'm accused of being a phony, of grandstanding. One thing I've learned about this business, you really don't make a lot of friends."

Listening to Phil describe a typical day in his life as a GM – the mere nuts and bolts of the job, minus the larger emotional pressures – was, in itself, enough to elevate blood pressure: "Start out with an hour's freeway driving," he said. "Then maybe three or four meetings with various people – my boss, my coach, an agent, p.r. people. This morning I spent a *very* tough two hours with an agent, hammering out a contract. I might spend six or seven hours on the phone in a given day. Sometimes more. On a game day, I don't get home till about midnight, at which point I'll often turn on the TV and watch more hockey. Then maybe I'll be on the phone with some-body from the West – Rogie Vachon in L.A., Pat Quinn in Vancouver, Glen Sather in Edmonton. It's often three a.m. before I get to bed."

The previous night (not a game night), Phil had watched parts of four NHL games on television and fielded a dozen or more work-related phone calls, two of them lasting an hour or more. "I don't even *like* the telephone," he grimaced, "but I'm on it all the time! I can't get off it! It's part of the job! I've even got one in my car! In the summer, I take a portable with me to the golf course! In fact, I was on the golf course last year when I got a call from Czechoslovakia, telling me that this Czech player Horova was coming over. He wanted to know what I was willing to pay him! On the golf course! I've had calls from agents at two in the morning!"

Phil estimated that, between the phone and the television, he was being robbed of perhaps 80 per cent of the time that he might otherwise spend happily with his wife and daughter. "Last weekend, my little girl said to me, 'Daddy, do we *have* to watch hockey again?' And the answer is, Yes, it's part of being a GM. I have to know the league inside out if I'm going to trade successfully. It's a twenty-four-hour-a-day job. Seven days a week."

Phil's life in New York began when he was traded from the Boston Bruins to the New York Rangers in 1975. He had been perhaps the greatest forward in the history of the Bruin franchise. During nine years with the team, he won five scoring championships, two Stanley Cups, and two Hart Trophies as the league's most valuable player. He was named to eight all-star teams and, in 1970-71, scored a then-incon-ceivable 76 goals (152 points). "The thing about Phil," said a former teammate, "was that he wasn't a pretty skater like Orr or Hull. He kind of lumbered along, and for that reason he never got quite the acclaim he deserved. But once he was near the net, nobody was better. If you could get the puck to him, he was strong enough not just to control it but to muscle free and get a shot. A lot of fancy little forwards can dazzle the fans, but when it comes to doing what a forward is supposed to do, which is putting the puck behind the goalie, they can't do it. Phil could do it."

He could do it so well, in fact, that he had every reason to believe he'd be a Bruin forever. The story is told that when he got the news of his trade he sat on the bed in a Vancouver hotel room and wept. "If you tell me I'm traded to New York," he told his coach, Don Cherry, "I'll jump out that window."

According to Phil, it took him two years following the trade to accept that he was no longer a Bruin. "I'd look in the mirror with the New York sweater on, and I'd say, Hey, wait a minute – where's the Boston crest? When finally I did accept that I was alive and well and living in New York, my first thought was, How on earth am I going to cope with all this *traffic*?"

Phil submits that his real acceptance of the Big Apple came when he and his wife Donna moved from the house they'd bought on Long Island to an apartment at 59th Street and Second Avenue. "From that point on we loved this city," he smiled. "Loved the restaurants, loved the theatre – I'd never attended the theatre. I got to like the musicals. I saw *Cats* twice – saw *They're Playing Our Song* three or four times. I went to numerous openings of Neil Simon plays because I got to know Neil through his producer, Manny Eisenberg. One night I invited Neil and his wife Marsha Mason to a hockey game. They came, and they liked it. Donna and I went out for dinner with them afterwards."

One morning in the middle of winter, 1981, Phil woke up with a feeling he had never experienced before: he was fed up with playing hockey. "I was supposed to go to practice that morning," he recalled, "and I said to Donna, 'Ya know, this is a drag.' She'd had no advance warning. I just didn't feel like it anymore. I'd always promised myself that if I stopped enjoying what I was doing I'd get out of it. And I'd stopped enjoying it. That was it.''

Donna contends that, well before his retirement, Phil had shown a distinct inclination toward front-office work. "I wouldn't exactly call it a vision of the future," she says, "but he used to say he'd like to be a general manager some day."

The first step to that goal came quickly when, a few days after calling it quits, Phil was invited to become the Rangers' assistant general manager under GM Craig Patrick. "That lasted three weeks," said Phil with unbridled disgust. "I didn't like it at all. I wanted to be involved, but I didn't *do* anything." Phil's relationship with his boss hit bottom one night when, during a game, he was yelling at a referee and was told by Patrick to keep quiet. "I turned to him, and I said, 'Whaddaya mean?' He said, 'We yell too much at them.' I said, 'It's part of the game, for cryin' out loud! I'm not swearing at him!' All I'd said was, 'Shake your head, your eyes are stuck! Get in the game!' Craig didn't *ask* me not to yell, he *told* me."

Following the game, Phil explained to Patrick that he didn't think their relationship was going to work. "I said, 'I like you very much, Craig, but unless I leave now I'm going to start second guessing you, and I don't want to do that.' And I also knew that I had a broadcasting job if I wanted it. Some time before, I'd been asked by Sonny Werblin, the head man here at Gulf Sports – they own the Rangers – if I'd be interested in broadcasting Ranger games when I finished playing. So the following season I started that."

During five years as a broadcaster, Phil also cast his net in several other occupational directions, one of which was restaurant ownership. "We called the place 'Sticks,' " he said. "It was on 79th Street, and, as far as the food and atmosphere went, it was a good place – we had line-ups outside. But after about a year, Bang, I found out that my partner – a guy to whom I'd given my trust and who was running the day-today operation – was robbing the place blind. Suddenly, he took off, just vanished, and we had to close down. I paid off my part of the loan that we'd taken out to finance the place, and now I'm stuck paying his part, too, because I'm Phil Esposito; I have a reputation to protect. The bank can't find this guy. 'Sticks' was a nice place and all that, but I'm not the type of guy to hang around a restaurant – I'm not a big partier; I'm a married man. To really watch what was going on I'd have had to be there all the time. Live and learn. That was a very expensive lesson. I lost a lot of money."

Phil also lost money, at least initially, on his investment in the Sault Ste. Marie Greyhounds, a Junior hockey team, one of whose founders was Phil's father. Although he and his partners recently sold the team at a reported profit, they endured several years of heavy losses, including a one-year deficit in excess of $100,000.

Phil got involved as well in a designer clothing operation called Colors and was on the verge of introducing a range of big-and-tall clothes called "the Espo line" when the company was sold and Phil was dropped from its plans. He said, "I didn't have money in that one, just my name. When you get down to it, I really don't have a whole lot to sell except Phil Esposito. My name is good, and I owe that to hockey – I know that. And I *protect* my name and image. For instance, if Donna and I go to a party and there are drugs around, we get outa there."

As their various business ventures were ravelling and un-ravelling during the early and mid-1980s, Phil and Donna put a prodigious amount of time and effort into the creation of the Phil Esposito Foundation, set up to help former players who were down on their luck. "We worked day and night to get it going," says Donna. "And it wasn't that we got paid, either. In fact, it cost us money. Phil simply decided that he wanted to give something back to the game. We completely devoted ourselves to it. I worked behind the scenes, book-keeping, letter-writing, and so on. Phil took care of the public end. It was wonderful. It worked. I mean, there are a lot of ex-players who are lost – they don't *have* the ambition that a guy like Phil has. And certainly no one's knocking at their door saying, 'What would you like to do with your life? – let us help you.' A lot of them turn to drinking or drugs. They've lost something that is very important to them. Suddenly they're not a part of this big family of players, with everything scheduled and organized for them. And of course most of them are too proud to ask for help. They walk into restaurants, and the manager says, 'Oh, come on in! Great to see you!' They're treated like celebrities, and they're ashamed to admit they're hurting. Their dignity is on the line. The foundation *helped* them. It allowed them to keep their troubles within the family, get turned around, and go out to face the world without anybody knowing what was happening. We put on hockey games and tournaments to raise money. And we got a lot of generous donations."

Phil said, "I never called the games old-timers' games. I called the guys Masters of Hockey. I thought it was asinine to call Bobby Orr an old-timer. And I didn't feel like an old-timer myself. We rented the Garden for $65,000 one time – that's what it cost to rent the place for one game – and we ended up making $60,000. Then we went to Maple Leaf Gardens and made $80,000. In the end, we got eighty guys jobs and gave financial help to a lot of others, including a number of guys who were sick and unable to work. Once, we flew a fella's family to him because he needed a blood transfusion, and only they could supply the blood."

Eventually, Phil approached the National Hockey League and attempted to get it involved with the foundation. "We needed a broader base for operating the thing," he said. But the league would have nothing to do with it. "And it seemed they were fighting it just because it was me," said Phil. "They seemed to imply that the only reason I was doing this was for my own glorification, or to make a dollar, or something, which was completely untrue and which of course made Donna and I feel terrible after all the work we'd put in. I said, 'Call it the National Hockey League Foundation, I don't care.'

The only reason I called it the Phil Esposito Foundation in the first place was so that people would associate it with a name they recognized and would be more likely to support it. One time I went to meet with [NHL president] John Ziegler, and he said, 'Well, Phil, we do have a retirement fund; we call it a Crisis Fund. It helps guys out a little if they're in trouble, pays for funerals, that sort of thing.' I said, 'John, why is that news to me? How come I've never heard of this fund; I've been in the league twenty-five years! Why is it such a secret?' He said, 'Well, we don't like to toot our own horn about it.'

In the end, Phil and Donna allowed the foundation to lapse. "Without help," Phil said, "we just couldn't keep it going. The good thing that came of it is that every NHL team has now started an alumni association; they put on games and try to take care of their own people. Some of the owners pitch in, too."

In February of 1986, Phil was approached by the Rangers' owners, who asked quietly whether he'd be interested in becoming the team's general manager. Craig Patrick still held the post but would be fired within months. When the job was offered formally to Phil in June, he took it. Although he asked for a five-year contract he was permitted only three years. He said, "My thinking was that it would take five years to turn the team around, to make it what I wanted it to be. One thing I was able to get in the contract was that I had the complete right to hire and fire coaches, scouts, players, whoever. They didn't like it, but they put it in there." Phil noted, however, that he never actually had that freedom. "And that bothered me," he said. "I felt I needed it to do a proper job."

It also bothered Phil that the media hounded him at times over his penchant for making trades. He said, "I told them at a press conference the day I took the job, 'Hold onto your hats, folks. I'm going to do a lot of things here, and I'm going to do them quickly. You're going to think I'm insane, but I have a purpose. We're going to win here.' I explained this all to them, but then the minute I began making trades they started howling, *Esposito has no rhyme or reason! He's going off in all directions!* It was only when the team started moving up in the standings that they started talking differently. Since *as far back as I can remember,* I've always had to *prove* myself, no matter what I've done. I scored seventy-six goals in 1971, and yet nobody thought I was a great player until after the '72 series with the Russians. The question was, How good will he be without Bobby Orr? – Bobby was hurt for the series. I did just fine. . . . I had to prove myself again during my first year as a broadcaster. I had people saying, I can't believe the way he talks on the air! He can't *talk* that way on the air! I used to talk exactly the way I talk in day-to-day life – right off the cuff. Honest commentary. My producer used to get livid! He didn't like that style. Then they all realized that it was working, that people liked it.

"Now I'm being doubted as a GM. Nothing comes easy to me – it's all hard work."

Asked about the effects of the New York environment on his personality, Phil conceded that it has altered, perhaps toughened him. "Although I think becoming a general manager has changed me more than the city has," he said. "It's made me into a totally obsessive workaholic. New York itself is often misunderstood. When people think of it they think only of the muggings and murders and so on. But most of New York is beautiful – it's gorgeous! And the surrounding area is beautiful. Our area, up around Bedford Village, is fantastic! We've got over four acres of land. I was up at 5:30 this morning, and there were three deer in my backyard. Don't get me wrong – New York will eat you up and spit you out if you're not tough. Mentally tough. That's what you've got to be. But no matter *where* you are, or what you do, you've got to be strong mentally to succeed. There's more pressure in New York for one reason only – the pace of the city. Everything is fast here. Everything *has* to be fast here, because it's the capital of the world, at least as far as I'm concerned. Economically, for sure. New York runs the world. If you're not quick, you're going to get gobbled up."

Three hours after I spoke to Phil that afternoon, the Rangers faced off against the Winnipeg Jets a few hundred feet from Phil's office. They were gobbled up, losing decisively to a team that they should have handled with ease. It was their seventh loss in eight games. A strong season thus far was beginning to crumble.

In the aftermath of the game, the Ranger dressing room was like the Seventh Salon of the Masque of the Red Death. The only missing factor was Death itself. A half-dozen reporters tiptoed around, daring not ask their questions too loudly for fear of violating the solemnity of the hour. Even in the corridor outside there was a festering, viral gloom in the air. Team officials and functionaries, their faces a foot long, padded gravely about, while Phil met in an anteroom with his coaches and several senior players. The only people seemingly unaffected were a few of the younger Rangers, who emerged from the dressing room chirping among themselves, two or three of them exchanging jocular pleasantries with members of the Jets, who were filing from their own room down the hall.

Presently, Phil emerged from his private tête-à-tête, showing the strain of a long day but nonetheless polite to those around him. He stopped in briefly at a reception for goaltender Ed Giacomin, whose number had been retired in a pre-game ceremony, and ten minutes later was at the wheel of his compact Lincoln, peeling north out of Manhattan.

It is an hour's drive from the Garden to Phil and Donna's home in Upper Westchester County, and for the first few miles of the drive Phil said little. But as he hit the south Bronx his frustration over the evening's carnage began to vent itself. "A game like that just upsets me *so much*," he said. "I feel *angry* at the effort my players put out, and at the fact that they weren't properly prepared mentally. We didn't have *one guy* out here tonight who was into the game. *Not one guy.* That's the coach's fault. It's his job to get these guys ready. And I'm

angry at him for not going in there after the second period
and blasting them. He should have been in there losing his
marbles, throwing things at the wall. Sometimes players
respond to that. I kept saying to myself, Why isn't he doing
this? I know he wasn't because I was down at the dressing
room. I wanted to do it myself, but it's not my place. So what
do I do? I call Donna. She says, 'You sound tense – are you
losing?' She doesn't watch it on TV; she's not a hockey fan at
all. She used to come to the games when I was playing, but
she's never cared that much. And I prefer it that way. She's
always been there for me when I needed her, but it's best for
our marriage that she doesn't become part of this hockey
scene. Then the pressure would be double for me. She'd
come to the games, and I'd worry about her. We'd be driving
home, and she'd be talking hockey – I'd go crazy. She'd point
things out about the game – maybe bad things, so-and-so
played awful, and she'd be right. I don't need that. I need
somebody just to sit and listen."

Phil paused for a moment and, as if uttering a perfectly
sequential thought, blurted, "You just can't *blow* games to
vastly inferior teams!"

As we hit the I-684 at Yonkers, Phil began to relax, eventually asking me if I had my tape recorder handy. He said,
"We might as well put a few things down." The night was
mild, and he reached up and opened the roof vent.

Expressing himself boldly and genuinely, for better or
worse, has always been the mark of the man. And as we
proceeded north into Westchester County that night, his
conversation broadened until, before long, he was moving
fluently, indiscriminately, from one subject to another,
apparently enjoying the psychological release of random
chatter. Here is a sampling of the night's thoughts and
revelations:

ON THE 1972 SERIES WITH THE SOVIETS: "The experience
wasn't as pleasant for me as it was for a lot of the guys. I
thought the Russians were pigs – on the ice, I mean. Imagine

them kicking our players with their skates! It was war for me. I've said this before, and I'm not very proud of it because I've never even killed an animal – I don't know how people can kill in a war – but there's no doubt in my mind that I'd have killed to win that series. It scares me, but it's true. And we did win. Our problem was that we only trained for ten days before the first game. We used to train for *six weeks* for NHL games! We weren't in shape until we got to Russia for the final four games. We could have played ten more games in Russia, and we would have won them all. We not only got into condition, we became a team, a team possessed, a team that refused to lose. I'd never reached that kind of emotional high before and have never reached it again."

ON PHYSICAL CONDITIONING: "During my playing days, I never did anything when it came to exercise off the ice. In training camp when they used to run, I'd hide in the bushes and throw water on my face. And that stupid stationary bicycle – I *hated* that thing. What a waste of time! I did my training on the ice. I'd come into camp maybe ten pounds too heavy, and by the end of camp I'd be at my playing weight, 210-212.

"My cardiovascular system is great. I had a test in Russia, and they couldn't believe how good my heart was. Two years ago I had another one – I've got the cardiovascular system of a twenty-five-year-old. It's hereditary. And I say that even though my dad died of a heart attack at sixty-three. He *ate* himself to death. He was only five-eleven, and he weighed 260. He ate sausages and salamis until they came out of his eyeballs. I eat junk but not the really bad kind – I eat popcorn."

ON RELAXATION: "The only relaxation I get anymore is golf, and that can be pretty intense in itself. But I like it. And yet I can't *play* it unless it's for money! I don't care if it's only a buck – I'll go for it. But if it's just for fun, I can take it or leave it."

ON HOCKEY STARDOM: "Sometimes I'm not sure there's all that much difference in talent between the stars and the lesser lights. But the guys with the most pride in what they do – with the most intensity and guts – come out on top. Take a guy like Gordie Howe – he's a very proud guy. No matter what he does, he takes pride in it. And that's done an awful lot for his career, both on and off the ice. I myself take a lot of pride in what I do. That's why I suffer so much over my work. I have full-scale anxiety attacks when things go wrong."

ON LUXURIOUS LIVING: "I need a good job because I like the good life, and I'm not ashamed to admit it. I love spending money. I figure, if you've gotta go, go first class or don't go at all. I'm not just talking about airplanes, but for nineteen years as a player I sat in 'economy,' and I'm so big that in those skinny little seats, with people beside me, I couldn't even lift my arm to eat. I used to promise myself that when it was all over I'd ride up front in comfort. Same with hotels – the teams used to stay in dives. We didn't have the best, believe me. I remember staying in a hotel in Washington that was absolutely the worst joint I've ever seen. It was freezing cold! And dirty! So I always take a good hotel when I travel. A Marriott or a Holiday Inn is just a room to me – I want a hotel to be like home. In New York, Donna and I like the Pierre – Donna took me there on my fortieth birthday; we had a suite. And we've stayed at the Plaza and at the Helmsley Palace – that was nice. . . . When I was broadcasting, one of the things I negotiated into my contract was that I always flew first class. They didn't want to give it to me, so I said, 'Okay, I'm not going to be a broadcaster then.' So they gave it to me."

Upper Westchester County is an area of narrow winding roads, of towns with shiplap houses, of cemeteries as old as the American Revolution. Its farms and villages, once a day's travel by stagecoach from Manhattan, over muddy roads, are now bedroom communities for the affluent slaves of New York. Mercedes-Benzes and BMWs sit in the lanes; pricey restaurants and fashion boutiques are the jewels of local commerce. This is not to suggest that twentieth-century gentrification has been unkind to the area: there are still neatly painted bandshells in the small-town parks, old wooden churches with proud spires on the main streets, unpainted sheds in the backyards. The grassy hills and dense stands of maple and oak are largely unmolested by civilization.

Although Phil and Donna's address is Mount Kisco, the town nearest their home is Bedford Village, a snoozy, anachronistic little place with backwater charm and no discernible industry. "I grew up in Swampscott, Massachusetts, just a short walk from the Atlantic," said Donna, on the day of my visit with her, "but even though there's no water here, this place has always reminded me of home. It's very New England – the houses, the white clapboard church with its steeple. When we built, I felt very comfortable up here."

The Espositos' house, designed by Donna, is an elegant structure built of grey-brown stone, with a large swimming pool out back and a scattering of exotic saplings on the hillside lawn in front. Except for that lawn and a rectangular clearing of perhaps two acres behind the house, the predominant surroundings are hardwood forest, heavily veined with horse trails. "Before we moved out here, I used to come out this way every day to ride," Donna said. "I still ride every morning. My horse, Sneakers, boards about a mile and a half from here. She and I compete; we're in what they call the Hunter division. We go around a course doing jumps, just small ones."

Donna, who appears to be in her mid-thirties, is a slim, pretty woman with longish blonde hair. She speaks in a gentle Bostonian accent and when asked about her background did not mention that she is a triplet. She is in many ways an ideal match for Phil – quiet, private, introspective, tending to bring forth a gentle side of him that many people do not get to see. The two met in California a dozen years ago, while Donna was working for Aetna Life and Casualty in San Francisco. "We'd been introduced years earlier in Boston," she said, "but I didn't remember it very well; Phil says he did. When we met again in California I thought his name sounded familiar, but maybe that was just because I was from Boston, and I would have heard it by chance on radio or television. I wasn't a hockey fan at all, and I'm still not, although I do appreciate the players' talents and the movement and excitement of the game."

Donna volunteered that she was attracted to Phil because of his "many-faceted" personality. "I realized right away," she said, "that he wasn't the sort of guy who was locked into one career or one frame of mind. He's a real individual – very outgoing, very confident. And very honourable and generous, too. Phil has a very good heart. All of these things impressed me."

Donna submitted that the same attributes enabled Phil to survive the transition out of active hockey without major disruptions. "The more you have going, the better off you are," she said. "If Phil ever left hockey completely, I'd have no worries about him. He goes into things so wholeheartedly, I'm sure he'd be a success at whatever he took up."

When the question was raised as to what he *might* take up if he left hockey completely, Phil reflected for a few seconds and said, "I'd probably do something in the public relations line. Right now I have a part-time p.r. job with the Sands Hotel and casino in Atlantic City, and I enjoy that. I drive over there from time to time – maybe once a month in summer, not so often in winter – and I meet the big players, do a little golfing. Sometimes I'll travel to Toronto or Montreal, wherever, and go to a party or a dinner put on by the Sands."

Confronted with the notion that his link to a major gambling establishment was somewhat out of whack with his concern for his public image, Phil was vociferous in explaining that the Sands is owned "not by mobsters" but by the reputable Pratt Corporation, owners of an international chain of hotels. "Why do people always think that gambling has to be tied in with drugs and so on?" he protested. "People who *work* for the Sands – or for any gambling outfit in New Jersey – have to get a licence. And I'll tell you, these employees are scrutinized before they get it. In my own case, the authorities went right through my records, and if I'd had one little bleep or blemish, I wouldn't have got a job. And the gamblers themselves aren't criminals! Most of them are wealthy lawyers or businessmen or brokers. Sure, there's the odd so-called shady character, but you get as many of them in Madison Square Garden as you do in Atlantic City. If I suspect somebody, I'll ask my bosses, and they might say, 'Yeah, stay away from him.' I mean, I don't even *go* around the gambling tables. I walk through, say Hi, and I'm gone. I stay up at the restaurant and the bar. Most of the time I'm in bed by midnight. But look at all this another way – do you know who the biggest promoters of gambling are? The *government*, that's who! They run more lotteries and gambling games than Atlantic City and Las Vegas put together!"

Defences and arguments aside, Phil's true vision of the future that day seemed closer to his family and to Bedford Village than to the gambling tables of Atlantic City. "What's important is right here," he said earnestly. "We've got our lives all tied up with this house and this community. We love the area. Donna's really enjoying it, and Cherise is at a great school. I was just over there to pick her up, and I watched her in the playground. It was fun! I never did that with my two daughters by my first wife – they're twenty-one and twenty-three now. As I was watching Cherise, I said to myself, I've gotta do whatever it takes to keep this going till I'm fifty-five (Phil is forty-eight now). By that time, I figure I'll be ready to let the work go, sell everything, do exactly what we want for the rest of our lives. On the other hand, if I feel I'm going to get sick, I'll cut out sooner. Worry is hard on me. When I get sick, it's generally because I'm worried. I'm not a *big* worrier – I don't worry about money, for instance. I always tell Donna, I can *get* money, because I'm not afraid to work. If we need something, I'll get it somehow. But sometimes I've got more than money on my mind."

Phil had more than money on his mind when, a month after my visit with him, he fired his coach, Michel Bergeron, starting a chain of events that would ultimately bring about his downfall as general manager of the New York Rangers. He himself took over as coach, leading the team through the final few games of the '88-89 season and into the Patrick Division playoffs against the Pittsburgh Penguins, a team with which the Rangers should have been evenly matched. As it turned out, they were not. They failed to win even a single game in the best-of-seven series and were the first team eliminated from the NHL playoffs. The common thinking was that, regardless of the Rangers' late-season slide in the standings, Phil had made a strategic error in firing his coach with the playoffs so near at hand; the upheaval had hurt the team's prospects. Apologists, however, say the Rangers would have done no better under Bergeron, given that the team's chances were already reduced by injuries to several key players.

On May 24, Phil's boss, Jack Diller, the executive vice-president of the Madison Square Garden Sports Group, entered Phil's office and announced that changes were being made and that Phil, too, was being fired. "I told him, 'Fine,' " said Phil. "He said, 'You don't seem that upset.' I said, 'I'm not. Whatever you think you have to do, you have to do. I did what *I* had to do when I fired Michel.' Then I said, 'Am I going to get paid?' He said, 'No problem.' See, I still had fifteen months to go in my contract."

On the day following the firing, the Toronto *Globe and Mail* speculated that Phil's contract was worth some $300,000 a year to him. The newspaper also speculated – and Phil agreed – that he had been fired not over his dismissal of Michel Bergeron but because Ranger executives felt he did not present the "corporate image" they considered appropriate to the general manager's role: too flamboyant, too outspoken, too much his own man. In a closing note, the story said that Phil and Donna were about to put their house up for sale.

Nearly five weeks passed before I spoke to Phil by phone. I had been reluctant to call, to disturb what I imagined was probably something of a wake in Bedford Village.

I could not have been more in error. Or more surprised to find Phil hale and chipper and bubbly with optimism about the future. "I've formed a new company," he announced. "Espac Associates. Contracting management."

Phil explained enthusiastically that Espac is a partnership linking him to the Scabia Construction Company of New York and Defeo Brothers Demolition of Boston. He said, "My job is to initiate business for these guys – construction, demolition, whatever people want. I guess you could say I'm a kind of agency. I've already contracted the construction of two new buildings. Having a great time. Great money, too. And of course I'm still getting paid by the Rangers."

Phil expressed no resentment toward his former employers, although he did admit to frustration that he had not been given the five years he felt he needed to put together a winner. "Other than that, I have no negative feelings about it," he said. "The stress is gone! I'm relaxed for a change. People come up to me and say, 'Phil, you look terrific!' I *feel* terrific."

The tough part, Phil allowed, would come in September, when for the first time in forty-three years he would not be revving up for a new hockey season. "I know I'm going to miss it terribly," he said. "And the further the winter goes along, the worse it's going to get. I just hope I can take it."

Was the house up for sale?

"Who said that?"

"The *Globe and Mail* said that *you* said it."

"What I said was that if another job in hockey came along, and it involved a move, *then* we'd put the house up for sale." Without skipping a beat, Phil revealed that if he *didn't* get back into hockey, he and Donna were thinking of buying a small farm somewhere. "Don't get me wrong," he said. "We love our place here. But it's way too big for the three of us.

We'd like a place where we can have some animals for Cherise and where Donna can keep her horse. We've been thinking about Florida, maybe even California. Could be anywhere, though."

Never one to think small, Phil disclosed that, if the dream of a farm came to pass, he hoped to construct a 500-yard golf fairway on the property. "I'd have a green at each end, and nine tees at various points along the sides. You could play to either green from each tee, giving you eighteen different approaches. . . . But, as I said, this is only if I don't get back into hockey."

And what were the chances of getting back into hockey?

"We'll just have to wait and see," said Phil.

In the meantime, was there anything he wanted to add to the story I was about to construct?

He thought for a moment, chuckled, and said, "Just tell the readers that if anybody needs a building put up, or needs one demolished, to let me know. I'll be happy to take care of it.

"Otherwise, that's about it."

5

Take the I-75 north out of Atlanta, drive for twenty minutes, and you'll find yourself in Marietta, Georgia, a sprawling patch of up-scale suburbia built on red Georgia clay and shaded by green Georgia pines. Marietta is a suburb of large parking lots, crowded shopping plazas, and, like every other place in Georgia, shocking summer heat (every enclosed space in the municipality is air-conditioned almost to the point of refrigeration). Signs of affluence are everywhere along the four-lane thoroughfares that circumscribe the residential subdivisions: swank corporate palaces, pricey restaurants and boutiques, up-market department stores such as Macy's and Rich's. The subdivisions themselves exude affluence, with their well-built houses and large lots.

One such subdivision – a cluster of forty or fifty homes with thick lawns and swaying pines – bears the name Woodlawn Common. It is an unlikely place to find a couple of expatriate Canadians (a far less likely place than, say, Florida or Arizona or California, where Canadians gather in herds). It is an especially unlikely place to find a couple once addicted to the cold-weather sport of ice-skating. Yet at the centre of

Woodlawn Common sits a luxurious, moderately sized house belonging to ex-Montrealers Bernie and Marlene Geoffrion.

The house and its lot are almost impossibly well kept; neither stick nor stone nor molecule of soil is out of place. The exterior walls are unblemished stucco, and the Bermuda grass lawn seems not so much mowed as shaved; it is as thick and soft as broadloom.

There are two cars in the Geoffrion driveway, a beige Cadillac Seville and a beige Mercedes 380 SL. His and hers. As you come up behind the cars, you notice that they are not quite typical luxury cars, in that each bears a discreet bumper sticker: one a message, "Jesus is Lord," the other a wordless emblem, the stylized fish symbolic of Christianity. Another message hangs above the door that leads into the house from the interior of the garage: "As for me and my house, we will serve the Lord."

The garage is no ordinary garage. Its floor is covered in green indoor-outdoor carpeting, and the work table along one wall supports a variety of elaborately decorated baskets in various stages of completion. The creations are Marlene's – manufactured in a dexterous, painstaking process, involving paints, lacquers, wicker, cotton bows, and chintz appliqués. She sells the finished products at a lucrative price to a growing number of private customers.

Even while she works, Marlene dresses in bright, fashionable clothes, in keeping with her upbeat personality. On this particular afternoon she is showing a modified pixie look – green velour pants, a green and white cotton sweater, troubadour boots. She is festooned in gold jewellery. She is a handsome, outgoing woman, a thoughtful woman, whose energetic beauty is internal as well as external. She is not only a complement but a pleasantly obliging foil to her husband's ever-present sense of humour and showmanship. Marlene observes casually that if Bernie had not become a hockey player he would probably have become an entertainer. To be sure, he is an actor – a walking catalogue of funnyfaces, gestures, mock put-downs, and *soto voce* asides. He is also, according to Marlene, an "absolute perfectionist," taking as much care with the placement of a stamp on an envelope as he takes with the cut and colour of his clothes or the state of his lawn. On almost any day of the year, he is impeccably dressed and deeply tanned; he gives the impression of having just stepped out of a travel ad.

Like Marlene, Bernie takes obvious pride in the plush decor, the signal oppulence of their home. He *enjoys* the thickly upholstered furniture, the ivory-coloured broadloom, the cathedral ceiling that soars above the living room to a height of twenty-five feet. Marlene has decorated the place in colours with names as euphonic as they are fashionable: "peaches & cream" and "seafoam green." There are floral arrangements throughout the house, as well as a variety of Marlene's baskets.

It is not until you reach the upstairs television room, however, that you get a hint of the source of the surrounding comforts. There, beneath the television, are videotaped highlights of the five Montreal Canadien Stanley Cup victories of the 1950s – victories in which Bernie played an integral role. More significantly, there are videos of the thirty-odd television commercials – both French and English – that Bernie has made for Miller Lite Beer. "Miller has been extremely good to Bernie," confides Marlene. And Bernie has been good to Miller. For well over a decade, he has been the brewery's chief advertising ambassador, as well as a sort of inspirational guru to its employees. There are a few Miller Lites in the Geoffrion refrigerator, and on the sitting-room wall is a large, Miller-sponsored drawing of Bernie. It is the master version of a smaller publicity print that Bernie signs and disperses to admirers. Beside the Lite beer logo in the print's lower right-hand corner, he frequently inscribes the words, "God loves you" and the Biblical reference "John 3:16."

Although affluent surroundings were not unknown to Marlene during her formative years, the couple's current circumstances are a far cry from those in which Bernie grew up in the east end of Montreal. And yet they are by no means beyond what he imagined for himself. For even in the depths of the Depression, when few Montrealers had any real prospects beyond the earning and spending of their next five dollars, little Bernie Geoffrion had a vision of the future. He had seen his dad try unsuccessfully to scrape a living out of the hard-scrabble of the restaurant trade, and he was determined that life would be different for him. He used to tell his mother, "I'm gonna make it big, Mom; I'm gonna make it very big."

Unlike many dreamers, Bernie fuelled his vision with a colossal power of will. His unlikely ascent into Junior hockey at the age of fourteen epitomizes that power. "The coach of the Concordia Juniors in Montreal asked me to try out, so I reported to camp," he says. "But after the first practice, the president of the team grabbed my stuff and threw it out the door. He said, 'You'll never make it. Get out!' I started to cry. But I came back the next day. And after practice he threw my stuff out again. He said, 'You're finished!' And I cried again. But again the next day I came back. I crept back in and got my stuff on before he saw me. Three times he threw me out after practice, but I never got discouraged. I kept saying, I'm going to make it, I'm going to make it, I'm going to make it.

"Did I make it? – I made it. I was the youngest player in the league that year. I scored twenty goals."

The same willpower is evident in Bernie's cultivation of the slapshot, which he invented at age twelve. Repeat: *Bernie Geoffrion invented the slapshot – the staple of the modern hockey player's arsenal – at the age of twelve!* One day when he was playing for Immaculate Conception School he misfired on what should have been an easy goal and was so incensed that he drew his stick back and gave the puck a vicious smack. He says, "I saw the thing take off, and it stuck in my head that maybe I could shoot that way! So every day after school I went out on the rink and fired 200 pucks. Nobody knew. I'd come down my right wing and let that thing go. Bang! Bang! Bang! But I never used it in a game until a couple of years later when I was sure I could score goals with it. When finally I used it in Junior, the goaltenders were ducking. They'd never seen anything like it."

When Bernie made a three-game trial appearance with the Montreal Canadiens late in the 1951 season, pro goaltenders, too, were caught off guard by his unconventional shooting weapon. He says, "My first game was against Chuck Rayner of the New York Rangers. In the second period, I beat him with a slapper; he never saw it. I was so happy I was crazy – dancing all over the ice. Next game against Chicago I scored on another slapper. Got another one the next day in New York."

The following season, Bernie scored thirty goals for the Canadiens and was named Rookie of the Year by the NHL. One of his rewards from the league was a silver tea service, the fate of which, twenty-five years later, exemplifies another facet of Bernie's personality: decisiveness. "It was all tarnished and we didn't want it on display anymore," he explains. "I said to Marlene, 'Let's go have it assessed – maybe it's worth something.' The price of silver was high then. I took it to a jeweller and was told it was worthless copper. I was so angry that the NHL had given us cheap junk I threw the tray in the garbage. And the teapot with it. And the cream and sugar, too."

In the world of professional hockey, where conformity and homogeneity are widely prized and practised, Bernie Geoffrion was (and is) something of a phenomenon – not only in terms of talent and will but in the quotidian practices that so often provide the truest window on a man's personality. On game days during the fifties and sixties, for instance, when most players napped through the afternoon, Bernie preferred to go into the basement of his home and listen to recordings of the great Enrico Caruso. While in New York, he gained sustenance at the Metropolitan Opera. ("I'd sit in the last row of a house that seats 5,000.") He himself is a singer of middling talent. "I once sang on a TV show with Danny Vaughan, Shirley Harmer, and Perry Como. When I got to the rehearsal, the producer said, 'Where's your music?' I said, 'What music?' The orchestra leader said, 'What key?' I said, 'The key to my house.' I sang 'C'est Magnifique.' Anything to make a buck. I cut a record once – it went nowhere." On one occasion, while he was with the Canadiens, Bernie sang at a resort at Mont Tremblant, Quebec. "All the guys were there – Rocket was there. He said, 'Bernie, are you sure you know the words? Are you sure you can do it?' I said, 'If I forget the words, I'll make them up.' I only knew seven songs. That was it. No requests. End of ballgame."

Marlene Geoffrion, too, is an unusual human being, with a tragic and disturbing past. She was three years old when they buried her illustrious father, Howie Morenz. Morenz had been the greatest hockey player of the 1920s and 1930s, and was often referred to as "the Babe Ruth of hockey." His somewhat mysterious death while recovering from a broken leg in a Montreal hospital in 1937 sent his wife Mary on a downward spiral into alcoholism, his daughter Marlene into a decade of pathos and sorrow. "My mother lost a lot of the insurance money that had come from my dad's death," Marlene recalls quietly. "Finally, they had to hold a benefit night for her at the Forum, so that she could afford to put her kids somewhere and go to work."

"Somewhere" turned out to be a Montreal orphanage, where for nearly three years Marlene pined for her mother's weekly visits.

In 1940, Mary Morenz met and married a millionaire, and Marlene was removed from the orphanage and brought home to live. She began attending a convent school. "I was the proverbial poor little rich girl. I had everything I wanted materially but very little spiritual support from my mother and stepfather."

Still suffering the loss of her first husband, Mary Morenz died of alcoholism at the age of forty-one. Fourteen-year-old Marlene continued to live with her stepfather, an older man.

Within months, she took up figure skating and gave herself to it with the same passionate energy that her future husband had given himself to hockey. She says, "I practised all winter after school and full-time during the summer. At the age of eighteen, when I was just about to turn professional – it was 1951, I guess – I was invited to put on a solo exhibiton at an ice carnival at the Montreal Forum. Just before I skated, several young hockey players were introduced to the crowd as the Canadiens' stars of the future."

Among the young stars was Bernie Geoffrion, recently dubbed "Boom Boom" in honour of his slapshot. "I skated out and tripped on a Dixie Cup top that someone had thrown, and went sliding across the ice on my backside," laughs Marlene. "I looked up and this gorgeous guy with bright blue eyes was smirking down at me.

"When I'd finished and had come out of the dressing room, here was my brother talking to this handsome creature who was on the ice when I fell. He said, 'Come here, Marlene – meet Boom Boom Geoffrion.' I wanted to get back at him, so I said, 'Boo Boo who?' "

Suffice it to say that love transcended ignition difficulties, and Marlene and Bernie were married in May of that year. Their first child, Linda, was born nine months later.

The Geoffrions today are a notably subdued version of the exciting young couple who met on the ice in 1951 and proceeded into a thunderbolt romance. Not that excitement has passed them by. As much as possible, they pass it by. Bernie is fifty-eight, Marlene fifty-six. They rise early in the morning – Boomer as early as five a.m. – and begin their day with a three-mile walk. "Boom golfs three days a week," says Marlene, "but he reserves Mondays and Thursdays for home, so that we can do things together. I do my baskets – Boom often helps me – and I like knitting. . . . Often we just sit and relax when we're together."

On Wednesday nights, the pair attends a mid-week worship service at Parin Church of God, and on Sundays they attend church twice, morning and evening. "We're really very private," says Marlene. "We don't like neighbours dropping in unannounced. We go to bed early. It's a quiet life, and we like it that way."

In the plush Geoffrion milieu, there is certainly no hint of the drama and commotion of the past. Everything is in its place – physically, emotionally, spiritually. And yet when Bernie and Marlene open their mouths and begin to reminisce, the feverish decades that followed their marriage gradually come to life: the fierce glories of the hockey wars; the bitter deceits that followed Bernie's retirement from the Montreal Canadiens in 1965; the pair's stirring conversion to Christianity. At times as he talks, Bernie rises to his feet and acts out a scene from his past – strutting, gesticulating, shunning an adversary, throwing an elbow. Marlene, too, becomes animated; her eyebrows lift, her hands flutter and flow.

Their lives together have been a novel, a drama – sometimes painful, sometimes funny, occasionally triumphal. They relate that drama with the authority of those who know who they are and where they've been. And, in this case, where they're going.

Bernie: As a young guy, my desire was so great, so intense, that by the time I was twenty-three I'd developed a stomach ulcer as big as a quarter. I used to vomit blood between periods, during games. Newspaper men used to say, Boomer's two men – one jovial, one moody. They didn't know I had the ulcer and that when it was burning I was in no mood to have fun. I was suffering.

Even so, my career developed. I loved playing for the Canadiens. For fourteen years they were good to me. It was what happened in 1964 that hurt. Actually, it started in 1962. The previous year, I'd had fifty goals, tied the Rocket's record; it was a big thing. Then in '62, I only had twenty-five or twenty-eight, which was still good in the old six-team league. But the Canadiens' management started to say I was going down hill. See, they knew that Yvan Cournoyer was coming up from Junior – he was a right winger, a good one, and they wanted him to take my place. Anyway, they said to me, "Boomer, what would you like to do when you finish hockey?" I said, "I'd like to coach." They said, "If you retire next year, you can coach the Quebec Aces." The Aces were the Canadiens' affiliate in the American League – Gerald Martineau was the owner; he was in thick with Premier Duplessis and all those guys in government.

I told them I wanted to coach, but for the time being I still wanted to play. And I did play another year or so. But they kept coming back with the coaching offer. So at thirty-four I said, "Okay, I'll take it – but on one condition: that I get to coach the Canadiens some day." David Molson, the owner, said, "Go to Quebec for two years, and you'll get the big team when you come back." They said Toe Blake would be quitting. I signed my retirement papers and told Marlene that I'd probably be coaching for fifteen years. My future was set.

I coached in Quebec for two seasons, and both years we finished first. And that was at a time when the American Hockey League was a real league – the Rochester Americans had half the Toronto Maple Leafs playing for them. I figured I'd done a job. I was on track.

Marlene: The night before we returned to Montreal after our second season in Quebec, the owner of the team, this guy Martineau, had us over for dinner and told Boom what a great job he'd done, and so on. The next morning on the road we stopped off at a restaurant to have breakfast with the kids, and Boom picked up a newspaper on the way out to the car. He glanced at it and he literally turned white. I said, "What's the matter?" He said, "Nothing." He folded up the paper when he got in, and I just figured he was in a bad mood over something he'd read. A while later I reached for the newspaper, and he grabbed it from me. But as he took it I saw the headline: BOOM BOOM GEOFFRION FIRED BY QUEBEC ACES.

Martineau *knew* he was going to fire him when we had dinner at his place. He'd already promised the job to an old friend. . . . When we reached Montreal, Boom phoned him and he just drilled the guy. The *insincerity* of some people in hockey is unbelievable! That was a really hard time for us, because Boom had done his best.

Bernie: In the back of my mind I knew Montreal would take care of me – they'd made a promise. But when a few weeks had passed, and they hadn't called, I told Marlene, "I've gotta do something!" So I went down to the Forum to see David Molson. I said, "I presume you've heard I lost my job. I'm coming to you about the promise you made me." He said, "Well, Toe Blake doesn't want to retire – sorry." They knew he wouldn't be retiring – I'm sure of it. But to get me out of Montreal, to make way for Cournoyer, they'd told me whatever I wanted to hear.

A few days later they offered me a coaching job with the Junior Canadiens – $6,000 a year, not even a living wage. I'd coached in the American League, and now I was being offered a Junior team! I got mad. I jumped up and told David Molson, "I'm coming out of retirement. Put my name in the waiver draft. You may not want me, but somebody will." Sure enough, they didn't put me on their eighteen-man protected list, didn't offer me zilch after I'd given them fourteen years' sweat and blood. Ballard offered me a four-year contract to go to Toronto, but New York had the first choice of unprotected players that year, and they drafted me. I met their general manager, Emile Francis, and I said, "Emile, I've got bad knees, a bad back, I'm old, I don't think I can make it." See, I didn't want to go to the Rangers; I wanted to go to Toronto. Emile said, "I don't care if you show up in a wheelchair – just show up."

A little while later I saw Dave Molson and I said, "I'm coming back to the Forum, and I'm going to whip your butt, Molson!" He got scared. He thought I was going to punch him. And I might have, too. Right then, I hated the Canadiens for reducing me to a *nobody*, a *nothing*. This was an organization that I very nearly gave my life for – literally! One morning in 1957, at practice, I got hit when I wasn't ready and fell unconscious – I had a perforated bowel. I very nearly died right on the ice. Bill Head, the trainer, saved my life, got me to the hospital. They operated right away. They called my mom, said I might not make it. They didn't call Marlene because she herself was in the hospital pregnant. . . . I barely made it through. It was almost the end of the season, and the Canadiens sent me to Florida for two weeks to regain my strength. I was a wreck, a ghost. When I got back, the doctor told me I'd be lucky to play the next year. But on the day the playoffs opened in Montreal, I said to Marlene, "Why don't you make me my steak." I always had a steak the day of a game. I told her it'd make me feel better. So she did, and we drove down to the Forum. Next thing Marlene knew I was out there taking my warm-up. She went bananas. She went and got Bill Head and brought him to the dressing room. He said, "You can't play, Boom." I said, "I'm playing. I feel great."

I scored two goals that night. But after the playoffs, I was so weak I could hardly walk, couldn't even play golf. It took me all summer to get my strength back.

Another time I had a cast on my leg. It was the last game of the '61 semifinals against the Black Hawks. We were on the train on the way to Chicago, and Doug Harvey said to me, "C'mon, Boomer, it's the last game, take this thing off. Try it." He went to the kitchen and got a big knife from the cook, and he peeled the cast off. And, oh boy, that leg hurt. I couldn't stand it. They had to shoot me up with pain killers. My leg was like cement – no feeling. So I went out on the power play, and, bang, right off, Bobby Hull came along and hit me on the knee. He never went for the puck – he went right for the knee. That was the end. I could hardly make it to the bench.

When I got back on the train and the pain killers wore off, I cried like a baby. We hadn't won the game, but I gave everything I had! That's what I did for the Montreal Canadiens. Mind you, I'm not bitter about my playing days. I chose to be a hockey player. At fifty-eight, I can't afford to sweat about the past. All I'm saying is that I could have been treated better at the end.

Anyway, when Emile Francis took me in the draft, I trained like a slave for four months – I had twenty-five pounds to lose. I never went out at night, got up at six every morning, went to the gym. I played handball with the Canadian handball champ to get my reflexes back. When I reported to training camp in Kingston, Ontario, I thought I was in shape. But when we started scrimmaging, I couldn't take it. We were going twice a day, morning and afternoon. It was all I could do to crawl home from practices and fall into bed. And my ulcer was just pumping.

Marlene: One night he phoned me and said, "I can't do it, I'll never make it." It was the saddest thing. Boom's heart had been broken when the Canadiens offered him the job with the Juniors, and this was to have restored his pride. I myself had told him he couldn't *possibly* come back after two years. And now here he was saying, "I made a mistake, I'm thirty-six, I'm too old." I said, "Hang on, Boom, you'll be okay. Hang on through training camp."

Bernie: That night I prayed for help, and the good Lord said, "What are you worried about, Boomer?" I said, "I don't know," and the next day I quit worrying. I felt free. I began to play better. I started pumping goals.

Three weeks later, I packed my family in a station wagon with a U-haul on the back, and off we went to New York. . . . The problem was the Rangers were a losing team. They had great players – Gilbert, Hadfield, Giacamon, Ratelle – but it never did them any good. I'd come from a team of winners, guys with discipline. So when I walked into the dressing room I sat down beside Rod Gilbert and said, "I'm nearly thirty-seven years old, Rod, and I'm going to get more goals than you this year." I wanted to give him a shot – get these guys off their cans.

When I returned to the Forum for the first time, Toe Blake sent out John Ferguson to cover me. I said to Fergie, "You can't cover me. I'm going to score two goals against you." We ended up winning 5–2 – I got two goals. I got nineteen for the year, and the Rangers made the playoffs for the first time in years. And they made the playoffs from that point on.

The next year I started in again, but I knew I couldn't do it anymore. One night I got hit, and the blood came shooting out of my mouth, right up from my stomach – bleeding ulcer. I went back to the bench; I was green. That was the end of my career.

When I was feeling better, Emile Francis said to me, "Would you like to coach the Rangers?" He'd been coaching himself. I said, "I'd love to."

I finished the year behind the bench, and by the beginning of the next season I had that team fired up. And I was fired up myself. We made the playoffs that year and nearly beat out the Canadiens. But halfway through the next season, my ulcers got so bad that one day I fell unconscious. Emile said "That's it, you're not coaching anymore." But he promised me that as long as he was with the team – he was president by this time – I'd be his right-hand man. Same salary.

Marlene: At that point Boom came to me and said that since we were going to be in New York for a long time, he wanted to build a house on Lido Beach on Long Island – right on the water. I liked the idea, so we went to see a contractor, and he started building. He said it would take six months – we were living in an apartment. But after six months, the house wasn't ready, and our lease at the apartment was up. So for the next two-three months Boom and the two boys slept in our neighbours' garage. Boom put some carpet on the floor and a couple of folding beds. My daughter and I stayed with another neighbour.

Bernie: In the meantime, I went to see the doctor about my ulcer, and he said, "Boomer, do you want to live a happy, comfortable life?" I said, "Doc, I'll do anything for that." He said, "Okay, we're going to have to take three-quarters of your stomach out." I didn't like the sound of it, but he told me that if I didn't have it done and the ulcer broke, it might kill me. So I went ahead with it, and by the time I came out of the hospital I'd lost twenty-eight pounds – I was a mess. We were just about to move into our new house when Emile Francis called and said, "Boomer, I think you're going to have to go back to Montreal – I'm going to make you a scout." I said, "Emile, what are you talking about? I played sixteen years, I was an all-star, and now you want me to crawl around those cold little arenas up north?"

Marlene: I'd never seen Boom so depressed. He asked Emile if he couldn't just stay put and operate out of New York. Emile knew about the new house and all – I was good friends with his wife. But Emile said, "I'm afraid not, Boomer – in Montreal you'll be better posted to go to games in Canada." The cruelest thing was that *then* Boomer found out that his salary was to be cut in *half*! From $25,000 to $12,500. And this after the promise that he'd always be paid a full salary. He really felt betrayed. . . . So many of these guys like Boom bring honour to their teams and to the NHL, and when it's over and they should be reaping what they sowed, they're simply turned away. If it hadn't been for opportunities outside the NHL – the WHA, the brewing companies, and so on – some of these Hall-of-Famers would be in very rough shape. What's so disgusting is that it doesn't have to *be* that way. Other sports treat their Hall-of-Famers much better than hockey does! I've always taken it as a token of the NHL's attitude toward its greats – a very small token but a token nonetheless – that the Hockey Hall of Fame ring is just a tiny little thing like a high school ring. And you have to pay for it yourself! At least you did when Boom was inducted. I sent them seventy-five dollars. The ring is so inconspicuous that when we started going on tour for Miller Lite with the great football and baseball players, who, incidentally, have *beautiful* Hall of Fame rings with big diamonds in them and so on, Boom was embarrassed to wear his. So on his fortieth birthday I decided to do something about it. I collected all his tie clips and cuff links and so on – anything that had diamonds in it – and I took them to a jeweller along with the ring, and I showed him how I wanted everything put together so that the Hall of Fame crest would be in one corner and the number 393 for how many goals he scored in another, and all the diamonds worked in, and so on. And I said to him, "Now show me the biggest square ring you've got." Well the biggest turned out to be a rectangle about an inch wide and and an inch and a half long. The jeweller said to me, "Marlene, this is going to look a little gaudy." I said, "The gaudier the better." There are men who love jewellery and men who don't. Well, Boom has just loved that ring – it's his pride and joy. When people say to him, "What's that ring?" he says, "That's my Hall of Fame ring." Nobody knows that it was designed and paid for by Marlene.

Bernie: We sold our new house, didn't make a dime on it, and moved into a place in Dorval. I *hated* scouting! It was unbelievable! I was wasting my life watching kids' games! The miracle was that I maintained my vision of being somebody. I never got discouraged. I said to Marlene, "You and the kids stick with me, and we'll get outa here. You won't believe what's going to happen to us."

By this time the league had expanded, and after a year or so of scouting I got a call from Cliff Fletcher, general manager of the new Atlanta Flames. He said, "Boomer, how would you like to come and coach the Flames?" I said, "You must be crazy! Nobody knows a puck from a stick down there!"

Marlene: When Boom came home and told me where we were going, I said, "*Atlanta*! It's the other end of the world!" I figured it was going to be awfully hard. But we came down, and they had a big press conference. We met all these southern girls, and I said to myself, Boomer's not coming down *here* by himself. This woman came up to me with her thick southern accent and said, "Oh, Marleeeene, yer jus gonna luuuuv it down here! After two years, you'll nehhhver wanta go back to Caaaanada!" And it was true. What made it easier for us is that our children followed us. Linda and Bob and their families live here in Atlanta, and Danny lives further south in Fort Lauderdale.

Bernie: My first job when I got here was trying to sell season tickets. Boosting the team. I was on every radio and TV show in Georgia. I carted films around to high schools and colleges. Our arena wasn't even finished. Our offices were in trailers. Even so, we sold 10,000 season tickets.

I ended up coaching a bunch of old veterans from other teams that year. All the media said we weren't going to win five games. I told my players, "Don't worry about it – they know nothing. Play the game on the ice, not in the newspapers."

We won twenty-five games that year. The next year we won thirty-five. We made the playoffs every year. Those players had big hearts for me. They'd go through the wall for me.

Eventually Cliff and I had some differences, and I resigned as coach. But don't be mistaken, I still regard Cliff as a very good man. In fact, he's such a good guy that, a year or so after I quit, he said to me, "Why don't you come back and help broadcast games?" I said, "Great!" I love broadcasting. I became an analyst. But when I stopped coaching, the Flames had a problem – season ticket sales dropped from 10,000 to 4,500. I want to be humble when I say this, but back then I owned Atlanta. I could have done anything I wanted down here. I loved the people, they loved me.

When the team moved to Calgary in 1980, Cliff said, "You wanta come with us?" I said, "No way. Atlanta is home." I went to see Ted Turner, the owner of the Atlanta Braves, and I said, "I don't have a job, Ted – hire me." He's a good guy. He said, "Look, Hockey Puck – he used to call me Hockey Puck – go in the office and tell them to put you on the payroll." I was supposed to do promotion for the Braves – sell season tickets, that sort of thing. Ted paid me better than the National Hockey League ever did, but after a year he had to let me go, because I wasn't doing anything, didn't sell one season ticket.

To make ends meet, I went to work for a Miller beer distributorship. This was before I started making commercials. I went around on a truck selling beer to hotels and bars. I wasn't even the driver. Sixteen years in the NHL, a Hall-of-Famer, and I was the driver's *assistant*. In the meantime, indoor soccer had started up here, so a guy asked me if I'd be the TV analyst for the local team. I said, "No problem," and I quit the beer truck. I couldn't pronounce the names of those European soccer players, but who cares? Then the soccer team went belly up. Fortunately, kick boxing had started up on TV, and a guy from ESPN called me, asked me to be the analyst. I used to wear a tux to the fights – guys kicking each other in the teeth.

When kick boxing folded, I was out of a job again. Although not in reality, because in 1976 when I was broadcasting for the Flames I'd had a call from a guy called Marty Blackman in New York. He said, "Boomer, how would you like to come up here and make a Miller Lite beer commercial?" I said, "I'll be there." And, zap, I was on the plane with Marlene.

What I got paid for that one commercial – thirty seconds! – it would have taken three years to earn with the Canadiens. It was a great commercial – it was about hockey. Since then, I've done twenty-three more – one a year solo, one a year with other athletes. Plus some in French.

A few years later, Miller had a huge eleven-day convention in Houston. (Let me say that I have one gift that the Lord gave me – I can motivate people.) At that convention, I was supposed to do two motivational talks, twenty-five minutes each. I ended up doing fifty-one of them. And when those guys got out of there, they were ready to do some selling. Then Miller said, "Boomer, how would you like to work full-time for us?"

In 1981 I signed a contract with them. I have separate agreements for my commercials and my motivational work. When they need me somewhere, they call me up, send me over the plane tickets, and a limo picks me up. First class. Marlene travels with me. I've been all over North America for them. I'm better known now, by far, than when I was playing pro hockey.

If I'd been discouraged twenty-five years ago, I wouldn't be where I am today. But I'm never down for long, and that's a gift from God. I believe in God – I'm a born-again Christian. Did I mention that? I gave my life to Christ ten years ago. He died on the cross for my sins at the age of thirty-three. A lot of people are going to say, "Boomer's crazy." That's their problem. I'm the happiest man in the world. I read the Bible every day. I keep one in the car. And I'll tell you, if I hadn't found God, I don't know where I'd be today. Eleven years ago, my wife almost left me. I was a smart alec. I thought I knew everything, running around all the time. Christ gave me back my marriage.

Marlene: And it wouldn't have happened if it hadn't been for Jennifer Kea, the wife of one of Boom's players here in Atlanta. She invited me to a Bible study one day, and I thought, *a Bible study* – Boom and I were Catholics, and Catholics don't even *read* the Bible. To make a long story short, I ended up going, mainly because it was a rainy day and I didn't have anything else to do. As it turned out, it was a beautiful group of gals – hockey wives, some football wives. When the study began, the girl in charge said, "Open your Bibles to Ecclesiastes, chapter 9." I thought, I don't even know how to *spell* Ecclesiastes, let alone where it is in the Bible. Here I was one of the oldest ones there, and I felt so stupid. At any rate, one of the verses the gal read says that husbands are a gift from God. The first thing I wondered when I heard this was whether or not God was into exchanges or refunds. As Boom said, our marriage was just about on the rocks at that point. I mean, anybody *looking* at Boom and me would have thought we were getting along famously, but on a deeper level we weren't communicating at all. I sometimes told the kids that I could have divorced their father two or three times a year. But until this particularly crushing time, we'd always made a point of keeping it together.

When I got home from the Bible study, I decided I was going to look into this business of Christianity, and I began reading my Bible. I opened it up to the Book of John and saw, "If you abide in me, and my words abide in you, you can ask anything you want." Because of this difficulty in our lives, I decided I was going to make a list of things – twelve things, as it turned out – that I wanted God's help with. I figured, if the Lord doesn't answer twelve, at least he'll come through with six if He's listening. Most of the things I asked about had to do with Boom – I wanted to see him make changes in his life.

Almost right away, those twelve items began to get answers. I kept going to the Bible study, and one day as I was coming home on the I-75 I said, "Lord, I don't know what's going on, but I want to know you better, and I want my husband to know you." I said, "If you can put this messed up marriage back together, I'll really know you're there."

And He did. Nowadays, Boomer phones me from out of town and says, "I really miss you, and I can't wait to get home." And he's an entirely different man when he *is* home. I used to wait on Boom hand and foot. Now he does a lot for himself – happily. Not that I resented doing things for him – cooking, cleaning, whatever. I think men need a certain amount of that; it makes them feel important. Of course, *I'm* more considerate of *him* now, too. One weekend he went away and left me sixty dollars for myself, and, instead of blowing it, which would have taken about two seconds, I went out and bought him a nice shirt and tie. When he came home he complained that he didn't need it, but I said, "Go put it on," and he did, and I said, "The blue *really* brings out the blue in your eyes." He felt great. Boom comes across like a big tough guy, but down deep he's a pussycat. He's got a tender, loving heart. You can't say that of a lot of husbands.

After that morning on the I-75, I got my courage up and told Boom that I'd accepted Christ. He looked at me as if to say, Isn't *that* great! And I said, "You know, Ed and Jennifer Kea have a Bible study for couples every Monday – maybe you'd like to go with me." He said, "Yeah, fine." But as the Mondays passed, he always had some excuse.

Then one day he said to me, "You know I've been watching Ed Kea – there's something about that guy that is really different."

Bernie: He was thoughtful, he was loving, he had peace of mind. We'd travel by plane, and he'd sit there reading the Bible. All the guys would go to the back of the plane, have a couple of beers, and they'd get on his case – "Hey, Ed, what's happening in the Book?" It made me mad, and I wasn't even a Christian then. I got up during a flight one day and I said, "Let me tell you guys something. Maybe if you'd be more like this man, I wouldn't have so many problems with you." I opened some eyes. I know I did, because some of them became Christians – Jean Pronovost, Dan Bouchard, and Tommy Lysiak, for example. Tommy was down in the pits, drinking, everything, and he pulled himself up.

Marlene: Boom mentioned how impressed he was with Ed, and I said, "Well, you can have the same thing he's got. Why don't you come to the Bible study next Monday – I think it might help." So the next Monday we went. I was so nervous I forgot my glasses. We sat there and listened, and Boom liked the lesson. But then he didn't go again. . . . One day Ed Kea said to me, "There's a seminar coming up in Arizona – three days at Camel Back. You could have a great holiday and meet some Christians. It'd be just the thing for Boomer." And I thought, Sure, can you imagine Boomer at an all-Christian seminar for three days?

Bernie: In the meantime, I saw a big difference in Marlene. She was quieter, less anxious. She always had her nose in the Bible, making notes – hour after hour. When I saw the change, I said to myself, This book must work. . . . I went away for a few days, and when I got back, there were pamphlets for this seminar all over the kitchen, the bathroom, the bedroom, everywhere. Marlene said, "If you want to go, Boom, Ed Kea is going to sponsor us, pay our way." . . . I should say that, just before that, the chaplain of the Christian Football Players' Association had given me a book called *Twelve Men in the Huddle* – the testimonies of twelve football players. Ron Pritchard was in it – I knew him. He'd been into drugs, alcohol, broads, everything! I started reading his testimony, and I couldn't believe that this guy had turned his life around. I told Marlene, "Let's go to Arizona." So we arrive, a hundred degrees – 500 Christians. I figured, okay, two hours of seminars a day, and the rest of the time I'm on vacation. Then I look at the agenda – the *whole day, every day, is taken up except for fifteen-minute breaks*! When we got settled in our room, we went down to the pool, and I told Marlene, "I'll be back, I'm going for a beer." She said, "Boom, please, not here." So a while later I said, "I've gotta go to the men's room." Instead I go for a beer – in a cup instead of a glass. I didn't want to offend the Christians.

Marlene: Throughout the week, there were choices as to what speakers you wanted to hear on what topics. On the second last day, Dave Hookins was to speak on relationships, men, women, and marriage.

Bernie: I said, "That's the class I'm going to." And the guy gets up and he talks just like me – men-only stuff. All of a sudden, it was as if the Holy Spirit shone through him and zeroed right in on me. I was sitting in the back row, and for ten minutes he never took his eyes off me. He said, "If you were to die right now, do you know where you're going?" A little cloud of doubt settled on me – poof. I put my hand up, and said, "As sure as I'm sitting here I'm going to hell – I'm in communion with the devil. I'm a sinner."

From then on, I took notes like you wouldn't believe. I realized I'd had my priorities all wrong. I had to start putting God first, then my wife and children, and, last, my job. I'd always taken care of my public, my fans, before my wife and family.

On Saturday night before the closing banquet, it was announced that a great speaker was going to give his testimony. Nobody knew who it was. When the time came, the master of ceremonies said, "Ladies and gentlemen, welcome Mr. Ron Pritchard." Same guy as in the book – I knew him, and I knew that the Lord had sent him there for me.

As he gave his testimony, I cried my heart out, because I knew what a bad character he'd been, and I saw myself. When he finished, I stepped out for a Coke, and guess who's at the Coke machine – Ron Pritchard. He said, "Boom, how's it going? You wanta know the Lord? Let's go for a walk."

As we walked and talked, he said, "So, do you want to accept Christ?"

Marlene: Boomer told him, "Maybe in a few weeks." He's such a perfectionist he figured he'd better get his life cleaned up before he accepted the Lord.

Bernie: Ron said to me, "Don't put it off, Boom. Now's the time." I said, "Let's do it, Ron," and right then and there we prayed the prayer. I accepted Christ. I've been a different man ever since. I still enjoy a beer and I like to have fun, but I don't go to nightclubs, and I told Miller, "Don't send me to any more Spring Break stuff in Florida." I used to go down there for them, and, I'll tell you, I was ashamed of what I saw. Everything! Sex! Drugs! The worst! All in the open! It bugs me when people say, "God allows this to happen." God doesn't allow anything – people have free will. They make up their own minds.

Marlene: After we accepted the Lord, we laid it on the line with Him. We said, "If you don't want us working with Miller, you let us know."

Bernie: The day God says, "Get out," I'll get out. Right now, I'm reaching millions of people through my work. I don't preach, but I give my testimony. I tell it like it is. The Book says that you've gotta preach on the four corners of the world. Everybody says the world is round, but in the Bible it's got corners.

Marlene: What I love so much about Christianity is that it gives me such peace. For instance, I'm going in for a heart check-up soon – an arteriogram; I've been having some problems. Fifteen years ago I would have panicked over it. But now I know that if the Lord brought me this far he'll take care of me. I'm actually looking *forward* to seeing what's going to happen – to getting better. Even if I have to face surgery, I have no fear. I'm not afraid of death. It just doesn't happen to be on my agenda right now. My work on earth isn't done.

Bernie: I used to think that when I died, that was it – I'd take the big slide and go see all my old buddies burning. Now I'm heading somewhere else. I've had some heart problems my-self, but right now my heart – my *heart*, understand? my *soul* – is brand new. I'm not concerned.

Marlene: Fifteen years ago it would have taken a lot of guts for Boom to sit down in a restaurant, take my hand, and say, "Let's pray, give thanks for our food."

Bernie: Who gave the food to us? Not Joe Blow in the chef's hat but God. I don't care if people look. Some people say, "They're just showing off." But we'd rather show off with Jesus in our hearts than show off with nothing. . . . I give credit to Jesus Christ for saving my soul; to my wife for supporting me all these years; to Miller Beer for putting money in my pocket; and to Cliff Fletcher for bringing me to Atlanta. Without them, I wouldn't have anything I have today. I'm not a millionaire, but for a little guy from Quebec I've done fine. They don't laugh anymore when I go to Montreal.

6

. . . .

STOPS ALONG

THE WAY

"If you can't take stress," says Jill Mikita, "don't marry a professional hockey player."

Knowledgeably spoken.

Consider the evening of December 16, 1967. Jill was at home in Elmhurst, Illinois, paying casual attention to a televised hockey game between the Pittsburgh Penguins and the Chicago Black Hawks. She vacated her chair by the television and returned a minute later to the sight of her husband Stan's face filling a good portion of the twenty-one-inch screen. Actually only part of his face was showing. Nearly half of it was swathed in a blood-spattered towel. The shoulder and chest of his jersey were stained bright red. The ice resembled the aftermath of a knifing.

"I always worried about his eyes," says Jill, recalling the incident twenty-two years later. "He'd had a lot of cuts around the eyes, and my first thought was that he'd injured or lost his eye. Stan always knew that I'd be watching his road games on television, so when he'd get an injury he'd call me as soon as he could. That night it was twenty minutes before he called. I was two months pregnant at the time. Between the injury and the call, I went into shock and lost the baby."

As it turned out it was not Stan's eye that had been injured but his ear. In his own words, the ear had been "sliced off" and took thirty-five stitches to restore.

"I always allowed that injuries were a part of the game," says Jill. "And yet I was never quite ready for them when they happened. Then again, I wasn't one of these wives who went around worrying about them before they happened either. It may seem odd, but what bothered me more in a general way, caused me more day-to-day stress, was when the team got on a losing streak. Not that Stan ever brought his problems home. I *myself* wanted him to win, couldn't stand it when he didn't."

Jill allows that a lot of things can "get to you" if you're married to a professional athlete. "You're alone a lot, your family life isn't always normal, you have added responsibility for your children. . . . " On the verge of plunging deeper, she stops, as if her frankness had suddenly been kicked in the shin by some deeper urge for tact. "But you can't go around complaining," she smiles. "You knew what was involved when you got into it."

The same can not be said for a hockey player's children. Yet they, too, face hockey-related stresses and challenges. For the most part, even the least of these are not apparent to them until the age of seven or eight, when it is suddenly evident that their father spends an inordinate amount of time away from home. Play time. Story time. Holiday time. Indeed, it was only in recent years that the NHL ended it's Draconian practice of scheduling games on Christmas Eve and Christmas night, which forced players to be away from their families – sometimes a thousand miles away – at that time of year. But New Year's, Easter, birthdays, graduations, and any number of special family occasions are still up for grabs. "You might say I had a father, but I didn't always have a dad," reflects twenty-year-old Jane Mikita. "Every year, for instance, my elementary school had a father-daughter banquet, and in all my years at school, my dad was only able to attend once. And when he did go, people lined up for an hour to get his autograph. These were my friends. It was so weird."

Jane finds it equally weird that ten years after her dad's retirement, his career still impinges regularly on her life – not always positively. "At the place where I work downtown, 90 per cent of the people are men, and they're always, 'Like, wow, is your dad Stan Mikita?' I don't know how many times a day. . . . The other day a guy said to me, 'You get special treatment around here because of who your father is.' And I looked at this guy and said, 'You're wrong. And don't say that again.' "

Jane is an outgoing young woman of dark complexion and striking height – she is taller than either of her parents. Besides working, she attends the Chicago Academy of Design and Fashion Merchandising. She has inherited a healthy dollop of her mother Jill's assertiveness and is a model agent of Jill's view that Stan's fame as hockey player must be kept in perspective. "I mean, I'm proud of my dad for what he did," she says. "But, you know, it's not a big deal. People come up to me and say, 'What's your dad like at home? Does he cut the grass?' I've seen people drive slowly past the house, looking for my dad. I can't accept this, and yet in one way or another I've always got to deal with it."

Jane also has to deal with an occasional challenge to her identity. She says, "It really annoys me when somebody introduces me as 'Stan Mikita's daughter.' I always say, 'No, I'm Jill Mikita's daughter.' It may seem snotty, but it makes the point. In high school, I was on the golf team, and I did pretty well, and when articles were written about me, they always referred to me as 'Jane Mikita, daughter of famous ex-Black Hawk Stan Mikita.' Around some people, you're identity can just disappear."

Even more irksome to Jane are people who buddy up to her with the hope of meeting her father. "I once went on a date with a guy who said, 'When I take you home will I get to meet your dad?' I said, 'Look, pal, you're not taking me home.

When you ask me out, you go out with *me*. If you want to go out with my father, you ask *him*.

"My older sister Meg had a hard time always being identified with dad. And my older brother Scott gets it in his theatre reviews – he's a professional actor here in Chicago: 'Son of Stan Mikita.' Meg lives in Boston now, so she doesn't get it anymore.

"I want people to get to know *me* and get to know my mom and dad *through* me, not the other way around."

It hardly needs saying that the most persistent hazards of the hockey life are reserved for the players themselves. The physical pain alone can be an outrage. And yet it is routinely minimized by coaches, managers, and media, who measure it not on a scale of suffering but in lost games or minutes of games. Players regularly perform with broken jaws, broken noses, plate-sized bruises, multi-stitch cuts – injuries that, should they befall the average human being, might well prevent him from getting out of bed, let alone participating in a game that poet Al Purdy called a "combination of ballet and murder."

Stan Mikita is unequivocal in declaring pain the most oppressive aspect of professional hockey. "I once had a broken heel," he says, "and I remember waking up in the middle of the night literally crying in agony. I had so many injuries I can't name them – lacerations, broken bones, muscle tears; everybody gets them."

Jill Mikita reveals that Stan once played with a broken shoulder that had gone undiagnosed by team doctors. "They x-rayed it and told him it was fine," she says. "It was only later that an independent x-ray showed it was broken. Another time, he was having trouble with his arm. He had no strength in it. He was told by a team doctor that he had tennis elbow. But Stan didn't buy it. He went to other doctors, orthopedic people, and they told him his tricep muscle was torn off the bone. Stan told the Black Hawk management that this is what he'd found out, and that no matter what they thought, he was going to have surgery on it."

Even a player's retirement from the game seldom puts an end to the cumulative physical discomforts of his career. Stan suffers chronic back pain, the legacy of being sledgehammered into the boards nearly twenty years ago while jumping to avoid a bodycheck.

In a broader sense, retirement can *create* more discomforts than it relieves. Some players find it an emotional dead zone, a restless vacuum, bereft of the camaraderie and attention of the big-league game.

For others the problems are practical. "You've got to understand that the system never gave us any useful education," says Stan. "I'm not talking about typical schooling; most of us learned more playing hockey than we would have in a classroom. But we're ridiculously uneducated when it comes to making a living after our legs give out. See, in hockey, everything is done *for* you – airline reservations, hotel reservations; if you have an agent, even your business is often done for you. I've heard stories of guys who after years in the game don't even know how to book a flight. Our Black Hawk alumni group has tried to counteract some of this by bringing in speakers every month to address us on different topics. We're making this available to active players, too. I took a university course for six weeks in 1980 – Business 101. I was thirty-nine; I felt like a grandfather. I only wish I'd started at nineteen. My belief is that education should be mandatory for the young guys. We older guys have made our mistakes. I accept that I could have gone to college and didn't. I take responsibility for it. I regret it. It would have changed things for me after I quit."

As implied, Stan's retirement was by no means a stroll into the Peaceable Kingdom. After nearly ten years out of NHL hockey, he is only now happily finding his feet. Had he not been a man of strong will and intelligence – a man accustomed to surmounting obstacles – he would not have come as far as he has since playing his last NHL game in April of 1980.

Born Stanislav Gvoth, Stan faced his first major challenges as an eight-year-old boy in the village of Sokolce, Czechoslovakia. "My dad was a menial labourer in a textile factory," he recalls. "My mother worked in the fields during the summer." Stan's earliest memories are of going with his parents in late August to load hay and sometimes to pull potatoes outside the village.

During World War Two, Sokolce was occupied by the Germans, and young Stanislav's family was obliged to billet two of Hitler's soldiers. "We had a little two-room house," he says. "One room was a kitchen with a bath and an outhouse off of it; the other was for eating, sitting, sleeping. The whole place was about the size of our current living room. Anyway, one of these soldiers had lice, so we had to burn our bedding. We talked to the captain, and he gave us new billets, higher in rank, very clean. I remember going to the mess hall to bring back their lunch; I'd walk very gingerly so I wouldn't spill too much. I'd go out to target practice with them; they'd rest their guns on a fence post and let me pull the trigger."

Unknown to Stanislav, as the war consumed Europe, an uncle and aunt he had never met were quietly mapping his future in a faraway country. Joe and Anna Mikita had emigrated to St. Catharines, Ontario, during the 1920s. "When my older brother was born in 1937," says Stan, "my uncle wrote my mother a congratulatory note, joshing her that the next baby she had was his, that he'd come and take the child to Canada. He and my aunt couldn't have children of their own."

In 1940, Stanislav was born, and eight years later the Gvoths received a letter from Uncle Joe, informing them of his impending visit to Sokolce. "He showed up with gum and candy and toys, and we thought he was God," laughs Stan. "Everybody has dreams, and we always dreamed of going to

Canada or the United States. We thought the people over here lived in paradise, that they didn't have to work, that if they needed money they just plucked it off trees.

"My uncle was still keen on taking me with him back to Canada – in fact, I guess that was the main reason he'd come – but my mother kept putting him off as if he were joking. But he was very persistent, explaining what life was like in Canada and the opportunities that were available.

"One night, he and my mom and dad were sitting around talking about him adopting me. I was in bed in the other room, and I was hungry, so I asked for a piece of bread and jam. My mother wouldn't give it to me, and I started to cry. They thought I was crying because I'd overheard her saying that she wouldn't let me go to Canada. So she told my uncle, 'Okay, Joe, he can go.' That was that. As far as I knew I was just going for a visit."

It was not until Stanislav reached the French port of Le Havre, about to embark by ship for Montreal, that it occurred to him that he might never see his parents again. But his uncle reassured him that was not the case.

Not quite. "By the time I saw them again, I was playing for the Chicago Black Hawks," says Stan. "I'd just finished my first season, and I went back for a visit with my aunt and a cousin. By this time my sister Viera had been born – she was ten years old – and I'll never forget the first words my mom and dad said to us when we reached their place in the middle of the night. They took me aside and said, 'Watch what you say; we don't know whether your brother and sister are in the Communist Party.' Then they asked if I was angry at them for giving me up. I let them know right there that I couldn't thank them enough for having allowed me to go."

His gratitude notwithstanding, there were times along the way when young Stan would have been quite happy to put the boots to life in St. Catharines and return to Sokolce. After initial placement in grade three, he was quickly demoted to kindergarten, unable to speak more than a few words of English. "About all I knew was that my name in Slovak had been Stanislav and that now it was Stanley. Fortunately, an older Slovak girl in St. Catharines took me under her wing and became my tutor. Within a few weeks I'd learned enough English to go back to grade three. But even so, there was always somebody making fun of me for the way I spoke, or calling me a DP."

Stan has poignant memories of watching the neighbourhood boys play street hockey during his first winter in Canada. "For a few days I watched from the window, then from the porch, then from the sidewalk. Then one day they were short of people, and they asked me to play. . . . Once I got involved in sports and in school, and made some friends, I pretty well forgot about home. And of course I loved my new mother and father. I'm not saying I didn't have homesick moments. In fact, for about two years after I got here I had an occasional fantasy that one day I'd join the Canadian Air Force and steal a plane and fly home. I figured it was the only way I was going to get there."

Although he had come to terms with his adoption many years earlier, it was not until 1964 that Stan caught a glimpse of the parental emotion – the extraordinary bittersweet commitment – that made the adoption possible. "I walked into my daughter Meg's bedroom one night when she was tiny, looked at her in her crib, and I just wondered how anybody could give up a child. Then it hit me that it must have taken an awful lot of love for my parents to give me up. They knew that after the war, with communism taking over, with all the poverty and destruction, there was very little for me in Czechoslovakia. And they were right – I'm sure my life wouldn't have amounted to much over there."

Over here, Stan's life has amounted to far more than he ever could have imagined. The physical evidence alone is impressive. The Mikitas live in an expansive five-bedroom home in the affluent Chicago suburb of Oakbrook. The beige brick façade of the place is fronted by tall white pillars, creating an architectural effect that is part colonial, part baronial, part southern antebellum. A circular driveway arcs past the front door, and a swimming pool occupies the back-yard. The interior of the house is a comfy aggregation of marble, broadloom, and wood panelling that Stan admits would at one time have seemed like a palace to him.

If anything, the plush surroundings belie Stan and Jill's essentially unassuming view of the world. The two are straight-thinking, hard-working people whose sense of order encompasses a deep belief in family togetherness and family responsibility. There is a manifest sense of warmth and caring among Jill and Stan and their children. At the same time, there are no free rides for the kids. At Jill and Stan's insistence – and in spite of the family's relative affluence – all of the Mikita children have held part-time jobs while attending high school. "When they get to college or university, we pay their tuition, nothing more," says Jill. "I don't like that sense of self-importance that some athletes' kids get, so I've always tried to make ours realize that they're just normal people, that they have to make it on their own. Naturally, you want them to do well, but not on the back of their father's reputation."

The struggle to impose normality upon the scions has had its low points and its laughs. Jill says, "When Meg, our oldest, was five years old she had her father sign some of the little postcards that the Hawks make up for each player. The next day I caught her outside selling the autographed cards for a nickel. So I brought her in and did my best to let her know why you didn't do these things. I thought I got the point across. But then a few days later I caught her out there signing *her* name and selling it. The funny thing was that, without realizing it, she was signing 'Gem,' her name spelled backwards."

Jill's rigorously unassuming attitudes are rooted in the hard-working ethnic neighbourhoods of Berwyn and Cicero on Chicago's west side, where she grew up. Her father was a welder, her mother what she describes as "a life-long house-wife." Jill studied physical education at the University of

Illinois, and by the age of twenty was doing full-time organizational work for Congressman Harold Collier of the Tenth District. "It was the sort of job I'm good at," she says. "I'm a very orderly person. Always have been – in everything I do." The self-assessment is beyond dispute. The Mikita home is impeccably scrubbed and vacuumed. The books are shelved, the flowers arranged with a florist's fastidious touch. Jill herself is neatly, fashionably turned out, morning, noon, and evening. In summer, she rises at 4:30 a.m. (no alarm clock necessary) to do her housework and to prepare the evening's dinner. By 7:30 a.m. she is at her favourite spot on earth, the first tee of the Medinah Country Club, fifteen miles from home. She golfs six days a week and would make it seven but for one reason: the club is closed on Mondays.

In winter she replaces golf with bridge, another game that, by her own admission, she could happily play seven days a week. In the corner of the den a sturdy, official-looking bridge table is encircled by chairs, ready and poised for occupants. There is a suggestion that a game could break out at any moment. Another bridge table sits in Stan's office.

Stan shares his wife's fascination with golf and bridge, and to a degree her sense of neatness. His slacks are well creased, his shoes polished, his shirts and sweaters invariably neat and new. His hair is carefully combed. Facially, he bears more than a passing resemblance to the actor Charles Bronson – or at least to what Bronson looked like fifteen years ago. High cheekbones, dark narrow eyes, angular jaw. For a man who has been nicked and cut and stitched so many times, Stan's face is remarkably free of scar tissue. His only noticeable scars are two fine horizontal white lines that abut one another in the middle of his upper lip to form a rakish-looking (and nearly invisible) moustache. He wears granny-style reading glasses and has the vocabulary and language skills of an English teacher. "The vocabulary came from doing crossword puzzles," he volunteers. But you get the feeling while listening to him – to the grammar, the syntax, the orderly progression of thoughts and sentences – that the concern for language runs deeper than mere vocabulary.

"Oh, yes," says Jill, "he always wants to say the right things in just the right way. That's why he's such an excellent speaker. He plans his speeches very carefully, writes them out, and for two weeks before a speaking engagement he's an absolute nervous wreck. But when he gets up there he's incredible."

Stan's sensibilities have not always included his current penchant for orderly communication. When he ascended to the NHL as an eighteen-year-old in 1959, he immediately became the most lawless and penalized centreman in the game and remained so for some five years. "He was the worst little cuss that ever was," notes his former teammate Bobby Hull.

Stan says, "At my size – 160 pounds – a lot of people didn't expect me to be around long. I once said to Ted Lindsay, who was with the Hawks when I joined them and who was just a little bigger than me, 'How did you ever last so long?' And he said, 'I hit them before they hit me. If you do that, you've got the element of surprise on your side.' So I took his advice. I figured if I was going to stick around, I had to show them I could handle myself."

Hall of Fame defenceman Bill Gadsby recalls Stan as "a miserable little pain in the butt. . . . He'd cross-check you, he'd spear you in the belly. You'd be going around the back of the net, and he'd spear you in the calf – down you'd go. I used to watch the better players, pick out their bad habits, and do my best to exploit those habits. Stan had a very bad habit of passing to the left side and then looking to see if it was a good pass. If you came from his blind side, while his head was turned, you could really crank him a good one. I nailed him dozens of times, but I've got to give him credit, he always got back up. I remember hitting him hard during the playoffs one year and telling him, 'Boy, one of these times you're not going to get up.' And he said, 'Ah, get lost, you old man, that was no bodycheck at all.' I'd hit him some nights and he'd have to crawl to the bench. But he'd always be back for the next shift. He had a lot of guts."

Stan's indifference to the rulebook was often matched by his indifference toward his fans. "He and I were always arguing about the way he treated these people," says Bobby Hull. "I'd tell him he should pay a little more attention to them. He'd say, 'Why should I? I don't owe them anything.' I used to tell him, 'Stan, the people you ignore on your way up are the same people you'll be passing on the way back down. When you're finished, you can take one step out of the limelight or you can take a whole big drop.' Oh, he was bad – cocky. I think actually he had a bit of a complex, coming from Czechoslovakia when he was very young, fighting his way, *thinking* he had to fight his way, up the ladder. I'm sure he was called a DP more times than he was called Stan. We'd argue and argue, and finally he'd say, 'Ah, I'm a better player than you are anyway.' And I'd say, 'Yeah, you're a better player, but that doesn't make you any less of a prick.' And he wouldn't know what to say.

"I'd come out after a game, and people would be after me, 'Where's Stan? Where's Mikita?' And I'd cover for him – I'd say he had to go home quickly or something. Then I'd get fed up with this, and I'd tell him to wisen up, I was sick of making excuses for him. He'd smarten up for a while, then he'd go back to his old ways, and I'd have to beat on him again. . . . As far as actual hockey was concerned, he used to tell me, 'If I were you, Bob, I'd spear this guy and hack that guy.' "

Stan's first encounter with Gordie Howe epitomized his attitude toward opposition players. And theirs toward him. "I'd always heard of Mr. Howe," he says, "and one night I decided to take a run at him. Unfortunately, my stick came up a little higher than it should have, and I cut him under the eye for five or six stitches. He went in to get sewn up and came back with a little mouse below his eye. The next time he skated by me he said, 'It's a long season, kid.' Anyway, I didn't think much about it; I probably laughed at him and went about my business.

"Nothing happened the next five or six games, then one night we were playing in Detroit, and we were both turning in the Red Wings' end of the rink. The last thing I remember was him going by me. When I woke up a few minutes later, flat out on the ice, there was Gordie looking down at me. He was a little concerned – concerned that he hadn't killed me, maybe – and he said quietly, 'Did you get the number of that truck, kid?'

"They carried me back to the bench, and Dennis Dejordy, our second goalie, told me that as Gordie had skated by me he'd slipped his right hand up under his armpit, pulled his fist out of his glove and given me a quick pop flush on the chin. Dennis was probably the only person in the arena who'd seen it. A minute later, Gordie skated by the bench and said, 'We're even, Stan.' And from that point on we left one another alone."

In 1966, Stan made radical changes to his game. "He was taking an awful beating from guys who'd go back at him," says Bill Gadsby. "I guess it was getting pretty hard to take, and he decided to clean up his act."

While not denying that he was being worn down physically, Stan outlines other motives for the tranformation. "One morning I came home from a road game, and my daughter Meg, who was two at the time, said, 'Daddy, I watched you play last night.' And I said, 'What did you think?' And she said, 'Oh, Daddy, you were so good. But sometimes when the whistle blew and all the players went one way, you had to go all the way across the ice by yourself.' I said, 'I was going to the penalty box.' And she said, 'But, Daddy, you were there for such a long time.' I thought, What kind of an impression is this for a little girl to have of her father? I thought, I'm going to have to make some changes. At about the same time, I started looking at my penalties and realized that a lot of them were cheap and unnecessary – holding, hooking, tripping, that sort of thing. And I was getting a lot of misconducts, too, for yapping at the referees. The first thing I decided to do was keep my mouth shut. Second, I was going to cut down on the cheap penalties."

The following season, Stan won not only the Art Ross Trophy for leading the NHL in scoring and the Hart Trophy as the league's most valuable player, but the Lady Byng Trophy for sportsmanship and gentlemanly play. He repeated the three-prize *coup* the following year, 1968.

One thing about the Mikita style did not change. From the time Stan entered the league in 1959, he had about him an inordinate, sometimes inane sense of the theatre of what he was doing. "We were in the entertainment business, and sometimes you had to be a bit of a showman," he says. "Sometimes nobody caught your act except your wife or your teammates."

Sometimes the entire arena caught it, as they did at the Montreal Forum on November 4, 1962, when Stan gave his most memorable performance. "I'd gotten into a little scrap with Claude Larose," he says. "And when we got into the penalty box, we looked at one another, and he said, 'You no-good DP!' And I said, 'You no-good pea soup!' And we just started swinging again. When we sat down, the crowd started getting on me, *really* getting on me. In Montreal, they always called me *'Le Petit Diable,'* the Little Devil. They'd say 'Shoo, Mikita, shoo!' Anyway, I turned around to acknowledge them, kind of stood up and bowed, and their noise grew, one section, then another. I thought they sounded pretty good; they were like an orchestra. So I stood up on the bench, facing them, and started conducting. The noise really swelled now. The whole building. So I stood right up on the boards to conduct my orchestra.

"Another night a guy took a dive on me, the ref called a penalty, and, in fun as I went to serve it, I took a dive of my own and slid on my belly over to the box."

Unlike some players, whose careers have left them with prolonged grudges against their former employers, Stan holds no significant resentments against the Black Hawks. In fact, he can name only two disillusioning incidents from his twenty years in the organization. "One thing I didn't like was the way Billy Reay, our coach, got fired in 1977. Management slipped a letter under the door of his office and another under his door at home. Unfortunately, he was on the road at the time, so his wife got the letter at home. She heard it arrive at three or four in the morning. . . . And I didn't like it when Bob Pulford took over as general manager and wanted me to take a big cut in pay. I'll admit that by the late 1970s my skills weren't what they had been, but I was still playing thirty minutes a game." In time, Pulford backed off, and Stan played his last two seasons at a salary commensurate with his achievements and experience.

"When I left hockey, our income dropped quite drastically," he says. "But our expenses were still the same. So we had to curb a few things. For instance, we sold three condos we had in Florida. We'd been using one ourselves and renting out the other two. . . . Today, I've still got to work to meet expenses, but we did put away enough of our hockey money to be fairly comfortable financially."

Finances aside, retirement for Stan was by no means what he and Jill might have imagined or hoped for. "There was no real transition for him," says Jill. "He just went from one thing he loved, hockey, to another thing he loved, golf. Unbeknownst to us, the golf would become a hundred times harder on us than hockey had ever been."

Stan's baptism into the golf business had come a year before his retirement, when he was invited to work with the golf pro at a new course owned by Kemper Sports, an affiliate of the Kemper Insurance Company. The course, at Longrove, Illinois, is a forty-five-minute drive from the Mikitas' home in Oakbrook.

"My first summer there," says Stan, "I really just followed the pro around for a couple of months, trying to get some idea of whether I'd like the work. The next spring, after my last season with the Hawks, the management of Kemper Sports invited me to go full-time, and I did. I was basically assistant club pro, a kind of general manager of the place."

Even today, there is an almost palpable anxiety in Jill's voice as she recalls Stan's years with Kemper. "He had a tremendous amount of responsibility – everything from the restaurant to the people on the tees to the locker rooms to public relations, greeting everybody as they came in. He knew everybody's name, and this is a public course, pay-as-you-play. He'd leave here at five in the morning, get to the course at six, and maybe come home at ten or eleven at night. When he played hockey he never brought his occupation into the house. When he was a golf pro, he got to the point where he was so edgy, so totally exhausted with the job, that we'd hear him come in, and we'd scatter. We'd pretend we were sleeping. We didn't want to talk about it with him, because as soon as he started talking, all his built-up anxiety spilled out on us. This got worse as he went along – the last two years, '85 and '86, were the worst.

"I finally said to Stan, 'I've paid my dues with hockey, I've been alone a lot, and that was fine; I knew when we married that I'd be spending time on my own. But this is ridiculous!' In reality, though, it wasn't so much being alone that I resented; it was the way Stan was being abused. The pressure on him was so intense that he was treating the golf course as if he owned it. If there were twenty divots out of a fairway, and the golfers who'd caused them had moved on to the next hole, he'd go out there and tell them to go back and replace them or to get off the golf course. Now, these are things that a golf pro shouldn't have to worry about."

By the summer of 1986, the pot was about to boil over, and Stan realized that he had to make a decision on his future, and make it soon. "My whole personality was being warped," he says. "I'm not saying the pressure on me was all external – some of it I put on myself. I did want the job to go smoothly, wanted the place to look nice. But the effort I was putting in was just affecting our lives way too much."

Stan's abrupt resignation that August was a well-noted event in Chicago. Not only was Stan himself still newsworthy as a Hall of Fame Black Hawk, but the golf course, too, had gained a popular reputation in the area. In fact, at the time of the resignation, the course was hosting the Illinois PGA tournament, the first PGA event for which Stan was an eligible player. "Things had become intolerable for me by this time," he says. "There were the workload problems as well as personality conflicts at the club. After my first day of play in the tournament, I told the boss that if he didn't do something by the time I left the course the next day, I'd be gone. The next day when I came in from the last green, I asked if there were any messages for me. When I was told there weren't, I said, 'Fine,' and I went in and started clearing out my office. There were newspaper reporters covering the tournament, and when they saw what I was doing, they said, 'What's going on?' I told them, 'No comment.'

"The next day I see in the paper, 'MIKITA RESIGNS.' The reporters had gone to the fellow who was running Kemper Sports – I'd rather not mention his name – and had asked about my leaving the club. He was quoted as saying that I'd left because I had 'personal problems.' Well, you know what the implications of that are – am I a drug user? an alcoholic? do I beat my wife and kids? is a divorce imminent? Nothing was specified. It was all open to speculation? I demanded a retraction."

Jill Mikita, who describes herself as "ruthless – like a lioness" when it comes to protecting the privacy and dignity of her family, was as upset as anyone over the incident. "It left us so vulnerable!" she exclaims. "In the meantime, this same gentleman we're talking about called here and said, 'Jill, this is so-and-so. Is Stan available?' For years, I've known when Stan wants to talk to somebody and when he doesn't, and I just said, 'No, he's not.' And he said, 'Well, I just want

(Clockwise from left) Jane, Stan, Jill, Chris, Meg, Scott, and the family pet
Mandy, Christmas 1988.

Jill and Stan Mikita.

Bobby Hull, the first NHL player to score more than fifty goals in a season, with his sons Bobby Jr. (left) and Blake.

The Golden Jet.

Bob and Deborah with Colleen Howe, 1988.

A pair of nines.

The Canadiens' all-time dream team at the Forum, 1984 (clockwise): the late Jacques Plante, Larry Robinson, Toe Blake, Jean Beliveau, Dickie Moore, the late Aurele Joliat, Doug Harvey, Maurice Richard, and Bob Gainey.

The Rocket and Lucille arriving at
Rideau Hall.

The Rocket (or "Rock," as he was
known to his teammates) in his office at
S. Albert Fuels.

The Howes on their wedding day, 1953.

Mark, Colleen, and Edna Gadsby share a thrilling moment during the 1963-64 season.

Three generations – Gordie, Travis, and Mark – at the '86 all-star game in Hartford, Connecticut.

The Howe team.

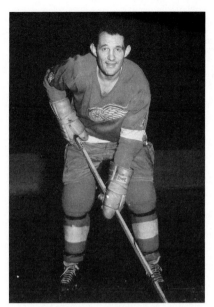

Bill Gadsby during the last season
of his career, 1966. He later returned
to coach the Red Wings (below).

Bill and Edna Gadsby pose with their four "hall-of-famers" at a Detroit Red Wings skating party in 1965, and, below, at Sandy's wedding in 1983.

you to know that I didn't say what the papers said I did – I was misquoted.' "

A retraction appeared the following day, but Stan has never accepted the stated rationale for it. "The papers said they'd misquoted the guy, but they hadn't. He'd said what he was reported to have said. The papers were simply put under pressure to retract. I've seen the guy since then. I nodded my head to him, hello."

The months that followed were not easy for the Mikitas. "We were just floating, no direction," says Jill. "Stan had no idea what he was going to do, or even what he might *like* to do. Our finances were okay for a while, but not exactly great, with two kids in college."

Stan was forty-five years old and, by his own assessment, "had no real qualifications. I knew how to play hockey, and I knew a little bit about the golf business. But I was so turned off by golf I didn't want anything to do with it. A number of my friends in pro golf phoned and offered me jobs teaching and so on, and I'll never forget them for it. But there was just no way. I mean, I still loved playing the game, but I *did not want to have to make a living at it.* And I couldn't exactly make a hockey comeback."

One thing did go in Stan's favour during the few months following his resignation – Kemper Sports decided to pay his salary from August to November. Stan contends that the decision was based on guilt over the statements that had appeared in the press. "I was never really paid all that well for golf anyway," he confides. "I was barely covering expenses."

By early autumn, the Mikita family had begun to feel unforeseen effects from Stan's career inactivity. "He'd never been around that much for the kids, but now he started to play serious father," explains Jill. "It was difficult for the kids – in fact, it made them kind of resentful. Suddenly, here was Stan asking them where they were going, what time they were going to be home, this sort of thing. Our oldest boy, Scott, would come home from college, and he wasn't accustomed to this. See, I'd always taken care of discipline, and the kids were used to me. I'm not saying Stan was wrong in taking up this responsibility. It just came along a little too late to be effective. But it was certainly part of our growing process."

As the weeks passed, Stan began talking to business friends, attempting to get some idea of what they thought his strengths might be if he went into business. "And I'd get the typical answers, that all I had to do was make up my mind, that I could do whatever I wanted, and so on, which didn't help much. I didn't want to get into something and go belly up because I didn't know what I was doing.

"One day I was talking to a friend, and the idea of a car dealership came up. It seemed like a good possibility, so we pursued it for a few months. But the more I thought about it, the more I saw potential problems. For example, I really don't delegate authority very well. I'd discovered this in the golf business, where I was always doing things myself instead of getting others to do them. *I wanted things done right.* But I realized that in the car business, if somebody who worked for me didn't put a muffler on properly, and a customer complained, I wouldn't be able to fix that muffler myself. At least in golf, I knew how to put things right if they screwed up. . . . What's more, the dealership would have been an hour's drive from here – that's a long way."

Jill was perhaps more convinced than Stan that the car business would be a disaster. "I'd always felt that our first obligation at that point was to finish educating our children. And I've always figured I could go to work if necessary – it wouldn't faze me in the least. So I wasn't thinking so much about finances. I just felt that a car dealership would be no better than golf in terms of the pressure it put on Stan. I could see the sixteen-hour days again, and I just shuddered."

In the end it was neither cars nor golf balls or hockey pucks but the petro-alchemic miracle of the twentieth century that renewed Stan's career ambitions. He describes his re-entry into the job market:

"We were in Florida that Christmas – we had a little place outside Tampa – and Glen Skov, a former teammate of mine, was down there. He'd been in the plastics business for twenty-five years, and he'd quit his job at about the same time I'd quit golf. One day we were having a beer, and we kind of looked at one another, and he said, 'What are *you* going to do?' And I said, 'What are *you* going to do?' And he said, 'I'm going to rep for a plastics colouring company in the Chicago area.' Up to that point, he'd managed a similar company's production plant. He said, 'I'm thinking of getting a partner and representing four or five lines – colourings *and* plastics.' Glen didn't want to work particularly long hours, and I know I didn't. So when we got back home, I let the car thing go, called Glen, and we had lunch. He explained what the business was, and I said, 'I've never been in sales.' He said, 'Don't worry, I'll teach you. You can follow me around for a while.' I said, 'I don't know the first thing about plastics either.' He said, 'You don't have to. You don't tell the customer what he wants, he tells you. You write it down and go to the supplier and say, "Here's what the guy wants – how much is it going to cost?" ' We don't sell an end product. We sell bulk plastic and we sell the colouring chips that go into it."

Stan has spent the better part of the past two years learning the ins and outs of the plastics business. He speaks of his work with rare enthusiasm, holding forth in an industrial dialect replete with the mysteries of "sheet extrusion," "blow moulding," and "profile extrusion."

It is something of an irony that, in a field as dynamic as plastics – in a century of computers and spaceships – Stan's fortunes may well rest with the future of the humble outhouse. "One of our biggest customers is a port-a-potty maker, a john maker – outdoor craphouses," he smiles. "We represent the sheet extruder who makes the plastic for the roof and sides of these things. And we represent the colour maker – you can't have a transparent craphouse. We also represent a profile extruder who makes little corner strappings that hold these contraptions together. And we represent an injection-moulding company that makes the plastic door latches. We don't have anything to do with the plastic holding bowls beneath the seats, the place where all the chemicals and so on go, but we hope they'll eventually be made by a blow moulder we represent. The only other parts are a pipe to take the stink out – it's made by profile extrusion – and the air vents, which we're looking to make by injection moulding."

Stan is optimistic in pointing out that with new laws being passed across the U.S., contractors, large farmers, and other outdoor employers will be obliged to have one on-site "pot" for every ten workers. He says, "We're looking for a boom here. I'm having a heck of a good time. Every day I learn something new. Going from golf to this is like coming out into the daylight."

Jill, too, is happy, because Stan is happy. She says, "I enjoy seeing him doing something he likes. At the beginning he was less sure of himself. But Stan is bright, and he enjoys people. He's in the place he ought to be. And I'm having a ball just acting as his secretary – mostly just answering the phone and doing some typing."

Jill is also pleased that, after twenty-five years of spending more time on her own than she might have cared to, Stan's endeavours are providing plenty of time for togetherness. "Only very rarely does he have to be at a certain place at a certain time," she says. "This year we went to every one of our son Christopher's soccer games. And we have more time for things like the theatre – we love going to the theatre. Stan really enjoys the lighter stuff. He says that Shakespeare's a bit obscure for him, yet when our son Scott was in college, we attended one of his Shakespeare classes, and it was absolutely fascinating to both of us. Later this month, we're all going to *Swan Lake*, the ballet. We go to the opera and the art galleries. We simply enjoy the arts. When we were in Amsterdam a few years ago, we spent hours and hours walking through the art museums."

Stan admits that during his playing days he didn't have time for the arts. "My whole life was consumed by hockey and other sports. So this has been quite a turnaround for me."

The fact that Stan works at home has undoubtedly aided his contribution to family unity. He is as honest as a Quaker, and willingly confesses that he can't afford a separate office at this point. Then again, he hardly needs one. He has a spacious bivouac in the front corner of the house that many executives would kill for: big window, big hardwood desk, plush carpet and furniture. On the walls, among the framed photos and magazine covers and memoribilia, there are dozens of citations – "for dedication," "for tireless service," "for outstanding work," "for exceptional leadership" (among other things, Stan has operated a hockey school for the hearing-impaired for the past sixteen years). One commendation is signed by the late U.S. Senator Everett Dirksen, "with best wishes to a champion." On the end wall hangs a handsome oil painting of Stan in his red Black Hawk jersey. Replicas of the Hart Trophy, Lady Byng Trophy, Art Ross Trophy, and Stanley Cup sit on a nearby shelf.

On the wall opposite Stan's desk hangs a framed newspaper report about the night in 1980 when the Black Hawks retired Stan's number (he was the first player in the history of the team to be so honoured). The account quotes the closing lines of his speech that night: "I have one more duty, and that comes from the heart. I'd like to pay tribute to someone who besides giving me love and affection gave me the greatest commodity in life. He took me out of a communist country and gave me something I think we're all striving for. He gave me freedom. I'd like to pay tribute to the greatest guy I know – my pop."

It is a long trip from Sokolce, Czechoslovakia, to Oakbrook, Illinois, but Stan has not forgotten the stops along the way.

7

Bob and Deborah Hull

. . . .

A KIND OF DREAM

THE POWER: "Do you know what I used to think when I was playing? I used to think that I must be going to die soon, and that these people were just allowing me to do these things before I died. It was a kind of dream. So many people would have loved to live my life. As to what it all meant, I don't know, I can't say. In many ways it was magical – does magic have meaning? I do know that when I'd pick up the puck behind my own goal and start up the ice with my jersey fluttering and go the whole length of the rink and slap one in the net – when I did that, if the fans had sat there twiddling their thumbs, I'd have felt it was all for nought. But to hear those people, to almost *feel* them charging down the ice with me was the greatest feeling in the world. I can't tell you how it felt to have power over 20,000 people in that way."

THE PRAGMATIST: "The problem with leaving the game was not being able to find any replacement for it – anything that was even a distant second to it in terms of excitement. I searched around for a while, but eventually I had to accept that I wasn't *going* to find anything that I could go at with the same energy that I'd always gone at hockey. It just wasn't there. So I've been biding my time from then to now – almost ten years. I mean there's always been the cattle, but beyond that I've never wanted to get involved with anything, jump in with both feet and then find out I didn't like it. So I said, I'll just do this and that, stay busy, make a buck here, a buck there, wait until that one thing comes along again. With a little patience maybe it will. Maybe it never will. Maybe I'll just continue for another five years or so, if I live that long, doing a bit of this, a bit of that. There's always something that comes along to pad the bank book."

THE WOMAN: "There's nothing I'd love more than to see Bob back in hockey, because he adores it, just like he adores his cattle. He's so obsessive and so creative about it, I just know that he could do something wonderful if he was given the chance. But for that to happen, hockey people would have to start treating him like a human being. I've been around Mr. Wirtz and his buddies a number of times, and I think they really respect Bob's athletic abilities and achievements. In fact, they see him as this athletic god. But they just don't take his views or opinions seriously. They don't have any regard for his intelligence – it runs entirely counter to theirs. It's sad, because Bob could do so much for hockey. He's available, they could use him, but they don't."

To get to Bob and Deborah Hull's, you drive south from Belleville, Ontario, across the bridge that spans the Bay of Quinte, and out onto the sprawling rural island that forms Prince Edward County. From the village of Rossmore you follow an ever-narrowing series of roads across sparsely populated, low-lying pasture and woodland. There is something primitive, even haunting about the landscape. It is not so much farm land as an amalgam of moor and range, close-cropped and dotted with cedars that emerge from the ground like random pegs in a game board. Chunks of limestone dot the sparse soil.

If you follow your directions closely they will eventually lead to a tastefully modest beige bungalow that sits within twenty metres of the Bay of Quinte on the island's north side.

Two sturdy brick pillars greet the visitor at the end of the driveway, and close to the house sits a white Chrysler New Yorker. The place is shaded by tall blue spruces and, while carefully groomed, has a summery insouciance about it, a cottage-like quality, accentuated by the vast body of water that laps up to the shoreline in front. In the distance, across that water, is a low ridge of mainland; and out of sight, somewhere to the northwest, are the remains of Point Anne, once a lively company town where Bob's father worked in the cement plant and where the young phenom grew up with his ten brothers and sisters. There is an air of wistful relinquishment in Bob's voice as he explains that, with the cement plant gone, Point Anne is "practically a ghost town."

Bob bought the lakeside house in 1959 and, since then, has occupied it sporadically, mostly during summers. At one time he farmed neighbouring land, and it was here nearly three decades ago that an enterprising photographer shot the famous beefcake photo of the brawny young Black Hawk pitching hay.

Today, Bob shares the house with his thirty-seven-year-old wife Deborah and his nine-year-old daughter from a previous relationship. In the two years since her arrival, Deborah has worked hard to put her signature on the place, refurbishing it room by room (six down, four to go). "My father was a contractor," she smiles, "and I used to love going to the new houses and driving nails and so on. My idea of a good time around here is tearing up a room and putting it back together the way I want it."

Deborah is a pretty woman in a pleasingly unconventional way. She has a high forehead and fine sandy-blonde hair, cut off with geometric precision at the nape of her neck. Her face is a study in focus (she has a way of looking at you that gives the impression she is either intensely interested in or intensely sceptical of what you are saying). She wears no make-up and her somewhat studious mien is accented by a pair of stylish red-framed glasses.

Her tastes in decor are a discreet hybrid of rural charm and old-world refinement. Regency hardwoods are crossed with Quimper china and back-country antiques. It is only in the newly finished rec room and bar – an artfully converted garage – that she has acceded to a more vernacular style, well suited to the room's use as a showplace for Bob's trophies and mementoes. Here, hockey photos share wall space with photos of champion bulls. And along one wall are perhaps fifty bronzed pucks, representing a variety of Bob's goal-scoring achievements. By no means, however, are all of the mementoes of his spectacular career given wall space, or even preferential lodging. Some twenty-five landmark sticks – commemorating a 50th goal, a 500th goal, a first WHA goal – are stuffed helter-skelter into the furnace room. Some are marked with ballpoint or pencil scratchings indicating what achievement they represent; some are unmarked. ("I haven't got a clue what they all are," laughs Bob.) The more intimate pieces of his gear – the shin pads and shoulder pads and elbow pads, all of which he wore from day one in Chicago to the day of his retirement twenty-three years later – are in a canvas bag in a portable garden shed in the backyard. In the name of literature, Bob retreats to the shed and produces the fossilized equipment, declaring as he pulls a few pieces from the bag that it is "held together with dust" – not very cohesive dust, as it turns out. The shoulder pads, threadbare relics that would surely provide no more protection than the shoulder pads in an average Armani sports coat, fall into two pieces as he attempts to untangle their laces and straps. The cracked shin pads are wadded up with cotton batting and look like something a pick-up player might dig out of his basement for a game at the community rink. "Actually, my legs never took that bad a beating," Bob muses as he throws the shin guards back in the bag. "But my arms! I always defended with my left arm as I cut toward the goal on my backhand, and, oh, it got an awful pounding."

In his fifty-first year, Bob himself is much better preserved than his equipment. Although he has not played hockey in more than nine years, he has not forfeited the physique that, throughout his career, made him one of hockey's strongest competitors. His chest is a boulder of muscle, his forearms as big around as fenceposts. Nor has he forfeited the Duracell smile that once signalled his role as hockey's most gregarious ambassador. He maintains a rich open laugh (which occasionally ascends into a mischievous cackle) and a bear's helping of boyish charm.

But there is also a pensiveness to Bob these days – a more shadowy sense of himself than has perhaps been present in the past. During a day of conversation, he several times makes reference to his mortality, as if it has been on his mind. Asked about the references, he passes them off, purporting not to have noticed that he has made them. They may be a function of his age; but it is difficult not to speculate that they are equally, subliminally, connected to the death of his and Deborah's infant son Ryan four years ago.

All of which is not to suggest that Bob has been anything less than a complex human being in the past. He has always had a broad emotional contour – part of which is a capacity for impetuosity – and a broad, poetic range of expression. His conversation is laced with graphic verbs and vivid turns of phrase. Nowhere is his lyricism more evident or appealling than in his evocation of working on his relatives' farm near Marysville, Ontario, as a boy. "It was just across the water here," he says, giving his head a cursory toss in the direction of the bay. "From the age of ten on, I spent my entire summer holiday there, haying, then thrashing – oh, I loved that thrashing; they used to stook thrash. I loved pitching on the sheaves. Then the older fellas used to have me carrying grain the length of those big Ontario barns and dumping it in the bins. They used to fill those bran sacks to the top with wheat, so that I could hardly get a handhold on them. The older guys used to laugh watching me stagger around trying to get those big sacks on my shoulder. They must have weighed 150 pounds each – and me just a pup. It's a wonder my guts didn't bust. But I loved it anyway. . . . And the meals! Oh, they were just heaven! See, the farmers along the road from about Shannonville to Marysville used to exchange help at thrashing time. I'd take the team and wagon and go wherever the thrashing machine was. And the gals on these farms would always try to outdo one another at mealtime – they'd have anything from *beef* to *pork* to *chicken* to *duck* to *lamb*, and about sixteen different pies and cakes; it was just fantastic the way those farm girls could cook. And I loved to eat – I *needed* it, I was working so hard. I was very ambitious as a kid – on the dogtrot all the time, never walked anywhere. I remember once during thrashing I was out in the field pitching sheaves with two older farmers, and they jawed all morning and smoked their pipes, never took their pitch forks off their shoulders. I'd run from one shock to the next and, before they'd get there, the sheaves were all on the wagon. At noon hour these older fellas came in for dinner at my mom's cousin's – her name was Hemmy Topping – and I'll never forget them saying, '*Hemmy*, you better get that kid out of that field or he's gonna *kill* himself!' And here they'd done absolutely nothing to help me all morning!

"I loved those summers. That's where my love of agriculture and cattle comes from. And also from just driving through the country in the old 1930 Model A Ford, with my mom and dad and sisters and brothers. I'd see those old red-and-white Herefords out there on that green meadow, and they looked kinda nice to me, and I thought that if I was ever able to afford some, I'd buy 'em. And as soon as I could, I did."

Since 1959, Bob has farmed, either on his own or with partners, in half a dozen locations in Ontario, Saskatchewan, and Manitoba. He is currently part-owner of a good-sized Hereford breeding operation, through which he shares cattle with the owners of three central Ontario farms. Although he has no formal schooling in agriculture, he has learned his lessons well enough that, not long ago, he was invited to lecture on Hereford breeding at the Agricultural College of the University of Guelph. He is an unofficial spokesman for the Polled Hereford industry and an internationally respected judge of quality cattle. "It's an art," he says, "and I've worked hard at it for thirty years."

And never harder than now, although no longer at the end of a hay rake or manure shovel as in years gone by. Nowadays, Bob logs endless miles of travel selling the unlikely commodity, bull semen. "That and my breeding program, B and C Polled Herefords," he says. He produces his engagement calendar – "my little book": a roughed-up and extremely unofficial looking promotional handout from a greeting card company – and flips through it, calculating that he spends at least a hundred days a year on the road in aid of semen sales. "We sell all over the U.S., Europe, South America, Japan – I'm doing more travelling now than I did when I was playing hockey. I go to sales, shows, to visit herds, sometimes just to keep abreast of what's going on, seeing which of our bulls are doing the job. It all takes lots of time, lots of effort, lots of money. A lot of money comes in, a lot goes out." Which might suggest a rather narrow margin of profitability. But Bob considers the breeding business less risky than most farming (which is perhaps not saying much in an industry that regularly bankrupts even its thriftiest practitioners). "This isn't the beef business, where you never know what you're going to get per pound. All our animals are pedigree. The only ones that go down to the golden arches are those that we don't feel are good enough to be breeding stock."

As effusive as Bob is about his business, it is not until he takes out his cattle photos – *stacks* of them – and begins to rhapsodize over bulls with names such as Rhett Butler, Excalibur, The Stick, High Noon, and Moonraker that you sense the true extent of his affection for his animals. "Here's High Noon's mommy – isn't she beautiful!" enthuses the doting squire, displaying a Kodacolour likeness of an animal that the average punter might mistake for any healthy Hereford cow. "And here's The Stick. Isn't he something!"

The Stick *is* something – or at least was until he broke his leg two summers ago and was reluctantly dispatched to bull heaven. "I knew he was special the moment I laid eyes on him," says Bob, who spotted him as a calf in a Connecticut field nearly a decade ago and bought him for $2,500. "He brought in more than $100,000 a year in semen sales for more than five years running. He was the daddy not only of *our* current operation but of a whole new breed of Polled Herefords. In fact, The Stick will probably go down in history as the most influential sire in the Polled Hereford industry. He had that kind of impact."

Never one to withhold praise (or its opposite, if he feels justified in dispensing it), Bob ascribes at least a corner of his niche in the Hockey Hall of Fame to his love and practice of agriculture. "I spent my summers throwing bales around and wrestling cattle, and it kept me in terrific shape. You've got to understand that the success of my game depended entirely on physical strength. I was powerful, I could skate, I could shoot."

Indeed, for hundreds of thousands of hockey fans during the 1960s and 1970s, Bob's magnificent skating and shooting were the very definition of the game of hockey at its best. Fitness king Lloyd Percival once measured Bob's shot at nearly 200 kilometres per hour. And his skating speed has seldom if ever been matched. Bob entered the NHL as an eighteen-year-old in 1957, and during twenty-three professional seasons was named to seventeen all-star teams, won four scoring championships, and was the first player to score more than fifty goals in an NHL season. In 1974-75, with the Winnipeg Jets, he scored a remarkable seventy-seven times. His signature move, the one for which his fans best remember him, was to accelerate across the blueline on the left wing (either with the puck or to receive a pass), to raise his stick to an exaggerated height and pound his terrifying slapshot at the net. When he wound up to shoot, a momentary paralysis would grip the crowd and undoubtedly the opposition goaltender. "When his shot hit you," says Hall of Fame goaltender Johnny Bower, "it was like being walloped with a sledgehammer." In the words of goaltender Les Binkley, "When the puck left his stick, it looked like a pea. Then as it picked up speed it looked smaller and smaller. Then you didn't see it anymore."

By no means, however, was Bob's impact on the game confined to his skills as a player. As much as anything, it was his radical defection from the Chicago Black Hawks to the Winnipeg Jets of the then-fragile World Hockey Association in 1972 that marked him as the most influential player of his generation. By signing with the Jets he gave instant credibility not only to his new team but to the entire WHA. In fact, had he not lent his formidable presence to the new league, whose solvency quotient at the time was approximately that of distilled water on marble, there would quite likely have been no WHA after a season or two; and the Winnipeg Jets, Edmonton Oilers, Quebec Nordiques, and Hartford Whalers would almost certainly not be part of the NHL today.

Of more significance to his peers, Bob's daring migration dramatically altered the game's salary structure. In the competitive open market between the two leagues, many players increased their income four- and five-fold. Even journeyman players, who might have been earning $20,000 in the NHL, were given $100,000 contracts by WHA teams. Other NHL players were given large contracts not to defect. "We all owe him a lot," says Stan Mikita, who was courted by the new league but chose to remain with the NHL Chicago Black Hawks. "For a while there, every morning when I got out of bed, I tried to figure out where Bob would be, bowed down in that direction, and said, 'Thank you, Bob. Thank you for doing what you did.'"

Bill Wirtz, the owner of the Chicago Black Hawks and a senior NHL governor, once told Bob's brother Dennis that the all-star winger's defection cost the Black Hawks and the NHL a billion dollars over a ten-year period. "I didn't believe it," Bob scoffs. "But one day I mentioned it to Harvey Wineberg, my accountant in Chicago, and he said, 'Well let's see – the Hawks went from crowds of 22,000 down to an average of 8,000 . . .' Harvey just makes that old adding machine smoke. And by the time he went through salaries, loss of attendance, everything else, he tallied up a billion dollars. So you can understand that the NHL wasn't too happy with me."

By way of punishing the departed star – and a nasty spanking it turned out to be – the Black Hawks immediately obtained a court injunction preventing him from joining his new team. "I couldn't even practise with them," says Bob. "I missed eighteen games and, for weeks, didn't know whether I'd ever play again. Wirtz had the judge in his back pocket. The Hawks thought that because of a certain clause in the standard NHL contract their hold on me was perpetual – that they *owned* me. But when it came to a final ruling, a black judge in Philadelphia, a guy named Higginbottom, said, 'Nobody *owns* anybody!' And I was free to play."

In the meantime, the NHL approached the Ford Motor Company, CCM, and a number of other corporations that advertised on *Hockey Night in Canada* and that also held endorsement contracts with Bob, and told them that if they did not jettison Hull, the league would jettison them as sponsors. "If I hadn't been so busy trying to get settled in Winnipeg, I'd have sued them blind," says Bob. "But I had too much else going on at that point.

"Then there was the '72 series with the Russians – it was called a Canada-U.S.S.R. series, not an NHL series, but the organizers wouldn't let me play because I was no longer in the NHL. Bill Wirtz, Alan Eagleson (president of the NHL Players' Association), and Clarence Campbell (then NHL president) were behind that. Eagleson's *such* a fart, and Campbell was the crookedest old snake that ever was. He was the guy putting pressure on Ford and CCM to throw me out. He was acting for the league owners, of course. He was just a puppet."

Bob makes it clear that, even up to within days of his signing with the new league, he had no intention of leaving Chicago. "As far as I was concerned it was the greatest city in the world, with the greatest fans. But the Hawks were giving me contract hassles. They always had. Back in '67 when I'd signed my last contract, they'd promised to leverage my income and invest this and do that, and they'd never done anything about these promises. The foot-dragging went on for several years, and finally at training camp one year, I said, 'If you don't clear all this up I'm not going to be here at the start of the season.' And I wasn't. I sat out nearly twenty games."

During the one-man strike, Bob deeply antagonized his employers by calling Wirtz "a bumstead" and Hawks' general manager Tommy Ivan "a puppet" – names that found their way into the Chicago newspapers. "I had quite a go with the Wirtzes over it all," he chuckles. "I was talking to old Arthur and young Bill at one point, and I said something, and the old man objected, and Bill said to his father, 'But Bobby's right, Dad!' And the old man hollered, 'Shuddup, Bill!' And I said to him, 'Bill, you're forty-five years old – are you going to let that fat old putz tell you to shut up when you know you're right?' And he said in this whimpery voice, 'Well, you know, Bobby, he is my father.' And I said, 'What's the matter? – you're *right* , and he told you to shut up! I wouldn't take that from my father!' It was just a bad scene all around."

When it came to offering a new contract at the end of the 1972 season, the Black Hawks were as sluggish as ever. But this time Bob had a career option that had never before existed for NHL players. In fact, the WHA had made its initial pitch to him several months earlier: "I'd flown to Vancouver for a game in the middle of the season, and as we checked into our hotel, Bob Turner, an old teammate of mine, came up to me in the lobby. He said, 'Bobby, would you mind meeting a friend of mine from Winnipeg?' I said, 'Not at all. Who is he?' He said, 'Ben Hatskin – he's my boss; I'm in the pinball and vending machine business with him. He's across the street in the hotel.' I'd never heard of Ben Hatskin, but after I'd cleaned up, I went across the street with Bob, walked in, and there was big Ben. We talked for a couple of minutes, and suddenly he said, 'I want you to come and play for the Winnipeg Jets.' Just like that. Apparently they'd put the names of all the NHL players in a hat, and Winnipeg had drawn my name. Ben said, 'I'll give you $250,000 a year for as long as you want to play, and $100,000 a year after that, if you want to stay and coach.' I was making about $100,000 a year in Chicago. I said, 'That's an awful nice offer, Ben, and I appreciate it, but there are two problems – I've got half a season still to play with the Black Hawks before I even want to talk and, furthermore, I think I can get $250,000 a year in Chicago.' "

No sooner was Hull back in Chicago than phone calls began coming in from Hatskin's office – as many as two or three a day. Hatskin also began hectoring Bob's accountant, Harvey Wineberg. "When the playoffs ended it just got crazy," says Bob. "At that point, I was meeting with Arthur Morris, a lawyer who the Black Hawks had sicked on me to try to sign me up. He'd say, 'What do you want, Bob?' And I'd say, 'Look, Arthur, I've busted my tail for this organization for fifteen years. You guys have to try to sign *me*. You make me an offer, and I'll respond to it.'

"By this time the media was beginning to get excited about the WHA and how they were romancing me, the whole deal. The phone calls were coming in so thick and fast by now that finally I said to Harvey, 'Look, they've gotten their million dollars' worth of publicity out of this. Tell them to get lost! I'm sick of their badgering! I mean it! I'm not going!' An hour later, Harvey called back and said, 'They want to know what it *would* take to bring you to Winnipeg.' I said, 'There's no *way* I'm going to cart an extravagant wife and five kids across the continent to a city I've never even been to.' Harvey said, 'They *still* want to know what it'll take for you to go.' So I said, 'Harvey, I can get $250,000 a year in Chicago for the next five years.' I'd made up my mind that that was going to be my salary. I said, 'What if I go to Winnipeg for the same money, and the league folds. They're not going to want me back in Chicago or anywhere else – I'm out a million bucks.' So I said, 'Go tell them I want a million dollars up front.' This was just to scare them, to get rid of them. A while later Harvey called me back and said, 'They don't want us to do anything until we hear from them.' I said, 'You mean they're considering raising a million bucks?' He said, 'Yep!' I said, 'I should have asked for ten – *I don't want to go to Winnipeg!*'

"All I *ever* wanted was a contract from the Hawks! And they didn't offer one until well into June. They hand-delivered it – $250,000 a year for five years. And I said to the guy who brought it, 'You can take this back to Mr. Wirtz – it's too late.' A few days earlier, the WHA had been in touch to say they'd raised half a million. The next day they phoned to say they were at $750,000. At that point I said, 'I'm gone, Harvey. If they've got that much, Ben Hatskin himself will ante up the other $250,000. I've given my word that I'll go for a million.' "

The World Hockey Association was certainly no Jerusalem for the million-dollar man. The league expected a return on its money, and, within months, the pressure of promotional obligations – a steady schedule of interviews, speeches, and rubber chicken – had afflicted Bob with a painful ulcer. Playing conditions, too, took their toll: eight- and nine-day road trips on which as many eight games were scheduled; second-rate facilities and, in some cases, second-rate opponents. "It got pretty rough," says Bob, arching an eyebrow. "I mean, in Chicago, I was just a member of a team in a well-established league with a good reputation. In Winnipeg, I was with a league that had to take second and third dates in arenas that were sometimes just horrible. In New Jersey it was hilarious – we'd put on our equipment in the Holiday Inn, then bus over to the arena in our street shoes and go into a little dressing room in *shifts* to put our skates on. The room was so tiny we couldn't all go in at once. And the rink was tilted! By the end of a period, with the snow built up on the ice, you really had to be able to shoot the puck just to ice it.

"And of course they let in a lot of incompetent coaches and players. We used to call the Birmingham Bulls the Birmingham Circus. Most of them were just goons, kookaloos, brought in to harass the better players, and they had a kookaloo coach, Glen Sonmor. And, here, I was supposed to be promoting all this to the world!"

The ultimate hardship for jumping leagues – and, in a larger sense, for being such an inveterate individualist – would not be known to Bob for a number of years. In fact, it was not until sometime after the two leagues had amalgamated in 1979 and he had retired that it became clear there was no place for him, and probably never would be, in what was now the only game in town, the NHL. Asked if "blackballed" is too strong a word to describe his current status relative to the NHL, he quips, "It's probably not strong enough. Certainly there are powerful people in the league who don't want me around. Eagleson is one guy who's against me. And Bill Wirtz once said in print that there's no place for me in the Chicago organization. Then again, Bill may not even be in control in Chicago. I think that lugnut Eagleson's got him so wound up that he doesn't know in from out. I wouldn't *mind* working with the Blackhawks, because I wouldn't mind living in Chicago. But I doubt it could ever happen."

Bob also believes that his long-standing commitment to fair and creative play, to the eradication of violence and intimidation, is too radical, too impractical for most NHL organizations. "There are a lot of people in pro hockey who'll tell you that the fans enjoy blood. But, let me tell you, they only want blood if you give them bad hockey. They *will not stand* for mediocrity; blood is more exciting. But if you replace mediocrity with *good* hockey, they'll buy it. Soon that's all they'll want, and if anyone impedes that good hockey, it takes away from their entertainment, and they won't stand for that. If you're going to give people bad hockey then you'd better stick about fourteen fights in with it, because that's the only way they'll watch it."

Bob is equally convinced that his presence in an NHL organization would make others in the organization nervous about their jobs. "I don't want anybody's job! But I'll admit that I'd love to put together a bunch of guys who know how the game should be played. I don't need to be a coach or a manager, or even have a title – just let me loose."

Since it is extremely unlikely that Bob will be "let loose" in the NHL, he would seem to have but one route back to the game: another new league, a league that he himself might very well help create. "We did it before, we could do it again," he says nonchalantly. "I'm serious. I've batted it around with a few people. But we'd need somebody like a Mario Lemieux to make it work. When Mario was having contract troubles in Pittsburgh a while back, I thought, Boy, if only we had something in place right now. We've got the cities and the facilities. Look at Hamilton – great rink, lots of people. They haven't even got a team, and they're only two points behind the Maple Leafs. I'm sure we could get people to take on a team in Hamilton, and I'm pretty sure about Milwaukee, Indianapolis, Chicago, San Francisco, maybe the east coast. What we have to do is map it out, go visit potential owners, tell them, 'This is the way it's going to be done. This is the sort of entertainment you're going to be involved in.' Of course, some of these people will be waiting for an NHL franchise, and it's going to be tough to convince them that our hockey is going to be every bit as interesting, or *more* interesting than the NHL."

In contrast to the possibility of returning to hockey, Bob has also imagined a quieter, more genial life for himself as he approaches his fifty-first birthday. He says, "Sometimes I think I should just start enjoying what time I have left. I don't want to be patted in the face with a spade before I do a lot of the things I want to do. I'd certainly like to get to a point where I'm a little better organized than I am now – not so

much helter-skelter, here and there, cattle sales, appearances, endorsements. I get tired of it all, tired of the travel.
Whether I'll ever be able to shut down entirely and be happy,
I'm not sure. I know I can't stay here in the country for all that
long before I get an itch to get to the city. I guess that's my
problem – I still have this wound-up spring inside of me, tight
as a bowstring. Nervous energy. It compels me to keep going.
Probably the only way to release that energy is to channel it
into one all-consuming pursuit. And I don't mean cattle. As
much as I love the cattle business, it's never really demanded
or gotten my full energy or attention. It's not quite enough.
The problem lies in finding that all-absorbing pursuit. No
matter which way I look at it, the closest thing I can imagine
to it is hockey."

One afternoon during the winter of 1983, as he worked
around the house, Bob received a telephone call from a young
woman in Bensenville, Illinois, a western suburb of Chicago.
The young woman explained that she worked in advertising
for a drug store wholesale company and that her boss was the
sponsor of an annual hockey tournament for the hearing
impaired. She wanted to know whether Bob could be persuaded to attend this year's tournament?

"I hadn't even wanted to *make* the call," laughs Deborah.
"In fact, when my boss, who was a real promoter, told me to
call Bobby Hull, I blurted, 'I'm not calling Bobby Hull! There's
no way I'm getting on the phone and calling *the* Bobby Hull.'
I mean, Bob is this legendary character in Chicago, right? My
boss said, 'No, call him. I want to get him down here!' I kept
saying I wouldn't do it, but you can only say no to your boss
so many times.

"As it turned out, Bob initially agreed to attend. But then he
phoned and cancelled. Well, my boss just went through the
roof. He said, 'That is not acceptable, I will not hear of it, I
have to have him. Get him on the phone again, Debbie. Ask
him how much he wants.' I was pretty embarrassed by this

time, but I got Bob on the phone, and my boss spoke to him, and they settled on a fee for the appearance. As soon as he hung up, my boss said, 'Get the air ticket, get the cheque cut, and get it to him Federal Express, so he can't say no.'

"Before the tournament, I had a last phone conversation with Bob, and he said, 'I'll have to meet you when I get to town.' "

For a year following their meeting, Bob and Deborah saw one another every few months, during his visits to Chicago. "But we never saw one another or spoke between times," she says. "Who knows where he was? Just gone! But when he'd get to Chicago, he'd call, and we'd go out, eat, whatever."

At Easter, 1984, Bob surprised Deborah by asking her to return with him to Ontario. "By this time," she says, "I'd quit work in Bensenville, and I thought, What a great deal! I've never been to Canada. I have nothing to lose, everything to gain. I mean, I really did sincerely like the fella.

"So I came up here to the island – I remember driving in from Belleville, weaving and turning, and thinking, Where on earth am I going? It seemed so desolate.

"I ended up staying three months, then returned to Chicago, and Bob left for a trip to Alaska. When he got back he had a bunch of little gold nuggets from which he planned to make a ring for me. I thought, Oh, no, this guy's getting serious."

Over the years, marriage has not been an easy road for Bob. An ill-advised teenage marriage while he was playing Junior hockey in St. Catharines ended quickly in divorce, but not before producing a son. His subsequent marriage to Joanne in 1960 lasted nearly two decades and engendered four sons and a daughter before ending in a protracted, painful divorce. A relationship during the early 1980s produced another daughter and another difficult separation.

But Bob is nothing if not a man of the present. And on August 17, 1984, he and Deborah drove to Picton, Ontario, some fifteen miles from home, and took their vows. "Bob never remembers the date," winks Deborah, "and last summer I decided not to remind him. And sure enough it went past without him remembering. Then on August 19th, 20th, and 21st, we were in Toronto for the Arlington Million horse race, and we were sitting having dinner one night, and there was a guy from Chicago with us. This guy tells us how wonderful his wife is to let him come up here and not be home in Chicago on their anniversary. And Bob's going, 'Well, that is something! That's really nice!' And I say to him, 'Bob, I can't believe you're saying this! Our anniversary was three days ago, and you didn't even acknowledge it!' He would never have known if I hadn't told him. Mind you, he's very observant in other ways. He can be a real sweetheart."

Asked for an elaboration on Bob's personality, Deborah volunteers that there is a "very sensitive guy" behind Hull's sometimes rather prickly exterior. "I've seen him cry – he cries just like the rest. Of course, there's a tough guy in there, too – a very opinionated guy who believes it's his way or no way. Because his way is the *right* way. I don't know how many times I've heard him say that. His kids make fun of him over it. But he believes it! There's no way you can argue with him when he believes he's right. Although I do," she laughs. "I can be pretty strong-willed, too. I'm certainly not afraid to stand up for myself, although I can also be very accommodating and forgiving. I'm like Bob in that I'm usually pretty up-front in my attitudes."

Deborah is certainly up-front in describing the challenges of being married to a man who for millions of Americans and Canadians is practically a cultural icon. "It's not always easy to preserve my identity in this relationship," she says. "So often, for instance, people refer to me as 'Bobby Hull's wife.' I mean it may seem insignificant, but it's the sort of thing that robs me of my sense of self. Not long ago, one of Bob's friends was talking on the phone, and I heard him say, 'Well, Bobby Hull's wife is here.' And I screamed at him, 'Jay! I have a name! It's Debbie! I'd appreciate your using it!' Not that I want to be front and centre – I don't. But you can't allow yourself to become lost in another person. It just doesn't work."

Deborah also rues the lack of what she calls "private time" with Bob. "Almost everywhere we go, whatever we do, there are always other people involved. And of course there are always the autograph seekers. After six years with Bob, it's still amazing to me how much adulation he gets. As soon as he leaves the driveway he's public domain – people swarm over him."

To escape the swarm, Deborah hopes that one day she and Bob will own a home in Florida, where people are not so much aware of hockey and of Bob's glittering past. "Down there, it's possible for us to be out on the golf course and actually enjoy ourselves. . . . I'm not saying we don't do lots of enjoyable things now. We get out to dinner and, occasionally, to live theatre when we're in Chicago or New York. And I love going to events where there are other former players and their wives. We were in Calgary recently for a get-together, and we'll be in Phoenix next week for a charity golf event. I really like getting together with Jill Mikita, Colleen Howe, Evelyn Cournoyer, all the girls. They've been very good to me, accepting me, the new kid on the block."

You could talk to Deborah Hull for hours, about everything under the sun, and the subject of her son Ryan's death would never come up. She has made it clear in the past that she does not like talking about it – that it is too personal, too private. "It's like, Here's my heart; it's broken; take it," she once said. "It's just not something I care to discuss."

That is why when the subject is broached on a warm afternoon in early April of 1989, Deborah's intense, free-flowing candour comes as such a surprise. It is as if after four years of harbouring the pain in her heart, sharing it only with her closest friends, she is ready to let some of it go. "Talking about it is certainly less painful than it used to be," she says. "But there's still only one word to describe the effect it's had

on me, and that's 'devastating.' All the more so because Ryan
was in perfect health. He died on May 10, 1985 – he was eight
weeks old. I put him to bed one night at 11:30, and the next
morning he was dead. Sudden Infant Death syndrome. The
autopsy showed nothing.''

As Deborah feels her way through a maze of wrenching
memories and emotions, Bob stands across the room, leafing
through business papers, occasionally glancing up at her,
sombre-faced. But he shows no inclination to interrupt or add
to what she is saying. As much as he shares her pain, he
seems to allow that the story is hers to tell.

"It's changed my whole emotional make-up," she says. "I
just haven't handled it well at all. I guess if I'd taken the time
and gone through support groups and spent more time with
people who understood, it might have helped. But I didn't. I
did talk to people on the phone – on these hotline numbers
that you can call for various difficulties – but that didn't mean
anything to me. There was no comfort in it."

Deborah volunteers that a day has not passed since 1985
when she has not re-experienced the agony of Ryan's death.
"Every single day," she emphasizes. "Some days are worse
than others. In fact, the whole thing haunts me so much that
most of the time it bothers me just to *see* other little babies. I
know I can't pick them up and hold them. When Bob's kids
start having children, I don't know how it'll affect me to have
a baby around here. Even the thought of it is just too much for
me right now. I don't even want another one of my own. I
look at it in very black-and-white terms – where we are in our
lives, what our lifestyle is like – and I can't see it. I know how
it was when I *had* Ryan. Bob was away a lot, and he still is. He
was gone the day Ryan died. That's Bob's life – I'd never ask
him to change it or stop travelling. But I don't want to be left
while he goes – not anymore. And with an infant, I don't
have any choice; I'm left. I took a lot of comfort in my baby
when it was just him and me. But at that time we were living
in Chicago – see, we got a condo in Chicago about six months

after we were married. We spent winters there for our first
four years together. We spent summers here on the island.

"The point I'm making is that in Chicago I had friends, I
had family. I could pick up the phone and call someone. Or I
could go somewhere and not be lonely. Bob's being away a
lot didn't bother me. But now we're up here full-time, and it's
very isolated. I simply don't have anyone here when Bob's
gone. God forbid anything should happen to a baby out here.
I heard it took two hours for an ambulance to get here from
Belleville once. Knowing what I know, how could I possibly
have a baby here? Believe me, there are days when I really
wish I had my own. Oh, yes, there are. But it's a dream, and I
have to tell myself to snap out of it. It just wouldn't be good
family planning right now."

Deborah falls silent for a few seconds, then says quietly, "I
deal with it all day by day. I go over it and over it, and there's
nothing that can be done – nothing that *could* have been
done. We've gone through every move that we made with
Ryan the week before, trying to figure it out – detail, detail,
detail – but there's nothing. It's not there."

"It's been pretty rough for us," says Bob, looking up from
his work. "But I guess I'd have to say that I'm in a slightly
different position than Deborah, in that I have kids of my
own – I've had the feeling. Deborah's only had one."

"And he was such a pretty one," says Deborah, "styled
right after Bob. Big chest, nice big hands. And he was growing like crazy. He would have been a big boy."

Asked what effect Ryan's death has had on her sense of her
own mortality, Deborah reflects for a moment and says,
"You'd think it might have made me more accepting of it. But
in fact it's made me terrified of dying. Because I've seen
death; I know what it looks like. I think about it often, and it
makes me shiver. The one constructive thing I can say about
the whole experience is that it's made me realize how pre-
cious life is. Every single moment of it."

Asked how the experience has altered *his* view of mortality, Bob tells a story: "Deborah and I were in Hawaii four

years ago. Almost no one knew we were there. One night the telephone rang in our hotel room. A guy said, 'My name is detective so-and-so, FBI. I hate to be the bearer of bad news . . .' Right away it went through my head, Which one of the kids is it? I never thought about anybody else – just, Which one of the kids? The guy said, 'Your mother has passed away.' Well, I just fell back on the bed in relief. She was eighty years old. I loved my mom very much, but she'd lived a good life. Ryan was different. Never had a chance.

"I'll tell you one thing, I don't take life for granted anymore. I used to live as if time was never going to run out. Now I've seen it run out, and I know how valuable it is. You've got to do what you can to make it count."

8

• • • • • • • • • • • •

IN THE MOOD

Some facts about the Rocket:

- He has a recurring dream that, at age sixty-seven, he has renewed his contract with the Canadiens and has returned to play in the NHL. His opponents are contemporary players such as Wayne Gretzky, Mario Lemieux, and Mark Messier. He can still manoeuvre. He can still put the puck in the net. He re-establishes all his old records.
- He rises daily at 7:30 or 8:00 a.m. and, though he is not a heavy drinker, begins the day with two ounces of Dekuyper's gin, mixed with grapefruit juice and Vichy water. He sips it as he reads the newspaper.
- He does not enjoy reading about himself – has never looked closely at the encyclopedic scrapbooks his wife Lucille has kept on him since the early 1940s.
- He read his biography, *L'Idol d'un Peuple*, when it appeared in 1976. Despite having spent months co-operating on the writing of the biography, he was paid nothing for the rights to his story. He was given a free copy of the book.
- Every year, he gives away approximately 20,000 photos of himself, each one autographed. Some are supplied to him

by Grecian Formula hair colouring for men, which he uses and endorses, some by Molson Breweries, for whom he does public relations work, and some by S. Albert Fuels in Montreal, which he has represented since his playing days.

• He insists that he was never a good hockey player, that he was just a guy who worked hard at the game he loved.

It happened at the Montreal Forum during the seventh game of the 1952 semifinals between the Canadiens and the Boston Bruins. The Rocket was given a savage bodycheck by Boston defenceman Leo Labine and for several minutes lay on the ice unconscious, blood pouring from a bone-deep wound in his forehead. There was fear that his neck had been broken, and it was some time before he was removed from the ice and his forehead stitched shut.

During the third period of the game, still dizzy and barely able to stand, the Rocket insisted on returning to the Canadiens' bench. There he sat gazing silently across the ice and occasionally up at the clock. He inquired twice about the time remaining in the game, and when his teammate Elmer Lach told him four minutes, he turned to his coach Dick Irvin and told him he was ready to play. Irvin hesitated briefly, perhaps pondering consequences, and sent his injured star over the boards. The score was tied 1–1.

What followed was a mythic eruption of fierce talent, obsessive will, and strength gone crazy. The Rocket picked up the puck in his own end of the rink and headed up ice like a heat-seeking missile – past the Bruins' forechecking wingers, past their centreman, around one of their defencemen, and deep into the right-side corner of the rink. Still in manic overdrive, he surged out toward the front of the net, eluding Boston's other defenceman and coming into the range of goaltender Sugar Jim Henry. In the words of the late sports writer Andy O'Brien, "There was a flurry of sticks, Henry dove, Richard pulled the puck back and blasted the netting."

There is an almost gothic photo of the Rocket shaking hands with Sugar Jim following the game. The Rocket is staring as if out of a coma at the smaller goalie. His forehead is bandaged; blood still streams down his face. Sugar Jim is half bowed as if to say: "You win, Mr. Richard, you win."

When Canadiens' president Senator Donat Raymond entered the team dressing room and shook hands with the Rocket after the game, the legendary right-winger began to sob, then went into fitful convulsions that were only stilled when the team doctor injected him with a sedative. In the course of his long rush up the ice, he had had several opportunities to pass the puck; and it was not known until later that he had held onto it only because his vision had been too blurry to pick out a teammate to whom he could pass.

Maurice Richard is thought by many to be the most spirited professional that hockey has ever known – and the game's finest goal-scorer. In an era when scoring twenty goals was considered a mark of excellence, he several times scored more than twice that many and, once, during the 1944-45 season, scored fifty goals in fifty games, a record that stood for thirty-seven years. But it wasn't just the *number* of goals that the Rocket scored; it was the way he scored them. Hall of Fame goaltender Frank Brimsek once said, "He could shoot from any angle. You could play him for a shot to the upper corner and he'd wheel around and fire a backhander to the near, lower part of the net." Another Hall-of-Famer, goaltender Glen Hall, said of the Rocket, "When he skated in on net, his eyes would shine like a pair of searchlights. It was awesome to see him coming at you."

To be sure, it was the Rocket's eyes that signalled the spirit within. Even in publicity shots his eyes burned with an animal passion – the Rocket's Red Glare, it has been called. During the early 1950s, American novelist William Faulkner, on a special assignment for *Sports Illustrated* magazine, went to Madison Square Garden to watch a game between the New York Rangers and the Canadiens. A short time later, he wrote that one player, Richard, had stood out beyond the others with a "passionate, glittering, fatal, alien quality of snakes."

"No doubt, I was a fiery hockey player," grins the Rocket as he relaxes in the alumni lounge at the Montreal Forum. "I'm still fiery when I play sports. Golf, for instance. I used to be pretty good, but now I hate playing because I don't play enough to stay in practice, and I get mad when I make bad shots. Same in tennis – I hate to lose. I want to win. Even when I go fishing I like to catch more fish than anybody else. I don't get *mad* if I don't – not anymore – I just like to be on top. It comes naturally to me."

During his playing days, the Rocket's intensity frequently got him into more trouble than he could comfortably bail himself out of. "One night when we were playing Detroit I got into an argument with Ted Lindsay," he says. "We started swinging at one another, then Sid Abel came in, and I fought him, too. I tried to get up and fight again, and Gordie Howe started swinging at me. I took a good beating there."

The Rocket readily acknowledges that his temper was "too fast," that he did not have the necessary self-control to turn his back on provocation. "If I took a bad bodycheck, I had to retaliate, had to go after the guy right away – I never waited so much as a minute. And I never mellowed, even in the end."

The Rocket has not fully mellowed to this day. "When I go to a game now, I don't get excited unless it gets rough. I like the big bodychecks. When I see a dirty check against one of the Canadiens I wish I could be out there, especially if somebody I know well gets hit. . . . One night years ago a Maple Leaf defenceman, Kent Douglas, hit Bobby Rousseau over the head with his stick. I was sitting just above the passageway the players go through on their way to the dressing room at the Forum. When Douglas passed underneath I tried to hit him on the head with my fist. But I missed him."

It is a conspicuous paradox of the Rocket's genius that his worst sins and greatest achievements as a hockey player arose out of the same volcanic intensity at the core of his personality. When he talks about that intensity, however, it's as if he were speaking not so much of an internal force as of a powerful and unpredictable foreign energy that regularly settled on him for better or worse. "When it was going in my favour I was on top of the world! I was a winner!" he says. "When it went in the other direction . . . well . . . let's say I did some bad things. It hurt my career."

The career damage was never greater than in 1956 when, in a late-season game against the Bruins, the Rocket committed the ultimate hockey malfeasance of striking an official. The incident began when Bruin defenceman Hal Layco raised his stick and cut the Rocket over the eye. "I went after him, took a swing at him, then one of the linesmen grabbed me from behind and held me so I couldn't move." For several seconds Layco rained knuckles on his defenceless opponent's shoulders and skull. "I turned my head twice and told the linesman to let go of me, so I'd have a chance. The third time I turned, I took a poke at him. I knew I was in trouble."

Two days later, the president of the NHL, Clarence Campbell, countered with one of the severest punishments ever meted out by a league executive: suspension for the remainder of the season and for the entire post-season playoffs. The Canadiens were as good as finished. "They could have suspended me for ten, fifteen games the next season. I would have accepted that. But not the playoffs! We were in first place! Oh, I was mad."

Canadiens supporters were equally incensed by Campbell's decree. When the team returned to the Montreal Forum for its final game of the season, Campbell, who regularly attended the Canadiens' games, entered the arena and took his seat, ignoring a sustained assault of insults, boos, and projectiles. He had been warned by both the police and the mayor not to attend the game. At the end of the first period, with Detroit leading 3–0, a fan threw a smoke bomb that landed within yards of Campbell's feet. The game was cancelled immediately and awarded to Detroit.

"I wasn't sitting with Maurice," recalls the Rocket's wife, Lucille. "I was behind the other team's bench, where I'd been sitting every game for fifteen years. Maurice was beside the goal judge, right near Mr. Campbell.

"When they threw the bomb, Maurice went into [physiotherapist] Bill Head's room. A minute later, someone came up to me and said, 'Come, Lucille – join Maurice!' Clarence Campbell came in there, too. We stayed a good hour until things had calmed down."

As the well-guarded threesome huddled in the bowels of the Forum, thousands of angry fans raged down St. Catherines Street, throwing rocks, breaking store windows, destroying whatever lay in their path.

"We didn't win the Stanley Cup that year, and I didn't get my playoff money," says the Rocket. "The funny thing was that during my suspension I got so many invitations to attend banquets, referee games, and so on, I ended up putting more money in the bank than I would have if I'd been in uniform. Back then I got paid $150, $200 for an appearance."

The Rocket is convinced that, to this day, many people have not forgiven him for his intense, confrontational style of play. "Even people in Quebec!" he exclaims. "When I take the Metro to the Forum, there's always somebody staring at me. I say 'Hello!' and if they don't answer, I say, 'Hello, sir! I said hello to you!' Maybe they're just shy, but maybe they don't like me from my hockey days – how do I know? I'm very sensitive about it. If somebody *writes* something bad about me, it gets me right in the heart. And I'll tell you, a lot of writers have said terrible things. It's been hard on Lucille and the kids over the years."

Whatever discomfort the Rocket feels in looking back is by no means limited to the barbs and accusations of others. Twenty-nine years after his retirement, he is still bothered by what he has always seen as deficiencies in his style of play. For a man of extreme pride, the great goal-scorer is remarkably self-effacing about his talents. "Everybody always wanted to compare me to Gordie Howe," he explains, "but I was never a natural hockey player like Gordie. He was stronger, more fluid, better with the puck. I used to say to him, 'Gordie, you're much better than I am, but you don't have the drive to win games like I do.' I always had a big heart for scoring – oh, I loved scoring goals. But I had to work *hard* for them. I wasn't a good skater. I played right wing for one reason only – because I could turn better from the right, and it was easier for me to cut to the net from that side. A really good player can cut from both sides. See, I shoot from the left side; I should have played the left wing instead of the right, but I wasn't any good over there. Even from the right, I could usually only get around the defenceman by holding his arm or body to keep him away from me . . . I was just a guy who tried hard – all the time."

Game films from his career – even films in which he was clearly the star of the show – do little to raise the Rocket's opinion of his game. "When I see myself, I'd love to be able to say, 'Gee, I looked nice when I skated or scored!' But I honestly can't say it; I never did like my style. The one thing I could do was put the puck in the net. I was the best scorer, not the best player."

Asked who he considered better, the Rocket names several of his former teammates, none of whom had nearly his impact on the game. For one, he considers his brother Henri a more accomplished all-around player than himself. "I played with Henri and Dickie Moore my last five years with the Canadiens – both of them were better than I was. Henri could make a beautiful pass. It made hockey a pleasure."

The Rocket's love of scoring was surpassed only by his love of scoring in the third period, when a game was on the line. "My secret was that I always tried to keep enough strength for the end of the game. Conserve my energy. Sometimes you work too hard at the beginning, and at the end you're too tired; you don't feel like doing anything. Scoring in the first period was okay, but I preferred to score game winners."

The Rocket can name only one other tactical "secret" of his success: "When I had a breakaway I never used a shot or move that I'd used before. Always showed something different. Shot a little different. Faked a little different. Most players in my day made the same play every time. So the goalies knew what to expect. I tried to keep them guessing."

The question is put to Lucille: "What do *you* think made the Rocket such a great player?" She muses for a moment and says confidently, "Because he scored lots of goals."

On a mild evening in February, against the muted hum of the televised Miss U.S.A. pageant, the Rocket and Lucille sit in the living room of their limestone bungalow in north Montreal, reminiscing on nearly fifty years of life together. They have lived in the house since shortly before the "Richard Riot" of 1956. Immediately across the street flows La Rivière des Prairies, the "back river" as Maurice calls it, the north boundary of Montreal Island. Maurice knows the river well, having swum and fished in it as a boy. "Every morning I used to get up early, and, before I went to school, I'd go and set a line. I'd catch eels, suckers, pickerel – I'd lift the line before I went home at night. My mother liked that."

The interior of the Richards' seventy-five-year-old home is a richly endowed museum – verging on a temple – to the Rocket's career. It houses a dozen or more paintings of him in uniform – some exact likenesses, some folky and naive. It also houses trophies and knick-knacks and mementoes – on the mantel, on shelves, in a display case in the basement rec room. Some of the trophies go back to the Rocket's teenage days; others are the fanciful inventions of local clubs and charity organizations (to "Hockey's Man of the Age," to "Le Champion d'Histoire d'Hockey"). Others still are esteemed awards such as the Lou Marsh Trophy, presented to the Rocket in 1957 when he was chosen Canada's Athlete of the Year. In the living room, behind the Rocket's television chair, stands a six-foot marble goddess, a lamp, presented to him in

1954 by L'Ordre des Fils d'Italie du Canada. By Lucille's chair stands a lamp made of wrought iron and featuring tiny iron hockey sticks and an iron "500" welded into its shade. The unusual creation is a sentimental favourite of the Rocket's, hand-made for him after his 500th goal by the students of the technical high school where he attended classes as a teenager. An enormous family photo hangs above the fire-place – Lucille, Maurice, their seven children and seven grandchildren.

Lucille Richard is a warm, dignified woman, whose temperament bespeaks all the motherly skills that must have been required to raise her extensive brood. She is tolerant and circumspect, and yet she has a forthrightness about her – a quiet assurance of tone – that suggests she is not accustomed to brooking more than her share of nonsense. She is old-fashioned in that she has devoted her life to raising her family and to the support of her husband's career. During the Rocket's eighteen years with the Canadiens, she missed just two of his nearly 600 home games at the Montreal Forum. Even her summer holidays were spent accompanying him to the outposts of rural Quebec where, night after night during the 1950s, he refereed professional wrestling matches, attracting more applause and attention than the wrestlers themselves.

"I went along because it gave me time with Maurice," says Lucille. "I've always enjoyed travelling anyway ... I was alone a lot during the winter, and I did miss Maurice, but I wouldn't say it was difficult for me, because I understood and accepted the hockey life. I was born into hockey; my brother played hockey; we talked hockey at home; I married hockey; my five sons played hockey. I loved hockey. If I hadn't been able to take it, I wouldn't have been there."

The Rocket says, "Everybody thinks Lucille was alone a lot during my career. But right now, I'm away more than when I was playing. Last winter I refereed old-timers' games all over the country – dozens of them. During my playing days, I'd go to practice in the morning, and I'd be away on the weekends.

But overall I was probably at home more than if I'd been working in a plant or for a company."

There were times, Lucille admits, when even the acceptance of her lot did little to fill the emptiness of being on her own. She says, "Christmas and New Year's and the kids' birthdays were hard. But it's even harder to have Maurice away today. I'm getting older. My kids are all gone now. I need him more now. Sometimes he goes away with the old-timers for a week at a time. I could go if I wanted, but on the longer trips they go by bus – and it's not my group. When he goes by car for short trips, I go."

Like the Rocket, Lucille grew up in Montreal, where she was extraordinarily involved in the typically male domain of competitive hockey. It was hockey, in fact, that brought her and Maurice together during the late 1930s. She says, "My brother ran a hockey team, and Maurice played for him. I never missed a game."

Although her brother was nominally in charge of the team, Lucille recalls that it was more often than not her mother who ran the show. "She was always telling the players what to do, phoning them up to make sure they were out for games and practice, that sort of thing."

Lucille, too, did her share of phoning and enterprising. "We used to have the players to our house after the games. We'd have soft drinks and chips and peanuts. I'd have my girlfriends over, and we used to dance until four or five in the morning. I taught Maurice to dance the tango. One of his favourite songs was 'In the Mood.' "

At the time, Maurice was playing not just for Lucille's brother's team but for four or five other Montreal hockey clubs – so many that, in order to maintain his eligibility on certain rosters, he had to disguise his identity. "He was Maurice Richard on some teams," laughs Lucille, "Maurice Rochon on others. Oh, he was good. Everybody wanted him. He used to score six, seven goals a game."

Even so, neither Lucille nor Maurice ever imagined that he would one day play professional hockey, much less become the sport's biggest attraction. "My Junior team was the Verdun Maple Leafs, sponsored by the Canadiens," says the Rocket. "It was exciting being part of the organization, but back then the NHL was just a dream. No one I knew ever got close."

When the Rocket graduated from Junior hockey, he played eleven games for the Canadiens' Senior A team, then broke his ankle, snuffing any last hope he might have had for a pro career. Or so it seemed.

"While he was hurt he came to stay at our place for a few days," says Lucille. "He used to stay there because he and my brother were such close friends. One day he said to my mother, 'I'm lonesome this afternoon – I'd like to see a movie. Can I take Lucille?' I loved movies, so I went with him. We saw *Garden of Allah* at the Stella Theatre – Charles Boyer and Marlene Dietrich. It was our first date. I was sixteen."

The following year, Lucille and Maurice were engaged, and a year after that they were married. The same year, 1942, Maurice made his debut with the Montreal Canadiens. He says, "I'd followed them on radio since I was twelve or thirteen – Howie Morenz, Aurel Joliat, Pep Lepin, Toe Blake. But as a kid I could never go to the Forum – that was for people with money."

As rare as it might seem for a boy who had grown up in Montreal and had played four years in the Canadiens' organization, the Rocket had never seen the team play until he skated onto the ice in the club's famous red, white, and blue jersey.

It was during his second year with *Les Glorieux* that the young star earned the monicker that would become the most famous in the history of the sport. "One of our lines back then was Ray Getliffe, Murph Chamberlain, and Phil Watson," he recalls. "I scored so many goals against them in training camp that year that one of them started calling me 'Rocket'; then they all did. The press picked it up, and that was that."

By the mid-1950s the name was known wherever hockey was played throughout the world. It's fame was strikingly revealed when the Rocket attended the 1957 world hockey championship in Prague, Czechoslovakia. At the time, Czechoslovakian newspapers carried no news of the NHL, and television was practically non-existent in the country. Yet when Maurice entered the Prague arena for the tournament's first game, some 20,000 fans rose to their feet and, as if greeting a national hero, began screaming, "Rock-et... Rock-et... Rock-et!"

The Rocket speculates that the Czechs knew about him through occasional newsreels that might have reached the country. Certainly the newsreels of 1957 were replete with his achievements; it was earlier that year that he scored his 500th big-league goal, a nearly unaccountable total in the defence-minded NHL of the day.

"I always enjoyed that kind of attention; I liked the limelight," declares the Rocket without a trace of self-consciousness. "I liked meeting people and signing autographs. I often say today that if a time comes when nobody recognizes me, I won't go out anymore. But everywhere I go they still know me, even the kids eight, nine, ten years old. It surprises me. I quit twenty-nine years ago. But they've read the stories, seen the books, seen the films. In fact, they come to me for autographs more than to the guys who quit ten years ago. Even the press still talks about me. Every time a record is broken, they talk about the Rocket. It makes me happy. Hockey is my life – always will be."

For a man who has enjoyed his fame so thoroughly, the Rocket's recollections of the events and achievements that inspired that fame are at times curiously minimal, if not absent altogether. "Some people like to tell stories, but I'm not one of them," he says with a shrug. "A lot of the things that happened to me in hockey I don't even remember. I don't know how my goals went in unless I watch them on film."

His protestations notwithstanding, the Rocket creates the impression that he has not so much *forgotten* his stories as simply never formulated them in any tellable way. He never had to; his stories were always told for him – by fans, by television announcers, by writers. It was enough for the Rocket to *live* the stories. It was up to others to put them into words.

When the recollections *are* available to him, their focus is often not quite what you might expect. Asked, for instance, to name his finest memory of eighteen years with the Canadiens, the Rocket settles not on a Stanley Cup victory or an epochal goal but on a regular-season game during the early 1950s when he scored five goals against the Detroit Red Wings (it was by no means the only time he scored five goals in a game). And it is not so much the goals themselves that excite the Rocket's memory as the context in which they were scored. This time there *is* a story. "The night before, Lucille and the kids and I had moved from Desirables to Papineau Street. It took us most of the night, and once we got there we just put mattresses on the floor and dropped. I hardly got any sleep at all – an hour or two. When I went to the team meeting that morning, I told the coach, Dick Irvin, that I didn't think I could play – too tired. I said, 'Use somebody else.' He used me anyway, and every puck I shot that night went in. Five goals, three assists."

Lucille's favourite hockey memory is of another of the Rocket's five-goal nights, this one against the Toronto Maple Leafs toward the end of World War Two. She says, "Just before the game, their goalie, Paul Bibeault, passed in the alley beneath where I was sitting. I knew him because he'd once played for Montreal, and I said, 'Paul, be careful, Maurice is going to get a couple of goals tonight.' He looked at me and started laughing. After the game he passed beneath me again – didn't say a word."

Maurice and Lucille's most disquieting recollections are of the months immediately before and after the Rocket's retirement in 1960. On the surface the retirement was a simple and understandable development. "When I turned pro in 1942," says the Rocket, "I weighed 160 pounds. But every season I put on two, three pounds, so that by 1960 my playing weight was about 210. It affected my play. My reflexes weren't the same – too slow. I couldn't get out of the way of the bodychecks anymore. During each of my last three seasons, I had bad injuries. In '57 I had a cut tendon in the back of my ankle – I missed twenty-five games. The next year I had a broken cheekbone, the next a broken ankle. I hadn't had a serious injury in fourteen years until then. . . . Two or three times during my last five years I went on diets – salad, vegetables, not too much dessert, not too many beers. And I lost eleven, twelve, thirteen pounds. But then I always ended up feeling worse than when I started. Too weak. No strength. So I'd let my weight rise again, even though I knew I was too heavy. The problem was that I always tried to lose weight quickly just before the season. I should have lost it over two or three months during the summers. Then I would have had time to build my strength at a lower weight. But I used to go out too much in the summertime – I had all kinds of invitations to dinners, barbecues, cocktail parties. And I loved eating."

During the summer of 1960, Frank Selke, Sr., then general manager of the Canadiens, told the Rocket that if he were willing to retire he would be given a job in public relations with the team and would be paid his regular salary for three years. "He told me to think about it," says the Rocket, "and I thought about it all summer. Talked to the wife, talked to my kids. I knew that after all my injuries I'd have to lose at least twenty to twenty-five pounds to play again. Going to training camp at 210 was no good. But I went at that weight anyway, and I knew after a week that I couldn't keep going. My kids didn't want me to quit, but Lucille wouldn't say one way or the other."

"Deep down I think I wanted him to keep playing," she says. "But I knew it was important that he make up his own mind."

In early September of that year, a few weeks before the start of the season, the Rocket deserted the Canadiens' training camp and made a public announcement that his playing career was over. "Our oldest boy, Norman, cried like heck," says Lucille.

It is clear, however, that the Rocket was never entirely at peace with the decision. "I wasn't *ready* to retire in 1960," he reveals. "I would have loved to keep going, and probably should have tried harder."

There is a suggestion that Mr. Selke's offer of a job may have been accompanied by a subtle twist of the arm – in fact, may have been more along the lines of an offer that his one-time star couldn't refuse. But on this issue, the occasionally outspoken Rocket is an almost perfect diplomat – perhaps out of self-preservation. He has seen it before, one day's unconsidered comment reincarnated as the next day's hysterical newspaper story. After nearly thirty years of retirement, the Rocket's remarks still have headline potential in Montreal's racier tabloids. So he protects himself and those he chooses to protect. Asked point blank if he feels Frank Selke, Sr., persuaded him unfairly into retirement, he smiles faintly and says, "I could tell you what Mr. Selke said or thought – he's dead now – but his son is still alive. All I'll say is that I think I could have played two or three more years."

Whatever the case, when the Rocket signed his retirement papers he signed away his right to play for any other NHL team, perpetuating a form of indenture with which he had grown severely disenchanted during the final years of his career. "We were like slaves," he says, "both to our team and to the league. In Montreal, we used to ask for a $2,000 raise every year we won the Stanley Cup. They'd give us half – $1,000. If we didn't like what we got, there was nothing we could do, nowhere we could go. It was either sign or go home. Today, the players have more freedom. Not that I wanted to play anywhere else than Montreal – I just feel they should have paid us properly. I heard a rumour in the fifties that Connie Smythe in Toronto was willing to buy me from the Canadiens for $100,000 and pay me $100,000 a year, but I don't have proof of that."

In 1967, seven years after his retirement, the Rocket was asked by Sid Solomon, owner of the St. Louis Blues, an expansion team, to return to the NHL as a part-time player. It was assumed that his presence alone would be motivational to the talent-thin Blues. "But I didn't feel like it. I wasn't in good shape. I didn't want to make a fool of myself playing with the pros. Doug Harvey went to St. Louis, but he was a different kind of player than I was – slow motion. Everything was easy for him. My game was a lot faster."

The Rocket's term as a public relations representative for the Canadiens was a four-year exercise in frustration. "I was always thinking that I could still be playing," he admits. "I wanted to be on the ice. I missed the excitement."

"It was a very difficult adjustment," agrees Lucille. "We were used to going to games, going out afterwards, enjoying the fans, the other players' families. I never wanted Maurice to go back to playing, but I would have liked it if he'd had a better job at the Forum. He wasn't happy. After the first year we knew it."

"I was spending all my time at banquets, carnivals, hockey tournaments, charity functions, that sort of thing," says the Rocket. "It went on year-round – six or seven days a week. All over Canada. Sometimes in the States, too. I was booked solid two or three months in advance. I had no time at all for myself or for Lucille and the kids. It was way too much."

Two years passed before the Rocket protested openly to Frank Selke, Sr., making it clear that he needed a day or two to himself from time to time. Selke agreed to a lighter schedule and promised not to lower the Rocket's salary. A year later, however, for no stated reason, his pay was summarily chopped in half. "I continued on through that year," says the Rocket, "but I didn't do nearly as much. Then I quit altogether. I was upset. I told Selke, too. I said, 'Keep the job for yourself.' And I went home. It was the happiest moment of my twenty-nine years of retirement – telling them I wanted to be free to do what I wanted."

The Rocket takes pains to point out that, after years of coolness between himself and the Canadiens, he is again on good terms with the organization – in fact, has been for some time. The evidence is in a long-term promotional contract he has just renewed with the team's owner, Molson Breweries, which he has represented since 1981. "I do what I can for them," he says, "and they treat me very well." It is all but forgotten that, while playing for the Molson-owned club during the 1950s, the Rocket did promotional work for his employer's arch-rival, Dow Breweries. "I was with them for ten years," he says. "Molson's never said a thing. They were always good that way. Even when I spoke out against them, they said nothing. Same with the club – I often criticized them, certain players or the coach. I had a newspaper column in *Dimanche Matin* back then; I used to write about them. They never commented. Maybe they thought my criticism was fair. I thought it was fair."

Within months of leaving his public relations job with the Canadiens in 1964, the Rocket bought a run-down tavern on Montreal's St. Laurent Boulevard, refurbished it, and named it Tavern Number Nine, in honour of his old number. "I had a big sign outside saying '544 goals!' I'd go to the place every day for three or four hours. What I didn't like was that once I got in there I could never get out. There was always somebody asking me to sit at a table and drink beer and talk hockey. Besides, I used to get thieves in there, Mafia types. It wasn't that they gave me a hard time – in fact, they helped me at times; there was always somebody trying to collect 'protection,' and these guys would tell me, 'Don't pay anybody anything; don't worry about it.' Even so, I didn't care to have them around."

The Rocket sold the tavern after three years, for twice what he'd paid for it. Within months, he turned his attention (and his cash) to an old love, fishing, sinking his profits from the tavern into the purchase of General Fishing Lines, a small company, which he operated out of his home for twenty-three years. He says, "I used to buy line from a big company in the U.S. – fly line, monofilament, different test weights – and package it under my own trademark, 'Clipper.' I'd travel the province, distributing it to sporting goods stores. But I had to quit a couple of years ago, because all the big companies were undercutting my prices. With the cost of travel, it was too hard to compete."

There is something touching, almost poignant, about the basement room in the Richard home where, night after night during the winter, the Rocket would sit gluing metallic labels onto spools of fish line and stacking them in cupboards for the spring and summer. His plywood work table still occupies the middle of the floor, and the shelves are still stocked with a varied inventory of spinning line that will never be sold. Each spool bears a circular label that features a stylized trout and a microscopic rendering of the famous signature, 'Maurice Richard.'

Among the Rocket's other ventures of the 1960s and 1970s were a variety of advertising contracts for products as varied as Chrysler cars, Vitalis hair tonic, and Salada tea. None of his endorsements, however, has had as much exposure or staying power as his good-humoured television advertisements for Grecian Formula hair dye. The Rocket used the product before he began endorsing it and still uses it regularly. "Not the liquid but the cream," he emphasizes, as if instructing a tutorial in such matters, "– and always with a little water. But not *too* much water, or the grey won't disappear. When I started using it, it didn't work, because I was swimming in my pool every day. But when the summer was over, and I stopped swimming, I saw a big change. . . . Everywhere I go today, the kids tease me about the ad: 'The wife likes it!' 'Two minutes for looking so good!' "

"When he started the commercials," says Lucille, "he used to say that he left some grey on the sides 'because a woman likes a little grey.' Then he started saying, 'because the *wife* likes it.' I like that better."

The Rocket has done the ads for ten years, earning $14,000 a year from them, plus residuals. "So they must work," he says, "although this year they're only running them in French, so I'll only make $7,000."

The Rocket also does regular promotional work for S. Albert Fuels in Montreal – his association with them goes back some forty years – and writes a weekly newspaper column, as he has done since his playing days. "I started with *Dimanche Matin*," he says. "They helped me do the writing. But they went out of business four or five years ago, so now I'm with *La Presse*. I take notes during the week on whatever I'm thinking about – baseball, hockey, any sport at all – and I do my column for Sunday."

By his own assessment, the Rocket has always been comfortable financially. "Only once did I lose money. I had a two-year contract to promote natural gas, and I took the money and invested it in a store that sold gas appliances and equipment. But the gas company was giving the same stuff away free, so we didn't sell much." Otherwise, the Rocket has put his money into bonds, certificates, blue-chip investments that pay steady dividends. "I don't have to work," he admits, "I do it because I like it."

If his engagement calendar is any indication, the Rocket especially likes lacing on the blades and taking to the ice with a gang of former NHL stars for whom he has refereed games for nearly ten years. The drafty arenas and overheated dressing rooms of the old-timers' circuit are a long way from the big time, and travelling by bus has its discomforts, but as he approaches his sixty-eighth birthday, the Rocket asks nothing more in the way of hockey. As it is, he is probably the only referee in the history of the game to get louder and longer applause than the players themselves. "I played myself till I was fifty-seven, fifty-eight," he says, "but I sometimes went too hard trying to check somebody, or I'd make too big an effort to put the puck in the net. I'd get dizzy. I didn't want to risk a heart attack, so I started refereeing. Even now, I sometimes do too much. I ref fifty, sixty games a year, sometimes six or seven nights in a row. I'm slowing down. I get tired."

Lucille, too, admits to tiring easily these days. Since beating cancer five years ago, she has cut back significantly on her domestic activities. "I don't even make Christmas dinner anymore," she says wistfully. "Not since I was sick. My daughter does it now. We had twenty-six people this year."

"She still likes company," says the Rocket, "as long as they don't stay for meals. She gets too nervous. Barbecuing is fine – we're outdoors. I'm the cook then. I like that. And the kids help."

During the summer months, the Rocket also likes to do what he has always liked doing during the warm weather – fishing. "We have a place in St. Michel des Saints – a cabin in a fishing camp. We go up ten, twelve times a summer. I go mostly for trout – sometimes walleye or salmon."

Lucille does not fish – doesn't like the black flies and mosquitoes. "And they go by plane," she says distastefully. "I don't like those little planes. I don't mind the big ones."

When the Rocket goes fishing, Lucille makes the rounds of her sons' and daughters' homes – a few days here, a few there. Or else her sons and daughters and their families come home to her. "In summer they like to use the pool," she says.

Between fishing jaunts and old-timers' tours, the Richards do a substantial amount of travelling together. "There's nothing I love more," says Lucille. "I enjoyed going out for the opening of Expo '86 in Vancouver; we were with Frank Mahovlich and his wife. Last summer we were guests at the Calgary Stampede; that was fun, although they worked Maurice pretty hard." Lucille's favourite destination is Florida, where she and the Rocket go every winter. She says, "It's not always so great for Maurice. There are a lot of Canadians down there, and they're forever coming up to him on the beach and taking pictures and asking for autographs. One comes along, tells his friends, then they all come. When we go someplace to eat, we can't even get through our meal. Maurice gets sick of it. He likes the attention, but he likes to eat, too. One thing we very seldom do is go to restaurants here in Quebec. There's always somebody after us."

The Rocket prefers European vacations, on which he is less likely to be put upon by hockey fans. "Our nicest trip was to Italy a few years ago," he says. "We started in Rome and went everywhere by car – Capri, the Adriatic, then to France, Nice, St. Tropez. On most of our trips to Europe we don't even reserve hotels. We just stop where we like. We feel free."

Lucille reflects for a moment on her travels with the Rocket, then, as if some resonant chord has been touched within her, says, "We've had a very good life. We've been married forty-seven years. Not many couples are as happy as we are." She glances at the Rocket and adds, "Hockey has been good to us."

The Rocket declares that it could have been better.

"He was born thirty years too early," says Lucille. "But it was good anyway."

Again the Rocket declares that things weren't what they might have been – especially the money.

"Maurice made plenty," she says. "But then again, we needed it with seven kids. It cost a lot. Today, people have two kids, that's it. But we're happy with what we've got. Very happy."

"We'd better be," says the Rocket, and a faint smile transforms his face.

9

. . . .

THE FLOWER AND
THE GARDENER

If Colleen Howe's dream comes to pass, there will one day exist a life-sized talking model of her husband Gordie, clothed in the green and blue of the Hartford Whalers, or perhaps the red and white of the Detroit Red Wings. ("We haven't decided that yet.") The model's job will be to stand at the entrance to what Colleen envisions as "The World's Largest Exhibit of a Famous Athletic Family's Personal Memorabilia."

"When people enter the exhibit," she explains, "this figure of Gordie will welcome them and tell them a bit about his career – how many goals he scored, how many games he played, that sort of thing. Then the people will go on into this incredible collection of our family's athletic effects: jackets, photos, trophies, skates, jerseys, pucks, sticks, art, *everything*. At each station, they'll be able to press a button and hear Gordie's voice, or the voice of another family member, telling them something about what they're looking at – *these are the gloves I was wearing when I scored my 1,000th goal*, and so on."

For nearly forty years, Colleen has been collecting the immense volume of effects she intends to display. At the moment, she has them packaged, catalogued, photographed, and awaiting attention at a storage facility in Connecticut.

She says, "My plan is to get corporate sponsorship for this project. It's going to be expensive, and it's going to be a lot of hard work."

A glance at Colleen's résumé would suggest that she is no stranger to a lot of hard work. Among other things, she has: run for Congress; managed the first Junior A hockey club in the United States; written a book about her family; produced a series of hockey videotapes; owned a herd of Peruvian llamas (her CB handle at the time was Mama Llama); co-owned a restaurant; sold life insurance; co-managed a large team of Amway salespeople and Cambridge Diet Plan distributors; co-owned a hockey arena and a travel agency; owned a herd of pedigree cattle; and served as president of Howe Enterprises, through which she currently manages all Howe family business endeavours.

Lest it be thought that she was dogging it in her spare time, she has also raised four children and done extensive work for a variety of charities. "I got the most wonderful letter when I ran for Congress," she enthuses. "A lady sent me a donation and said, 'I'm putting my money behind you, because you can raise kids, work at the same time, and do all the other things I know you're doing. And I feel you'd do a lot better job running the country than the current government. At least, you wouldn't let us get a trillion dollars in debt.'

"I never saw myself as a housewife," declares Colleen. "I was a home engineer, a total camp director."

In the interest of accuracy, it might be pointed out that Colleen's energy is not that of a camp director but of an entire camp . . . of marathon runners. Her appointment calendar is the sort of document whose appearance alone is enough to make the average nine-to-fiver feel the need of a nap. She rises most days at five a.m., works seven days a week, and has been known to work all night. "When she ran for the Congressional ticket," says Gordie, "she wouldn't go to bed for two days at a time." (Recently, as Gordie watched a television documentary on the hammertop stork – a bird that, in the words of the documentary's narrator, "is constantly building, adding to the roof of its nest, plastering the walls" – he looked up and said softly, "If Colleen were a bird, that's what kind she'd be.")

Colleen owns hundreds of motivational tapes and has a bedside library that bristles with titles such as *Being the Best, The Other Guy Blinked, Don't Talk About It, Do It, How To Wake Up the Financial Genius Inside You,* and *How To Do Just About Anything.* Gordie's bedside literature consists of a couple of books on fishing and a book on sea shells.

Asked about the roots of her drive and gumption, Colleen reminisces for a minute, stops suddenly, and tells this story: "Just after I graduated from high school in 1950, I was interviewed for a file clerk's job at Bethlehem Steel. When I was asked why I thought I deserved the job over twenty other applicants, I said, 'Because filing requires a knowledge of the alphabet, and I'm the only one of all those girls who can say the alphabet backwards.' The guy who was interviewing me just roared. He said, 'Say it.' So I did. It was something my aunt had taught me when I was little – Z, Y, X, W, V and so on. I got the job."

Colleen goes on to say that, during her term with Bethlehem Steel, she often spent evenings at the Lucky Strike bowling alley a few blocks from her home near the Detroit Olympia. One night as she bowled, she noticed a dark-haired young man with a high forehead and rather gentle smile. "He was wearing a western-style suede jacket with fringe on the arms, and I thought, Boy is that guy ever good-looking. When he came over and asked if I had a ride home, I nearly died. Here, I had a friend's car, and couldn't accept. All the way home I just couldn't stop thinking about him. Fortunately, he got my phone number from the fella who ran the alley. I was *so excited* when he called the next night. Then he called every night that week! He'd talk for three hours at a stretch – about his home, his family, his childhood in Saskatoon, whatever. I felt as if I knew his whole family by the end of the week. It was really old-fashioned. The funny thing was that all through these conversations Gordie only mentioned hockey once, and I didn't pick up on it. I didn't have a clue that he was a professional hockey player – and here he'd been with the Red Wings five years! In fact, they'd just won the Stanley Cup."

Gordie says, "Finally I found the courage to ask her to a movie. Then in October she started coming to hockey games. I had a pair of tickets – one for my landlady, one for Colleen. I'd leave Colleen's at the ticket window, and she'd pick it up. I'd look for her from the ice."

On April 15, 1953, a week after the Red Wings had been eliminated from the Stanley Cup playoffs, Colleen and Gordie were married in Calvary Presbyterian Church in Detroit. "My only regret," says Gordie, "was that my roommate, Ted Lindsay, couldn't be my best man. He was Catholic, and they wouldn't allow it in a Protestant church."

Before the decade ended, Gordie had won five NHL scoring championships, had led the Red Wings to four Stanley Cups, and was widely recognized as the finest all-around player in hockey, some said the finest in the history of the game. The curious thing about Gordie was that, in spite of his vast talent, he didn't always *appear* to be doing that much on the ice. "My skating style was so smooth," he submits, "that a lot of people thought I was lazy." His stride was measured, his checking controlled, his shot a powerful but unexaggerated flick of the wrists. His strength and subtlety were such that he could often accomplish in one motion what other players took two or three moves to achieve. If, for instance, he was being checked from the right side (his shooting side), instead of shifting frantically, or whirling, or powering to a stop, he would often simply switch his stick to the other side of his body, change hands on it, and drill the puck ambidextrously from the left.

"You've also got to remember that I was crazy," says Gordie, in assessing his capabilities. "I was never afraid of getting hurt. And I was a good size, too. When I was a kid in Saskatoon, they called me the slope-shouldered giant. Everybody always seemed smaller than I was. Even if they were bigger they seemed smaller. And, oh, I was rough. It's one thing to be rough, but to be rough *and* crazy means the other guy is never going to get the last hit. Players knew that if they hit me, it was just a matter of time before I'd get them back. In the old league, we'd play a team fourteen times, so if a player did something dirty to me, I'd tell him I was going to get him. Sometimes I'd wait five, six, seven games. I'd play with him, tease him, but he knew that sooner or later he'd pay."

On occasion, Gordie's vengeance was less protracted, as Eddy Coleman of the Rangers found out during Gordie's early years as a pro. "He used to spike me in the back of the legs with his stick," recalls Gordie. "And I'd be bleeding. So I told him one night that if he touched me again he'd be very sorry, and he laughed at me. We went down the ice, and I flipped the puck over to Lindsay, who was going to the net all alone. Everybody's eyes were on him. Suddenly, I saw Coleman beside me and just turned around and nailed him with my gloved hand. Broke his cheekbone. A promise kept."

So as not to create any wrong impressions, Gordie makes it clear that under normal circumstances – that is, circumstances in which he was not in the process of a retributive strike – he found it impossible to cause anyone deliberate injury. He says, "Most of the time I played like an angel. I guess I could afford to after a while; almost everybody left me alone. Even the tough guys. There seemed to be a certain respect."

Given the tough defensive standards under which he played during his prime, Gordie's 1,071 career goals (NHL and WHA, including playoffs) are an almost unaccountable record for major-league hockey; his 975 regular-season goals are the equivalent of nearly twenty fifty-goal seasons. His thirty-two-year pro career – a career almost twice as long as the Rocket's, nearly three times as long as Bobby Orr's – is an unprecedented record for *any* major-league sport. By the time he retired at the age of fifty-two, Gordie had played NHL hockey in five decades. "People sometimes ask me how I lasted so long," he smiles. "And I always tell them the same thing: that I was totally in love with what I was doing. Even as a grown man, I could have played hockey all day. The sacrifices I made to keep my career going just never seemed that tough."

Today, at sixty-one, Gordie looks as if he could still take a turn at right wing. He is about fifteen pounds over his playing weight of 205, but the added cushioning is by no means sufficient to disguise the extraordinary ropes of muscle that form his shoulders and arms and thighs. The only true signs of his aging are his snowy white hair, a few facial wrinkles, and a plum-sized hummock of arthritis on the back of his left wrist. His feet are a startling composite of sinew and calluses and boot hide (the toenails resemble thick purple and yellow sea shells), but their condition is less the result of aging than of fifty years of stuffing them into skates and having them battered by the rough and tumble of the game.

The hands, by comparison, are soft and supple. In fact, in a curious way, the hands are a totem of their owner's personality. They are so pliant that when you grip one of them in a handshake, you might easily imagine a quarter inch of sheepskin beneath the surface of the wide palms and fingers. At the same time, you cannot help but sense the vice-grip power that lies just beneath the sheepskin (these are most certainly hands that could convert your knuckles to pulp should they decide to do so). Likewise, you cannot help but be aware of the formidable tenacity beneath the gentle exterior of Gordie's disposition. "Oh, there are very definitely the two sides there," says Colleen. "And they can be traced almost directly to his parents. Gordie's father was a very tough, very resilient, stubborn man. The family didn't have a lot, and sometimes to get money he had to ride horses bareback, run down coyotes for the bounty, that sort of thing. He had a bit of a mean streak, too, and of course this came through in Gordie when he played hockey. Gordie won't hesitate to tell you that he and his brothers and sisters were scared of their dad. One time Gordie was playing on a pair of stilts that his dad had told him not to go on, and when his dad caught him, Gordie jumped off so suddenly that he impaled himself on a picket fence and was badly injured.

"Gordie's mother, on the other hand, was an extremely tolerant, understanding woman, and there was *such* a love between Gordie and his mother. Even when I first met him he'd talk about how wonderful she was. She was totally unselfish; she'd give and give, constantly concerned about her family. I remember how she'd rub Gordie's back, just loved doing things that made people feel good. It was this unselfishness and patience of hers – this incredible generosity of spirit – that I've always seen in Gordie in his life off the ice."

Indeed, it is this generosity of spirit that over the years has elevated Gordie above the precincts of mere sports idolatry and earned him an enduring portion of public appreciation and respect. He is a man not only of honesty but of the profoundly common touch. He is seldom happier, for instance, than when he is signing an autograph for a child. Or a teenager. Or an adult. In fact, to watch Gordie sign autographs is to observe a perfect paradigm of his generosity in action. No matter how long the line-up of autograph seekers, he has a kind word, a joke, a reassuring smile for everyone.

During the 1960s, as an itinerant spokesman for Eaton's of Canada, Gordie would sometimes sign autographs from sunrise to midnight. "Literally!" he exclaims. "I'd be signing while I ate, while I watched TV, when I went to bed. I must have signed five million times." He recently signed the packaging on 35,000 copies of a series of instructional videos that he made with goaltender Ed Giacomin and his sons Mark, Marty, and Murray. "It took me thirty-six hours," he calculates. "I can sign about a thousand times an hour."

As if by uncanny prescience, Gordie realized at the age of eight that he would one day be dispensing his signature in volume. "My older brother Vern's wife says she can remember me writing my name several different ways, then tugging at my mother's skirt, asking which one she liked best. The one she chose, the one I still use, I practised like everything. When Mom said, 'What are you doing?' I said, 'That's for when I become famous.' "

Only once in more than forty years can Gordie remember being upset by an autograph request. "I was in the press box in Hartford the night my son Mark got pierced in the backside by the deflector plate on the net. When I saw him biting his hand I knew that he was badly injured. And I could see the blood, too. So I beat it out of there to get to the ice, and about halfway down the press table a guy held out a piece of paper to me and said, 'Sign this.' I looked at him and said, 'That's my son on that stretcher.' He said, 'It'll only take a minute.' At that point somebody else stepped in and told the guy to give it a rest.

"I guess there've been a few times when I've been too tired to keep signing, or have had to leave to catch a bus or a plane or something. When they can't get to me in person, I always hope they'll send a letter."

Many have. During the peak of his fame in Detroit, Gordie was receiving some 500 fan letters a week. Colleen acted as his secretary, scanning and categorizing every piece of mail that came in: "Some people wanted something for a charity auction (I'd take Gordie's old ties, and he'd sign them, and we'd send them out), some just wanted an autograph, some wanted a picture, some had *sent* something they wanted signed. Some people wrote *pages*, their life stories, and I'd have to skim these letters to see what the request was. There were some beautiful letters, too, of course. We answered all this mail at our own expense, postage and all. The Red Wings never offered a nickel." Colleen has saved every fan letter Gordie ever got, more than 250,000 pieces of mail, some of which will eventually go into the big exhibit of the family's memorabilia.

And has Gordie ever gotten tired of the requests, the autograph signing, the adulation? "Never," he says solemnly. "I worked too hard for the privilege."

Today, nearly ten years after his retirement from play, Gordie is not only one of the best-known and loved figures in the sporting world but also one of the most marketable. And Colleen is the ideal agent of that marketability. Where he is pliant, she is assertive; where he is quiet, she talks; where he waits, she scours the radar for action. She says, "Gordie's such a good guy, he can hardly ever bring himself to say no to people. So sometimes I have to be the bad guy, so to speak, if we're going to keep things in balance. Mind you, I don't deal rudely with people. I always try to find out what they want, and then give them what we can. I try to be as creative as possible."

With Colleen in charge of his appointments calendar, Gordie could hardly be busier. In addition to doing year-round public relations work for the Hartford Whalers, he acts as an international spokesman for the Rayovac Corporation and has promotional ties to three Detroit-based companies, Lumberjack Supply, Oliver's Pizza, and American Needle and Novelty, a hat manufacturer. He also makes as many as 100 banquet speeches a year and is in constant demand as a spokesman for charities and athletic endeavours. "Colleen gets it all planned out," he says. "All I have to do is show up."

"He's the flower, I'm the gardener," she laughs.

Gordie is indeed one of the rarest flowers the game has ever produced. Unfortunately, the game has not always seen fit to cultivate him as such. Through most of his twenty-five years with the Red Wings, for instance, his salary was nowhere near commensurate with the effort he was making on behalf of the team. "Had I made more back then," he says, "I wouldn't have to work so hard today. But you don't see that at the time, because you want so much to be a part of it. It just never occurred to us that someone else was making a small fortune off our talents."

Even if it had occurred to the players of the fifties and sixties, they were generally not secure enough in their jobs to raise the issue with management. Gordie says, "Anybody'd think I wouldn't have had the same insecurities as most players, but they're dead wrong. I had serious injuries early in my career. I wasn't sure I'd last. And I wasn't trained for anything else – I'd devoted my life to hockey. On top of that you've got to remember that, until 1967, there were only six teams in the NHL and that they 'owned' the rights to their players. You couldn't exactly pack up and move on if you didn't like the money you were making or the way you were being treated. If you balked – or weren't willing to play through injuries, say – there were always lots of players to take your job. And, of course, management used that to keep us in our place. My teammate Marty Pavelich once said, 'I never could understand Gordie Howe. Every training camp he'd show up worried about making the club.' I guess my true feelings showed. I'd go out there and work my butt off out of fear."

In 1945, Gordie had been ecstatic to sign for $2,300 a year, plus a team jacket, with the Red Wings' Omaha farm club. That year, he bought a car, a couple of new suits, and re-turned home to Saskatoon with $1,700 in his pocket.

The following year in Detroit his salary doubled, and, over the next dozen years, it proceeded upward in marginal incre-ments. But it was not until the late 1950s that he felt the first stirrings of his current disenchantment over what he was paid. "Here I was winning scoring championships, awards, Stanley Cups, and a friend of mine who sold insurance was making more than I was. He could afford to go away on weekends; I couldn't. He owned a boat; I only wished for one."

If there was financial hope for Gordie during the fifties it was that a pension plan had been introduced that would one day pay retired players $50 a month for every year of NHL service. "I remember thinking, That's pretty good," says Gordie. "If I last ten years, I could make around $500 a month at age forty-five – as much as I was making playing hockey."

Today, after the most distinguished career in the history of the sport, Gordie collects an NHL pension of some $1,300 a month, by far the largest pension for any player of his era. "What most people don't understand," says Colleen, "is that, because the pension is so puny, a lot of former players will have to work forever.

"Someone once said to us, 'Maybe things would be better if you'd deferred money way back when.' But how could we defer money in an era when our salary barely covered our expenses? We had four children to support! We had to scrimp. I made our clothes. I cut the kids' hair. We used skate exchanges. It was strictly no-frills. I mean, I couldn't even afford to make long distance calls to Gordie when he was on the road. Then again, hockey wives – at least those in Detroit – were pretty well prohibited from contacting their husbands on the road, anyway. The wives were just nobodies in the grand scheme. I remember once when I wanted to reach Gordie during the playoffs, I had to explain to the general manager what I wanted. *Just to talk to my husband.* As far as they were concerned, my only purpose in life was to make sure that Gordie was well fed, well rested, and well taken care of. Total support of his career. There were times when I'd drive to the train station to pick him up at two a.m., with two kids in the car, in a snowstorm. Or I'd drive him to the hospital in the middle of the night. And yet when I'd show up at the rink the next day, I'd be treated like a schlock."

In September of 1969 Gordie learned his harshest lesson about the ethics and operations of his long-time employers in Detroit. Bob Baun had come to the Red Wings from Oakland during the off-season and had joined the team at its training camp in Port Huron, Ontario. "One day he took me out for lunch," recalls Gordie, "and the first thing he said to me when we sat down was, 'You're a stupid son of gun, Gordie – I'm making almost twice as much money as you are.' This really stunned and hurt me, because I'd always had an agreement with the Red Wings that, because I was one of the best in the game, I'd always be the highest paid player on the team – in fact, the highest in the league. I was making $45,000 at the time; Baun was making $80,000. I owe a lot to Bob for setting me straight."

Gordie subsequently discovered that another Red Wing, Carl Brewer, was also making far more than he was. His first inclination was to quit hockey and go into the insurance business, where he'd been guaranteed a job on retirement. Ironically, the company that had offered the job was owned by Red Wings' owner Bruce Norris, who was primarily responsible for short-changing Gordie as a hockey player. "I phoned the manager of the agency," says Gordie, "and I said, 'How much will you pay me when I'm through?' And he said, 'Fifty thousand.' And I thought, For that kind of money, why should I beat my brains out here? I explained my situation to him, and he said, 'Before you do anything, let me phone Mr. Norris.' And he did. And, as a result, the Red Wings raised my salary to about $100,000. But they wouldn't have done it if I hadn't caught them out.

"What made it worse for me was that when Norris notified me of my raise, he said, 'I hope that makes Colleen happy.' I said, 'Colleen has never scored a goal or backchecked or taken a penalty in this league, Bruce, and it has nothing to do with her or her happiness. In fact, because you people have been lying to me indirectly, it doesn't even make *me* happy.' "

Beyond the large duplicities, Gordie was regularly affronted by a host of smaller deceits and antagonisms on the part of the Red Wings' ownership and management. "There were just so *many* things," he says. "For instance, a little while before I retired, my dental work was getting pretty bent up, and I wanted to get it fixed. But the Red Wings said to me, 'Don't get it done now. Wait till you retire and we'll fix it all up so it'll last forever. When the season was over, Colleen and I went away for a while, and when we came back, I asked them about the teeth, and they said, 'Oh, it's too late now. You're not with the club anymore.' They wouldn't put a new plate in for me. So the team dentist, Dr. Muske, said to me,

'Gordie, I heard them make that promise, and I'm embarrassed – I'll put the plate in for you at my own expense.' They just seemed to think so *little* of us."

It might have helped reshape Gordie's opinion of the club that, upon retirement, he was invited into the front office as a vice-president. But before long, that, too, turned sour. He says, "I'd always been told that when I was through playing, I'd be involved in running the team. And I guess I was naive enough to think that that was what they had in store for me. It turned out that in two years on the job all they ever asked me to do was run around and show my face at banquets and promotional functions – 'go represent the club,' they'd tell me. Half the time, they didn't even have the courtesy to tell me in advance where I'd be going. Some days I did nothing at all. It was pathetic. I was floundering."

"It didn't help matters," says Colleen, "that they gave him the tackiest little office in creation. It was a joke. When he had an interview or had to get his picture taken, they'd move him into someone else's office. They didn't even give him a secretary."

"One day," says Gordie, "they sent me out to an awards event being held by the Food Caterers of Michigan – the Red Wings had purchased a table. They told me, 'You won't have any responsibilities; just go sit at our table. Enjoy yourself.' So I showed up, and sure enough they'd bought a table for ten, but there was *nobody* sitting at it but me. So I just walked away from it. It turned out that I was the recipient of an award, and the Red Wings hadn't even told me. They knew – they just never bothered letting me know. They were so bush-league about it all. And if I complained, they'd say, 'What are you belly-aching about now?' "

Gordie came to refer to the club's attitude toward him as "The mushroom treatment . . . that's where they keep you in the dark and come in once in a while and throw manure on you."

Colleen says, "When Gordie resigned from this travesty of a job, and we were about to leave Detroit, we went down to say good-bye to some of our special friends at the Olympia. While we were there, Gordie picked up his final paycheque, and he opened it and started to laugh. He said, 'You're not going to believe this.' As a favour to Bruce Norris we always booked our travel through his travel agency, and the agency would bill us at the end of the month. And here they'd gone and deducted our last travel bill from Gordie's cheque. His pay had been reduced almost to nothing. That's what twenty-five years of commitment to that organization got us. Someone gave that order – make sure they're paid up before they leave this building."

Even today, Gordie and Colleen frequently run afoul of those who operate big-league hockey. In 1987, for example, they were invited by the Quebec Nordiques and the NHL to appear at *Rendez-Vous*, a two-game series between Soviet and NHL all-stars in Quebec City. "They offered to pay our expenses," says Colleen, "and a $100 fee – that's right, one hundred big ones for three days' work. I told them to forget the hundred dollars, but that we'd come because we wanted to see our son Mark play in the games. As it turned out, Mark was injured and couldn't play, but we went anyway, and we found out that the Rocket had blatantly refused to go and had finally been paid thousands of dollars to make an appearance. So had Guy Lafleur and Vladislav Tretiak. There were even athletes from other sports who had been paid to be there – Gary Carter, Wilt Chamberlain, Nancy Greene, Pélé the soccer player, and a number of others. One of these athletes told Gordie that he'd been paid $5,000 to attend. In fact, so much emphasis was put on these other athletes that attention was deflected away from the real stars of the show."

Colleen explains that Bernie Geoffrion was invited to attend *Rendez-Vous* for the same $100 fee that had been offered the Howes. "He told them, 'Look, I don't make a living from hockey anymore. Do you think I just sit here in Atlanta waiting for you to call?' He wouldn't do it for $100, but to accommodate them he contacted his sponsor, Miller Brewery, and they organized some paid events for him in Quebec and sent him. Bernie didn't score all those goals for Miller, but they take care of him, even when the hockey moguls won't. And he's grateful for it. But when he got to Quebec City he was so busy with his obligations to Miller, plus what the league wanted him to do – they were holding autograph sessions at the city armories, where they had a display of Hall of Fame artifacts set up – that he collapsed with the stress."

Gordie says, "He was just finishing his autograph-signing shift when he felt faint, and his chest started hurting. He said, 'Excuse me, I've got to go to the washroom and have a drink.' And suddenly he was on the floor. As it turned out, he was all right, but the episode might have been avoided if he'd just been treated in the same way that the organizers treated the big stars from other sports – if they hadn't been so insensitive. What made it all even harder to accept was that *Rendez-Vous* ended up making a big profit, and you can be sure some of it came from the admission charges to this Hall of Fame display."

Colleen says, "Gordie has done a great deal of work for change. And so have I. For one thing, we've tried to convince the league administration that when they put on a big production – whether it be an all-star gathering, a televised awards night, the Hall of Fame induction ceremony, whatever – and they pay so many technical and promotional and staff people to work on these things, they should also compensate the former players who show up and participate. So often the players who give these events their character are older fellas who don't always have a stable income. Then there are those who never show up at all, aren't even invited – great Hall-of-Famers, and they haven't been seen at a league function for years! The step that Gordie has taken is to tell the people in the league office that he is no longer available for league appearances unless he and any other players who appear are properly compensated."

"Not long ago," says Gordie, "I attended an NHL marketing meeting and discovered they'd scheduled twenty-one appearances for me without a word of consultation. I had to refuse them. I simply said, 'I work for the Hartford Whalers, not for the NHL.' "

Colleen says, "I've said to these people in the league office, 'Don't you see that a backlash will develop if you don't start paying a little more respect to some of these guys?' The sad truth is that the league is *far* more concerned that its corporate sponsors be taken care of than it is about the players who have made the league what it is. We ourselves *never* hear from them unless they want Gordie's services. We do get a Christmas card, but, for instance, we never get an invitation to the all-star game or the Hall of Fame dinner. Last year, we were taken to the Hall of Fame dinner by Avie Bennett, the publisher. He seemed shocked that we hadn't been invited by the league.

"At the last all-star game that Gordie *played* in, in 1980, I wasn't even given a seat. I had to roam the halls of the arena until one of the people from the league office saw me and rescued me. But I'll tell you, there wouldn't have been a corporate sponsor who didn't have a seat. After the game, a friend of ours from Chrysler said to us, 'Come on, we'll walk with you to the reception.' We said, 'What reception?' It was a thing the league was putting on for their corporate friends – the all-stars weren't invited. We've just never been able to figure this sort of thing out – do we cramp their style? Are they afraid the players are going to say something that will embarrass them? The corporate people would far rather meet players than NHL functionaries. As it turned out, nobody from the league asked us to leave, but they obviously hadn't planned on us being there. We felt about as welcome a dead mouse in a punch bowl."

What Gordie and Colleen didn't realize at the time was that the league had not even wanted Gordie to *play* in the 1980 all-star game. Colleen says, "Gordie found that out later from Scotty Bowman, the coach, who'd had to fight to have him on the team. The league said there were more deserving players, with better records. I mean, the game was to be held in

Detroit! It was almost certain to be Gordie's last all-star game. Bowman simply told them that it was important to hockey and to the people of Detroit that Gordie be there."

"It was the only game I ever played," says Gordie, "in which the opposing team was cheering for me to score. They were saying, 'C'mon, take a shot – put the sucker in.' Oh, I had a great time. And the fans loved it."

Colleen says, "Later that night as we lay in bed at the hotel, Gordie said, 'Isn't it funny how the people we've done the most for are the people who show the least regard for us? I don't even want to be around these people anymore. We can't operate like that.' " Colleen reflects for a moment and says, "Maybe we should have been a little tougher years ago. We've given way and given way to these people. Yet if I speak up, I'm labelled a troublemaker. When they say I'm difficult to get along with they mean I don't fall over dead like I'm supposed to when they do something they shouldn't have done."

Of all the things league officials shouldn't have done, few have piqued Colleen as much as their actions of February, 1982. "They made arrangements for several players, including Gordie, to have lunch with Ronald Reagan at the White House before the all-star game," she says. "But they made it crystal clear that no wives or female companions would be attending this function, that women simply weren't welcome. And this really bothered me; it stung me. It was the first time Gordie had been invited to the White House without us going as a couple. I've always said that players' families share in the bad times and should be welcome for the good times, too." In this case, Colleen's grievance was not just with the NHL but with Gordie. "He didn't agree with what was going on," she says, "but because he felt an obligation to attend and didn't take a stand on my behalf, it put a heavy strain on our relationship at the time. If I'd been invited to the White House for some reason, I never would have gone without him. I'd rather have offended the President than my partner in life. As it turned out, when Gordie got to the White House, he discovered that there *were* women there. We both felt badly deceived."

Gordie says, "Someone once told me he'd heard a league rep say, 'You don't want to deal with Gordie Howe because you'll have to deal with Colleen.' "

"And yet," says Colleen, "our business associates from outside the league deal with me all the time. And we've had a wonderful relationship with them. They don't see me as some sort of Yoko Ono or Jezebel. They treat me with respect and openness. What we want – what anybody wants, I guess – is to be with people who make us feel welcome and good about ourselves – the way the fans do. The fans have always been our salvation, and we love them for it."

It isn't surprising that Gordie and Colleen's fondest memories of hockey are not from their NHL days but from the six years Gordie spent in the World Hockey Association upon coming out of retirement after his two-year stint in the Red Wings' front office. In the WHA he was free of the restraints and narrow-mindedness with which the old league had bound him for decades. The move also gave him the opportunity to fulfil a long-held dream of playing with his sons Mark and Marty, both of whom were too young to sign with NHL teams at the time. What's more, it afforded him the generous remuneration that had for so long eluded him in Detroit. The contract that Colleen and a business adviser negotiated with the Houston Aeros during the summer of 1973 brought the family nearly $2.5 million in exchange for four years of service from Gordie and the two boys.

"The WHA was so much more relaxed than the NHL," says Gordie. "There just wasn't the pressure. Hockey was fun again. And I know the hockey was every bit as entertaining as what we played in the old league. I told the management in Houston that if I'd known it was going to be this much fun they wouldn't have had to pay me. And yet I never worked harder in my life. A lot of my enjoyment, of course, came from playing with the kids. It made the work seem easy."

Gordie considers it one of the saddest facets of his career that after four years with the Aeros, the franchise was sold, resulting in what he calls "financial problems and personality conflicts" that left the Howes no choice but to move on. He says, "When they asked us to take a big cut in pay, I knew it was over. It hurt more than ever because the kids were involved."

As they waved good-bye to Texas, there was some possibility that the Howes would return to Detroit. "It was either there or Boston," says Colleen. "The Red Wings asked us what we'd expect if we came back, and I gave them a proposal as to what Gordie would consider an ideal role in the organization. The general manager's job wasn't out of the question. The boys would play, of course, although their rights would have to be obtained from the NHL teams that owned them. The thing was we *wanted* to go back there – our hearts were still in Detroit. But just as our negotiations were climaxing after months of talks, Bruce Norris went out and hired Ted Lindsay as general manager without telling us he was even thinking of it. So we knew they had an agenda of their own, and we had no way of knowing what other surprises might be on it. As it turned out, Ted refused to negotiate with me, and refused to trade a draft pick to acquire Mark's rights, which were held by Montreal. That was that. We weren't going back. And I took the fall-out. The Detroit headlines said something like, *Colleen Howe makes decision to keep family out of Detroit.*

When negotiations with the Boston Bruins also fell through, the Howes of Houston became the Howes of Hartford, and Gordie and his sons enjoyed another three years in matching uniforms with the Hartford Whalers of the WHA. At the end of year two, however, the Whalers were absorbed into the NHL, and suddenly the Howes were back in the old neighbourhood.

Today, Gordie and Colleen maintain a 4,000-square-foot home and office on a wooded acreage just east of Hartford in Glastonbury, Connecticut. But in spite of their attachment to the home and to the area, their preferred residence – the place where Colleen says she spends the lion's share of her "inner" time – is on a twenty-mile-long peninsula that rises as straight as a spike into Lake Michigan's Grand Traverse Bay, a few miles north of Traverse City in northwest Michigan. It is a resplendent place, a state-of-the-art kind of place, with an exterior of treated cedar and architecture somewhere between Frank Lloyd Wright and Rubik's cube. The interior is a multi-level showpiece that features a sunken living room, a twenty-foot-high ceiling, and ubiquitous tracts of oak trim. Several generous expanses of plate glass look out onto the West Arm of Grand Traverse Bay – icy and sullen in winter, piercing blue in summer.

"We try to spend about three months a year up here," says Colleen. "A week here, a week there, whenever we can fit time in. As much as we can, we like to do our family entertaining up here. When our son Murray graduated from medical school, we brought our whole family in from everywhere, and a lot of old friends. We had quite a reunion. Another time we had fifty people out here on the lawn for a charity barbecue. Michigan is my roots, of course; it's the kids' roots. Strictly speaking it's not Gordie's roots, but it might as well be after all those years in Detroit."

As often as possible, the younger generations of Howes – three married sons, a married daughter, and seven grandchildren – make their way to Traverse City to spend time with Gordie and Colleen. But even when the scions and sprouts aren't in residence, they inhabit the place through numerous framed family photos: on shelves, on tables, on walls and bedroom bureaus.

When Gordie and Colleen are alone in the place during summer, one of their preferred activities is to take the power boat out to rugged Marion Island on the bay for an evening picnic. "Or we just drift and enjoy the water," Colleen says. "We also like sailing. And Gordie fishes further up the bay."

Colleen likes to get to the place even on her own and has been known to drive hundreds of miles for a weekend's respite. She says, "I love the tranquility. If I feel the need, I just crawl into bed early and sleep. Or I go for walks. Or read."

Even in this remote haven, however, Colleen cannot always resist the temptation to do a little business ("The phone is a wonderful tool!"). In fact, on a mild mid-winter Saturday she has succumbed to more than a little figuring and phoning. Throughout the afternoon she burns up the phone line, and as the day wears on, her pertinent papers and correspondence spread themselves gradually across the kitchen table and bedroom table and onto the bedroom floor. As she works, Gordie and a guest take a walk along the waterfront, picking their way through beached floes of ice, keeping their eyes peeled for "Petoskey stones," smoothed chunks of colony coral exclusive to the pebble beaches of northern Lake Michigan.

When Gordie and the guest return at sundown, Gordie plays solitaire for a while, eventually suggesting to Colleen that they make plans for dinner (they have not eaten since breakfast).

Within twenty minutes, the threesome is in the Howe's eight-seater van, and ten minutes later is casing the streets of Traverse City, trying to decide on a restaurant. Traverse City was built by the lumber barons of the nineteenth and early twentieth centuries, but it is now supported largely by tourism and by the Michigan oil industry. It has 20,000 inhabitants and ninety-three restaurants.

At Shelde's on Munson Avenue, the diners remove their coats and are escorted to a comfortably upholstered booth. Even before the waitress arrives to take their order, a heavy-set man from a neighbouring table approaches and addresses Gordie jovially as "Number Nine," explaining that he was present at Gordie's retirement festivities in 1972 at the Detroit Olympia. The man produces a paper placemat and asks if Gordie would mind signing it: "Make it out to Sam."

A minute later, a younger man approaches: "I was at the all-star game in 1980. Could I get you to sign this?"

When the man is just out of earshot, Gordie whispers, "So many people have told me they were at that all-star game, I figure there must have been half a million people there."

The next man to the table claims to have seen the first game Gordie played with his sons.

"They all have a story," says Gordie. "They saw me score my 500th goal; my 800th; saw me in the '62 playoffs; went to school with one of the kids. A ton of them went to school with *me*," he chuckles. "We must have had an awful big classroom.

"The other day a guy said he saw me play with Eddie Shore. I told him, 'If I'd played with Shore, I'd be a hundred years old!' The guy said, 'No, I saw ya.' All right then, he saw me."

During dinner, three more autograph seekers materialize beside the table, and when the first-course dishes have been cleared away, the manager appears with a complimentary dessert – a tasty (and enormously caloric) mound of apple pudding. The waitress moves in and, as if a major breach of protocol had been committed, explains, "I'm sorry – I didn't know who you were." What she'd have done had she known is not clear, although a minute later she returns with five sheets of paper: "Would you mind signing these for the guys in the kitchen?" She pauses just long enough and says, "To Carl, to Mike, to Terry, to Marty, and to Tony."

When it seems that everyone in the restaurant who cares must surely have an autograph, and Gordie is set to pay the bill, a woman tiptoes up to him with news that her husband would like an autograph and would like to shake Gordie's hand but is too shy to ask. "Where is he?" chirps Gordie, and she points across the room at a small, balding man – a Danny DeVito clone – wearing a sheepish smile. Gordie walks over to him, extends his hand, and says, "Nice to meet you." It is all the man can do to stammer, "I saw you in the all-star game in 1980."

On the way home, the talk turns to the future, to finances, to retirement – "final retirement," as Colleen calls it, to distinguish it from Gordie's two previous retirements from active hockey. Colleen reveals that she and Gordie are somewhat concerned that, at the moment, a major chunk of their income is derived from Gordie's personal appearances and services. An average week's work might well take him to as many as three or four cities, at the request of either the Hartford Whalers or any of the family's several corporate sponsors. "A time will come," says Colleen, "when he just isn't going to *want* to spend all this time travelling, or perhaps when he isn't *able* to." Colleen submits that she, too, will eventually want to cut back on her seven-day work weeks and extensive travel. "Right now I'm doing almost as much travelling as Gordie. By the end of the year we're both exhausted."

According to Colleen, the pair's "five-year plan" is to develop business interests that will gradually take the emphasis off Gordie's personal appearances and her own consuming labours and put it where it belongs – on golfing and snorkeling in Florida, where the two enjoy annual winter vacations; and on sailing, swimming, and fishing at Traverse City. "And, of course, on family," adds Colleen. To accomplish this, she and Gordie hope to develop increased amounts of "passive income" – earnings that can be nurtured without significant outlays of time or effort.

Gordie sums up his hopes for retirement in two words: total security. "I want financial comfort for myself and Colleen, I want to be debt-free, and I want to be able to assist the family if necessary, particularly some of the older members. I don't want a 150-foot yacht; I just want a home, a boat, and some time to enjoy them. Above all, we don't want to have to rely on anybody but ourselves."

But while Gordie is thinking relaxation, Colleen is girding for further productivity. Among other things, she has plans to collaborate on a pair of videos, one about Gordie's boyhood on the Prairies, the other a feature-length account of the life and times of the Howe family. The latter will be accompanied by a family biography that Colleen refers to simply as *Howe* or occasionally *Howe: the Book.*

"In the meantime," she says, "I'm working on affiliations with several corporations and expect that Gordie will be appearing in a national advertising campaign for one of them next year. And of course I want to get the display of Howe memorabilia going. . . . I guess I've got the next few years pretty well cut out for me. And I intend to enjoy them.

"God willing, our most exciting years are still ahead."

10

Bill and Edna Gadsby

• • • • • • • • • • • •

A NATURAL HIGH

It is a quiet February afternoon in the Detroit suburb of Southfield. In San Marina Villa, the attractive little subdivision that nestles in the crook of 12 Mile Road and Inkster Road – a subdivision of large lots and towering hardwoods – you could easily get the impression that *every* afternoon is a quiet afternoon in Southfield.

For the most part the impression is accurate. But on this particular afternoon the tranquility is nudged by an anonymous young woman in a blue wool coat. She steps tentatively off 12 Mile Road onto East Kalong Circle. She appears lost, frustrated. She is crying. She walks a ways and enters the driveway of a comfortable-looking two-storey brick house. She approaches the door and rings the bell.

In the family room at the rear of the house, Bill Gadsby, a seven-time NHL all-star, rises from his chair and steps jauntily to the front vestibule. He is a tall, angular man, with grey hair and a face that bears the scars of some 700 surgical stitches. His personality brings together hearty portions of boyish innocence and gladiatorial pride.

He swings open the door and listens sympathetically as the young woman explains that her car has run out of gas and that she needs a lift to the nearest station.

As she and Bill drive off, her crying intensifies and she reveals that she has no money – an anomaly, to be sure, in comfortable Southfield. But no problem. Within minutes, Bill has bought several gallons of gasoline at the local Total station and has deposited them in the fuel tank of her car.

The woman is about to drive off when it occurs to her to thank her benefactor and to suggest that some day she'll stop by and repay him his money. Some frosty Friday.

Back home Bill describes the incident to his wife Edna and to an afternoon guest. He terminates the description with a shake of the head and a muttered declaration: "Sometimes I don't understand this world." The comment might easily go unnoticed. But in Bill's case it resounds with an unintended echo, resonating back across twenty years of his life – years in which he and Edna have faced and surmounted a daunting array of challenges and setbacks: the sudden unexpected loss of a golf business in Edmonton in 1968, a business the two were counting on to carry them into retirement; Bill's mysterious summary dismissal as coach of the Detroit Red Wings in 1969; the investment and loss of a lifetime of savings in the automotive business in the early 1980s; another lost job in 1988, this time for reasons that Bill understands all too well. "Poison," as he puts it, "that junk I was putting in my body." Alcohol.

That he is firmly on his feet today is brash testimony to Bill Gadsby's resilience. As you get to know Bill, however, you can't help but realize that at least part of his resilience is a *shared* strength, a kind of collaborative energy that flows through and around him as it emanates from his wife Edna. A petite, gracious woman of superior inner strength, Edna transcends life's affronts not with a painkiller or a shrug but with a Godly conviction that truth and tolerance and optimism will carry the day. She has taught Bill and she has learned from Bill. She has learned *with* Bill.

Today, Bill and Edna's life is as peaceful as it has been in perhaps a decade. They occupy their comfortable home in much the way birds occupy a nest – padding, feathering, nestling. Edna's kitchen – and with due respect to feminism, it *is* Edna's kitchen – is a potpourri of folk art and pleasantly countrified decor. Some of the accoutrements come from the Country Junction, a gift shop where she works part-time in the local mall. Outside the window there are well-stocked birdfeeders that attract a parade of jays, chickadees, and songbirds – Bill is quick to identify a visiting finch. The Hall of Fame defenceman keeps a fire in the family-room hearth throughout the winter, not so much for warmth, he admits, as for atmosphere. In summer he rises early to garden, or perhaps to knock a few golf balls across the park-like terrain that adjoins the backyard. Several mounted trophy fish, at one time the pride of the rec room, hang outside on the back wall of the house.

You get the impression that there's no place Bill and Edna would rather be – and preferably in the company of their four married daughters and their families. "We never turn down a babysitting job on the weekend," enthuses Edna. "That's *my* Hall of Fame," says Bill, referring to a collection of framed photos of his nine grandchildren. He ponders four photos of himself arm in arm with his daughters on their respective wedding days and says quietly that walking them down the aisle was a greater thrill than anything he accomplished in twenty years in the NHL.

These days, the nerve centre of the house is Bill's office by the front door. The place is chock-a-block with the sort of amiable clutter that you might expect to accrue from forty years in and around big-league hockey: photos, plaques, citations. On this particular day the clutter is increased by hundreds of stamped, addressed envelopes containing applications and promotional literature for Bill's recently expanded summer hockey school. On the desk are two mounted bricks from the demolished Detroit Olympia, and on the wall by the window is a stark, almost otherworldly oil painting of Bill in his early days as a Chicago Black Hawk. "An art student came up to me one day in the late forties in Chicago," he says. "He asked if I'd mind if he painted my picture. I told him it'd be an honour. I'd like to know what happened to the guy, how he made out." On another wall hangs a framed cover photo from *Sports Illustrated* magazine showing Bill as a Detroit Red Wing digging his stick ferociously into the back of Stan Mikita's neck.

"Bill is an extremely gentle man – a tender man," says Edna. She reflects for a moment and adds, "completely the opposite of what he was on the ice."

Bill *is* a tender man – a churchgoing grandfather with a protective instinct that goes well beyond the feeding of small birds. Nowhere is his tenderness more evident than in the several hundred love letters he sent his wife and daughters during his years on the road playing hockey. From the recesses of the house, Edna brings forth an aging tin biscuit box painted in tiny coloured flowers. She dusts it off and lifts the lid on a lifetime of memories. She has every letter Bill ever wrote to her, the earliest dating back to her teenage years in Edmonton, when her young knight was an eighteen-year-old rookie with the Chicago Black Hawks.

"Darling," Bill wrote in November, 1947, five years before he and Edna were married. "Sorry I didn't phone you tonight, but I couldn't get through. I sure wanted to talk to you, Honey. Every day I love you more. I miss you so much. . . . It's been snowing here all day. You should be here to keep me warm. It would be nice, wouldn't it, Darling? I think about you constantly and look at your picture all day long."

Two years later, as a twenty-one-year-old, he wrote, "It isn't three minutes since I hung up the phone, Honey. I couldn't hear you very well. I guess because you're so far away. It was wonderful to hear your voice, although you sounded as if you had something on your mind. Is there anything, Honey? It reminded me of the night down at the golf course. Nothing on your mind, is there? . . . I'll probably think and dream about you all night. Can't think of anything better. Especially those dreams. Maybe they'll come true one day. I love you! I love you! I love you!"

Twenty years later, the missives were still coming. "... My love to all the children and to you, Darling. I love you and miss you more each year."

By no means are the letters exclusively sweetness and charm. More than a few reveal Bill's thirst for the sort of hockey that makes activists cry Foul!, mothers wring their hands. In February, 1948, he wrote, "We leave for New York today and for Toronto next Saturday. I figure it'll be a rough one against the Leafs – especially for me. In the game against them here I cut Teeder Kennedy for ten stitches across the eye with my stick. I nearly broke Howie Meeker's arm. There'll be some fun for sure. I'm looking forward to it."

"You had to be able to give it, and you had to be able to take it," says Bill today. "I remember one night in Toronto I hit Tim Horton – broke his leg and jaw. I was scared; the blood started coming out of his mouth and ear. The Toronto fans thought I elbowed him, but I didn't; I got him with my shoulder, and his leg twisted on the ice. It was the hardest bodycheck I ever threw. . . . The hardest one I ever *took* was from Bill Barilko. I didn't see him coming. It knocked us both out. I crawled to the bench. When they cut my sweater and underwear off, my shoulder bone was sticking out through the skin. . . . We used to get cut up and go right back out and play. I played once with a thirty-five-stitch cut in my chin – got stitched up and out I went. I was on tea and toast for two weeks. Lost fourteen pounds. Kept right on playing."

"The worst injury I ever saw Bill get was during the first game I went to at Madison Square Garden in '56," says Edna. "He got hit in the face with a stick. The point went up his nose and ripped most of his nose back from the bottom up. He was just *covered* with blood."

"The doctor put me on the rubbing table to stitch me up," recalls Bill. "He said, 'Son, this is really going to hurt.' And it did. I'll bet my fingerprints are still in that table. Yet it wasn't twenty minutes before I was back on the ice. Going home on the subway that night I was just a mess, all swollen up and bleeding – Rudolph the Red-Nosed Ranger. Sometimes I think they should have frozen us up before they stitched. I'm not always sure we got the medical care we deserved. You were always expected to be so tough.

"Overall, I broke my leg twice; had a very serious shoulder separation; had a slight separation on the other side; broke my nose maybe eleven times; had a few concussions; broke my fingers quite a few times. You really never get over these things. Today I have arthritis in my hands, sometimes in my hip. I have a hernia problem, although that's not necessarily from hockey. . . . I guess my worst difficulty over the years has been a bad back that I picked up in the late fifties in New York. Sometimes it just snaps; the muscles go into a spasm, and I can't move. One night a few years ago I sneezed in the bathroom, and it went on me, and I fell on the floor, paralysed. I've been in and out of traction in various hospitals fifteen times I guess. Ten or twelve days at a stretch."

From the time he was a boy in Calgary's North Hill, Bill was a rough and ready customer at the rink. "My dad worked for the CPR and was the manager of an industrial league team – all outdoor hockey. Even when I was six, eight, ten years old I'd go to practice with the men. Sometimes I'd get bumped around pretty good. We didn't have the money to buy skates every year, so I'd often have skates about three sizes too big with newspaper jammed in the toes. My dad would bring home cracked and broken sticks from the industrial league games, and we'd fix 'em up with scrap tin plating from the hardware store down the street."

In 1944, at the age of sixteen, Bill travelled north to play Junior hockey for the Edmonton Oil Kings. Within weeks, he was introduced to young Edna Anfindsen, a student at McTavish Business College. "We went out occasionally," says Edna, "and because I lived close to the rink, Bill would drop in as he walked home from his games. My mother would allow me to make him something to eat."

"It was good eating, too," smiles Bill. "Edna's dad was quite a hunter, and her mother'd put up jars of pheasant breasts and ducks and geese – real delicacies. I've told a lot of reporters that Edna won my heart with pheasant under glass – it was in glass jars."

As Bill and Edna recall their years together, their voices take on vigour, exuding a theatrical, almost script-like appeal.

Edna: When Bill was scouted and signed by Chicago it was exciting for *him*, but for me it was a disappointment – I felt I'd never see him again. Chicago was a big city, and so far away.

Bill: I remember hitting Michigan Avenue the first week I was there. I went down with Bert Olmstead and Metro Prestai. We were all from the Prairies. I'd never seen skyscrapers except in pictures – none of us had. And seeing Lake Michigan so close to the city just boggled the mind. It looked like an ocean. . . . In those days most of the single guys lived at the Midwest Athletic Club, a hotel at Hamlin and Madison. All the jockeys from Aqueduct and a lot of prize fighters stayed there – Marciano, Kid Gavilan, Jake LaMotta. And gangsters! There was a guy called Suitcase Smith who'd been a bodyguard for Al Capone, then for his brother Matty Capone. Suitcase used to carry a machine gun in his golf bag when he went golfing with these guys. The funny thing was that seven or eight police lieutenants lived at the hotel, too. And the whole second floor of the place was illegal gambling! I was pretty naive about it all, but I couldn't help getting to know some of the hoods – I lived in the place for six seasons. But none of them ever bothered us for inside gambling information, who was hurting, that sort of thing.

Edna: Bill dated lots of girls while he was away, and I dated other fellas, but I always knew that Bill was the man for me. And yet, while we were carrying on this long courtship – it was eight years from the time we met till the time we married – all my girlfriends were getting married, and I was starting to wonder if it would ever work out. Then in January of 1952, Bill called me from Chicago, told me he'd made a very big decision – he wanted to settle down, get married. He had a ring – would I come to Chicago to get it? Now you have to remember that in 1952 a nice girl didn't go to Chicago to meet her boyfriend. But my darling mother came to me – I still lived at home – and she said I had her and my dad's approval; it was all right if I went. So I took the train to Chicago. Bill and Doug Bentley were there to meet me when I pulled in. I stayed with Gus and Etta Bodnar, Bill's teammate and his wife. A week or so later I returned to Edmonton, and we were married that June. We were both twenty-five.

Bill: We had an awful polio epidemic in Alberta that summer. At the time, I was part-owner of a golf driving range in Edmonton, and a number of the young guys who worked for me came down with it. Some of them were paralysed for life. . . . The night before I left to go to North Bay for training camp, a bunch of my buddies had a party for me, and I didn't feel too good when I got up the next morning. I thought maybe I'd had a bit too much to drink. But the headache and stiffness didn't go away all the next day. On the plane to Toronto, my head just pounded all the way. I thought maybe I had the flu – oh, I was miserable. When I got to Toronto I ran into Bill Tobin, the owner and president of the Black Hawks, and Johnny Gotselig, who was coaching at the time. Bill said to me, "You don't look too good." Anyway, we flew on to Ottawa. Mr. Tobin had a limousine there, and we took it to North Bay – I had to stop three or four times to throw up.

A doctor in North Bay took fluid out of my spine and broke the news to me – I might have polio. Even the *word* polio terrified me. At that point, they whipped me to Ottawa by ambulance, where they confirmed that I had the disease. I was just devastated. Immediately they put me in the hospital in the isolation ward. There were guys in there in iron lungs – it really shook me up. I remember thinking about Edna – she'd told me before I left that she was pregnant, and I was worried about the baby.

After a week the doctor explained to me that the germ count in my blood was forty-eight. Paralysis came at fifty-two. I was determined that I was going to fight this thing with everything I had. I'd have my legs and arms going all day, exercising, moving, doing anything I could to stay active. I got a lot of medication, a lot of needles, and after ten or eleven days, they came to me and said, "You're fine; you're well enough to go to training camp." Oh, I was happy! Just overwhelmed with relief.

Edna: That first year in Chicago together was great, and by the time we returned for the next season, 1953, Brenda was about six months old. Bill had an apartment all set for us, but it wasn't ready when we arrived, so for a week or so we all went to Bill's old stomping ground, the Midwest Athletic Club.

Bill: One night we wanted to go out for dinner, and I asked Vic Lynn, one of the players who had three kids of his own, to babysit. We took the baby carriage and baby up to his room.

When we got back to the hotel, our baby carriage was sitting by the elevators in the lobby, with nobody around. We looked around, didn't see anybody, and I said to myself, I wonder if that rascal's in the bar.

Edna: We walked down there, and, sure enough, there's Vic, and there's Brenda sitting in the lap of this very handsome man who I'd never seen before. The one strange thing about him was that, as he was talking to us, he kept his hand over his glass. As we came out I asked why he did this and who this guy was. Bill told me he did it so that nobody could slip anything into his drink! I thought, Who *are* these people? I was surprised, to say the least, when Bill told me he was Matty Capone, Al Capone's brother, a notorious gangster. He lived right there in the hotel!

Bill: After nine pretty good seasons in Chicago, I was traded to the New York Rangers with Peter Conacher, for Nick Mikoski and Alan Stanley. When I got the news I was shocked. I phoned Frank Boucher, the general manager in New York, and I said I wasn't coming, and he said, "No, you get over here. We'll help you get a place to live."

Edna: My biggest concern at the time was how long Bill and I were going to be separated. When the trade occurred we'd already *been* separated for six weeks – me in Edmonton with Brenda, Bill at training camp. I'd just gotten to Chicago and gotten comfortable in our little brownstone, and now we had to uproot again. And by this time, I was pregnant with our second child. But off we went!

Bill: I must say, I never really liked the living conditions in New York. We were there seven years, and every year we'd have to get a new apartment – see, all through my career, we always returned to Edmonton for the summers, then back to hockey in the fall.

Edna: That was the hardest thing about being a hockey wife. The girls would start school in Edmonton in September when Bill went to training camp. Then six weeks later we'd leave our beautiful home in Edmonton, fly to New York on a weekend, and move into an apartment that was *just* livable. The girls would be in a new school on Monday, without missing a day. Same thing returning to Edmonton in the spring. I did a lot of packing and unpacking. On occasion we discussed me staying in Edmonton with the girls for the winter, but we always felt it was more important to stay together as a family. . . . I'm not saying I didn't *like* New York. I *loved* the theatre, for instance. We saw all the big musicals – *South Pacific, My Fair Lady, The King and I* . . . and I always enjoyed Bill's games. I went to every one of them.

Those were our productive years; we went to New York with one child, left with four – all born in Edmonton during the summers. It was a very exciting time for us – a big stimulating city, a lot of nice people.

Bill: And the money seemed awfully good back then. I was making about twice as much as my buddies back home. And I always had a new car – they didn't even *own* cars.

Edna: Bill made $11,000 the year we were married, and we saved $7,000 of it, because we wanted to buy a home. One of our dreams was to own a small home of our own, a place to go back to. We paid $12,500 for our first home in Edmonton.

Bill: In 1961, after six years in New York, I was traded to the Detroit Red Wings. The clubs I'd played for in Chicago and

New York had never really done all that well, so I was awfully happy to be with a better club. And I was happy to be back in a real hockey city. In New York you can walk down Fifth Avenue and nobody knows or cares who you are. In places like Chicago and Detroit, people have a feeling for their team. You've got some fans behind you.

Edna: It was during those years in Detroit that we started thinking about Bill's retirement. Our goal was to to have our home paid for, with a little money in the bank, and to have the golf business going strong in Edmonton. We'd had every-thing pretty carefully worked out, and it looked as if we were going to be happy when Bill finally quit in 1966. Unfor-tunately our plans blew up just like that. Bill's partner in the driving range died unexpectedly at forty-eight, and the driv-ing range had to be sold for estate purposes. Suddenly there we were, without any source of income – at least nothing of substance. . . . A short time later Bill was asked to coach the Junior Oil Kings, and he did that, but we felt very insecure about it – coaches come and go all the time. We weren't too badly off, mind you; we had some money in the bank, we owned a nice cottage near Edmonton and had two cars in the garage that were paid for. We still owed $6,000 on our house, but that wasn't a great deal.

Bill: That winter, the Red Wings weren't doing very well, and they started calling to see if I'd come out of retirement. Sid Abel called, and when I turned him down, Bruce Norris, the owner, called – first thing he said was, "Is this mon-eybags?" I said, "Whaddaya mean?" He said, "You won't come back for half a season for the kind of money we're offering you?" They were offering fifty thousand. I said, "Bruce, I'm not in shape – it'll take me a month to *get* in shape, and I'm not in a mood to play; I don't think I can help your hockey club." It made me mad. The previous year I'd had to fight like the dickens to get a small raise to maybe thirty thousand, and now they were offering me the moon to play half a season. But it was no go, I was tired of playing hockey.

Edna: I always felt they held it against Bill. They expected him to bite. . . . As it turned out, things didn't go well with the Oil Kings – Bill and the owner, Bill Hunter, didn't see eye to eye. Then, out of the blue, the Red Wings offered Bill the coaching job in Detroit. At that time we still felt good about the Red Wing organization. They'd been good to us while Bill was playing, and he was flattered to be offered the job. The problem was, I didn't want to pack up and move again. We'd just gotten settled for the first time after all those years of roaming around. The older girls didn't want to move either. And yet I knew that the job was an opportunity that Bill really couldn't afford to pass up. He just wouldn't have been happy if he'd turned it down. I thought about staying in Edmonton with the children while Bill was in Detroit – I'd fly down maybe once a month, and we'd all go down at Christmas. But Bill didn't feel that that was a very good life for him, and I agreed.

In the end we realized we were better off together, and away we went. It was the hardest move we ever made, because it closed the door on all the plans we'd made to settle in Edmonton. Naturally, we had no idea that coaching in Detroit would be so precarious. The Red Wings' coaches had always been with the team for a good long time. Sid Abel had been here for years. We were awfully naive – Bill didn't even have a contract, just a handshake.

Bill: They paid me twenty-five thousand that year. And I'll tell you, for what the job turned out to be, it wasn't much. A lot of the things that happened to me that year were down-right demeaning. One night in Pittsburgh Bruce Norris came down to the dressing room after the first period – he used to show up at road games once in a while – and he said, "I don't know what you're playing [Dean] Prentice for; he's not doing anything!" And I just couldn't believe it, because Dino was playing well – he'd had six goals in the past eight games. Bruce said, "I don't want to see him on the ice again tonight." When he left, I said to Sid Abel, our general manager, who'd been standing beside me, "What's going on?" And Sid said,

"I dunno, but you'd better do what he says." I was hurt, because I knew my hockey players, and Bruce was suggesting I didn't. Anyway, I didn't play Dino for most of the second period, and he kept looking down the bench at me, as if to say, What's the matter? I didn't feel good at all about it. But when we got a penalty near the end of the period, I put Dino and Bruce MacGregor out to kill it. They were two of the top penalty killers in the league. We killed the penalty, the period ended, and Bruce showed up again at the dressing room. He said, "Didn't you get my message? I don't want to see Prentice on the ice." So again I turn to Sid and say, "What's up? Have we got a trade going for Prentice or something? Are we supposed to keep him from getting hurt?" Sid said, "No, he just doesn't want him on the ice." My feeling was, If I can't play him, we might as well trade him. It really bothered me. I thought, Am I going to let myself get pushed around this way?

Afterwards on the bus, Dino came up to where I was sitting and said, "What's going on, Bill? How come you benched me?" I didn't know what to tell him. As far as he was concerned, I'd made the decision – I was the coach, it was my responsibility. So I said, "I didn't think you were hustling, I just didn't like the way you were playing tonight." He looked at me, and he said, "Bill, I don't know what I have to do for you." And he walked away. I felt terrible for a long time, lying to him. It was degrading to have to do it, yet if I told the truth it would have gotten around that I wasn't in charge of the team, and in a sense that would have been even more degrading.

When we were at the Olympia, Norris used to sit up in his private box with his cronies, and they'd get into the sauce. These guys would say to Bruce, "Why don't you do this or that with your players?" He'd be all juiced up, and he'd say, "Yeah, I'll show them who the boss is," and he'd phone down to the bench – he'd installed a phone down there. He'd say, "What's the matter with Bergman?" or "How come Bathgate's not shooting more?" This and that. There was a red light on the phone, and sometimes I wouldn't see it come on. But Lefty Wilson, the trainer, would see it and he'd say, "Bill, the phone's on." I got so sick and tired of that phone I yanked it right out of the wall one night. Norris saw me do it – he was right up in the corner of the rink looking down – but it was never mentioned. I couldn't be yakking with him during a game; I had other things to think about.

Edna: Bill was unhappy, and our two older girls were unhappy. In Edmonton they'd been able to play tennis, and walk to school and Sunday school. And now they had to take a bus to a big school where they didn't know anybody. They didn't adjust well at all.

For myself, being a coach's wife was entirely different than being a player's wife. It was expected that we wouldn't be friends with the players. It was so silly. Once I took Colleen Howe and Marie Mahovlich into the Red Wing alumni room, and apparently some people got upset – what was I doing fraternizing with *them* – were they special or something? They were good friends of mine from when Bill had played here!

Bill: We went home to Edmonton after that first year coaching, and I flew to Chicago to meet Bruce Norris, to find out if I was going to be back with the Red Wings the next year. Bruce said yes, certainly. We'd bought our house in Detroit by that time and were having someone take care of it for the summer.

Edna: The next September, things went much better. Bill had a successful training camp, and the girls were a little more settled. We were beginning to feel pretty good.

Bill: We beat Toronto in the opening game of the season, then we went to Chicago and played a great game, which we won 4–2. Afterwards, Bruce Norris came up to me, put his arm around me, and said, "Good work, Bill, you've really got these guys going." I was two feet off the floor.

The next day he called and said he wanted to see me in his office before our game with Minnesota that night. This wasn't unusual – we often chatted about the team. I walked into his office, and right off the bat he said, "Bill, I'm relieving you of your responsibilities as coach of the club." I thought he was kidding. I said, "Did I hear you right?" And he repeated what he'd told me. He said, "I just think we should make a change."

I was so stunned I just sat there looking at him. Finally, as it sunk in, I said, "Why are you doing this, Bruce? Why are you firing me?" Again he said, "I just think it's time for a change. I run a lot of corporations, I've had a lot of experience in this area, and I think I know when things need changing." I said, "Bruce, you have to give me a better reason than that!" But he just kept mumbling away – he'd had a couple of drinks, had a martini right in front of him. So I said, "Bruce, if you're not going to tell my why I'm fired, I'm going to go down and find out from Sid." So I walked out of his office, and who do I meet coming into the building but Edna.

Edna: His face was just ashen. I said, "Bill, what's the matter?" He told me, and I just crumbled. I said, "Let's go home."

Bill: But by now I was hot; I wanted some answers. I went down to the dressing room, and Sid was sitting in my little coach's office with Baz Bastien, his assistant. I said, "What's going on, Sid?" And he just threw up his arms and said, "I dunno – Bruce phoned me today, said he wanted to make a change." Now I was *really* mad. I said, "Doesn't anybody know what's going on? Shall I go and ask Lefty, the trainer?"

By this time the players were coming in from their warm-ups – I didn't know what to do, where to go. I was so angry and upset, I was just in a daze.

That night, Edna and I sat here at the kitchen table with Gordie and Colleen Howe and John and Jackie Curran – John was a friend who owned a crane company. He said to me, "What are you going to do, Bill?" And I said, "I don't know." He said, "Why don't you come and work for me?" And I told him I'd have to clear the air on this other business before I made any moves.

Edna: The next day we had media all over us – right here at the house! Reporters, television vans – it was unbelievable. Bill had always had good press and good rapport with the fans. In fact, for the first time in the history of the franchise, the fans picketed outside the Olympia to protest the firing of a coach. In the meantime, the reality of our situation was beginning to sink in. Here we were with no job, a mortgage, and no house or equity back home in Edmonton.

Bill: What hurt me most of all was that I was never given a reason for being fired. That was unfair. . . . I met Bruce Norris by chance in Key Largo in Florida maybe a year later. We were in a restaurant, and he walked in with his big entourage. Oh, was he surprised to see me! I'd had a few drinks, and I decided to go over to see him. Edna tried to hold me back, but I wanted to go – I still had the whole business in my craw. I walked up to him and said, "Bruce, can I see you for a minute?" He said, "Gee, Bill, I've got these people here; we're going to have dinner." I said, "It'll only take a minute – I want to see you down the hall here." He thought I was going to paste him. But he came with me, and I said, "Okay, Bruce, now, man to man, why did you fire me? I want to know – nobody's ever told me." He said, "Come and have lunch on my boat tomorrow and we'll talk about it." I said, "I want to know now." But he still wouldn't tell me. So I turned and walked away. That's the last I ever saw of him.

Edna: Bill's bitterness over this has surfaced from time to time in the years since. And that's not good. You've got to be able to forget and get on with your life. But, then again, over the years people have come up to Bill and reminded him of it, said things like, "I know who wanted you fired." . . . I myself sensed the truth about the matter before Bill did. I felt that Sid Abel was behind it, that he felt Bill wanted to move in and take his job as general manager. I liked Sid, I still like him, but that's what I felt; it was intuition. For one thing, Sid was very surprised when he heard we'd bought a house here. It was as if he didn't want Bill around in any permanent way. He *never did* give any real support to Bill. It was pretty obvious, but Bill didn't see it. Now, however, he's heard it from so many other people, I think he's convinced.

Bill: Two weeks later I got a letter from Bruce Norris saying that my salary would continue to the end of the year. But underneath his signature in pencil – in *pencil*, mind you – was a note that said, "If you make any derogatory remarks about the Detroit Red Wing hockey organization, your pay will cease as of that date." Apparently his lawyer had told him to put that in. Since I didn't have a written contract, I was at their mercy – fired and muzzled. And this from an organization to which I'd given my utmost for a good many years. Then they said that if I was going to draw my pay, I'd have to do something for it, so I did some scouting. Sid kept saying to me that we'd have to have lunch, talk about the firing. I said, "Just give me a call." He never called.

Edna: Many years later when Sid and his wife Gloria were leaving for Florida, she called to say good-bye. And she said she'd heard it rumoured that Sid was behind Bill's firing, but that it wasn't true. I said, "Gloria, it's all water under the bridge." I have no bitterness. And I think Bill has pretty well come to terms with it, too. It wasn't the end of the world.

We thought things over; we wondered if we should go back to Edmonton. But then Bill decided to take the job with John Curran's crane company, doing p.r. work. We felt it would help our stability not to have to move again.

Bill: I ended up working for John for twelve years. And I enjoyed it very much at first – I'd play golf with clients, take them to lunch, whatever. There were some terrific perks – for example, John would always allow us to use his big home in Florida. All our daughters honeymooned there, and we'd often go down for vacations. I had a good paycheque. I was making more than I'd ever made in hockey.

But then after a while, the work began to get repetitious. A lot of different people, but always the same situations. Eventually I found I just couldn't keep my interest up.

Edna: In 1979 I noticed a big change in Bill's drinking habits. He'd always liked a drink, but now he was having two or three drinks before we even left the house to go out. And he'd drink too much *while* we were out. He never really seemed drunk; he'd just get very morose, very unhappy. The country was in economic recession at that time, so the construction business was down, and he'd come home from work and say, "There isn't that much for me to do." Then he started saying he thought he'd like to get out on his own, have his own business. He and John weren't getting along very well at this point. Bill wasn't supposed to be drinking with the clients, but he was. And John knew this and brought it to Bill's attention. . . . Bill wasn't an alcoholic back then, but I was seeing enough signs of a problem that I went to a few Alanon meetings, for families of alcoholics. I told Bill about it, told him I thought he was drinking too much. He's always been such a gentle person, a wonderful family man. He'd never been a bar hopper, but now, for instance, after Red Wing alumni meetings, he'd go out drinking. This was so unlike him. . . . Things continued to disintegrate on the job, until finally, in 1982, Bill and John Curran parted ways.

Bill: Right away Edna and I started looking into buying a business. We considered a few things, but the first one that seemed suitable was a distributorship for metric nuts and bolts and other car parts and tools. It was a family-owned business, but the owner had cancer and was dying, and he wanted to sell. I looked at the books, had some business friends take a look, and we all thought the outfit was pretty stable. And it seemed to have lots of potential. We assumed that metrics were really going to catch on in the States. I figured with my connections I could build the business up. So Edna and I took the leap and invested all our savings. And we borrowed on top of that, which I'll admit was pretty scary for us. We were the types who'd never even used credit cards – well, we *had* credit cards, but we'd never let them run up. Our policy had always been that you saved your money, *then* bought what you wanted. We'd always been savers; we felt we had to be because the NHL pension fund was so crummy.

Edna: The original owner died about a year after we bought, but his wife stayed on with us to help out. But then she left, and there we were, two greenhorns, who knew virtually nothing about this field.

Bill: I was learning fast, but there were always problems. For instance, we only had two people working in the office, and they often wouldn't show up, so I'd have to handle the office myself, when I should have been out on the road selling.

Edna: Besides that, Bill wasn't in it very long before he realized that it wasn't really something he *liked*. There was a lot of pressure to sell, a lot of bidding for contracts, a lot of cutthroat. We should have gotten out six months after we got in, because all we were doing was throwing money away. But we kept thinking, Maybe if we get this bid, this contract, we can stay in.

Bill: What I *should* have been doing all along was something I understood. I should have been developing the little hockey school I'd begun to operate for a few weeks during the summers.

Edna: In the end we couldn't even sell the business. We felt lucky to find somebody to take it over, take on the bills and liabilities and back taxes. We lost pretty close to a hundred thousand dollars.

Bill: Things were pretty grim around here for a few months. Then in December of 1985, I went back to work for John Curran. The construction business was moving again, and he offered me my old job back.

Edna: It was the best Christmas gift we could have had. We had some income again; we could start paying back our debts, our lawyer's and accountant's fees, and so on. We skimped on everything else. . . . The first year went great. Bill was happy to be back. We went down south to his boss's home in Florida and everything. There was a lot of socializing down there, and Bill handled it very well.

But in the second year, he began having the same old problems with repetitiveness – calling on this person, calling on that person. More and more he'd come home before the work day was over, seemingly uninterested in what he was doing. He was lethargic and depressed, very argumentative, and I suspected he was drinking on the side again.

By this time I'd begun a little job at a craft shop in the mall near here. I'd needed a change, so I'd gone and gotten work two days a week. Anyway, I'd come home and I'd find Bill home, sound asleep in the chair at five in the afternoon. He wasn't interested in the old-timer games or the Red Wing Alumni anymore. When we went to any of our daughters' for dinner, he'd just want to eat and go right home again. This was highly unusual because we're such a close family, and Bill has always loved his children and grandchildren so much. He'd get very impatient with his grandchildren.

The truth was he'd become a closet drinker. He'd drink wine at dinner, that was fine, but then he'd have three or four drinks somewhere else – at one point he was keeping a bottle of vodka in the garage! I found it one day, and I said, "Bill, I can't *believe* it. If you want to drink, drink, but don't do it behind our backs." And he said, "No, no, no, I haven't been drinking out of that; I don't even know how long it's been out there." Then the girls started noticing that their dad had changed. They said, "He's sick, Mom – what's the matter? Why won't he go for a physical? He's not well." He certainly wasn't the man that you see here today. He was bitter about things – didn't like this, didn't like that. And socially, well, we'd go somewhere and I wouldn't see him for two or three hours – he didn't want me to see him drinking so much.

Bill: The thing that bothered me the most was that I couldn't quit. I'd get up in the morning, and I had to have a drink. I'd get home from work, had to have a couple of belts of vodka. I loved taking customers to lunch because I could have a couple of drinks without it seeming out of place. I felt so lousy without it, I was drinking just to feel normal.

Edna: One day in March of '88, I came home from my job, and Bill's company car wasn't here, so I came in expecting an empty house. But he was sitting here – I was so shocked to see him. The first thing I thought was that his car had been stolen. He was very depressed, and he said to me, "You'd better sit down, Edna." I sat down, and he said, "I've been fired." And I said, *"Oh, Bill."* And he told me the truth, that he'd been drinking on the job again.

Bill: I'd drink at noon with customers, I'd drink in the car, I'd drink anywhere. . . . All alcoholics are the same – they're sneaky and they're liars. I'd come home, and Edna'd ask if I'd been drinking. I'd say, "Oh, I had one glass of wine." Here, I'd had three or four martinis. I'd even stopped going to church with Edna – I couldn't be that long without a drink.

Edna: This was the low point of our lives. I said, "Bill, you have to do something – this can't go on." I'd always covered for him, which is the wrong thing. When the girls had asked if he was drinking I'd always say, "Oh, no." I'd tell Bill I was *going* to tell them – I'd threaten him with that. But he'd always say, "No, Edna, they've got families of their own – we mustn't burden them with it. I can handle it."

Needless to say, we had very little income after Bill lost his job. He was just sitting home all day, and he realized he had to go out and bring in some money, which made him even more depressed. He wasn't *well* enough to go to work. It broke my heart.

I talked it over with my daughters, who truly love Bill, and we figured we had to get him into treatment. My youngest, who's a nurse, said to me, "Do you think if I went with him, he'd have a physical?" What we wanted to do – it sounds very sneaky – was to find Bill's blood alcohol level high.

Eventually, we did persuade him to go for a physical. The doctor took a look at him and said his cholesterol level was a little high, but he didn't see any of the symptoms of alcoholism. So we decided that what AA calls "intervention" was necessary.

Bill: On Sunday, October 15, 1988, I reached a turning point in my life. Edna and I had finished dinner, and our four daughters and their husbands walked in the back door. I was sitting here at the table, and I said to Edna, "What are they doing here?" We're a close family – when our daughters are coming over I know about it. Edna said, "They want to have a little talk with you, Bill." So they sat down, and our daughter Brenda came right out and said, "Dad, we think you've got a drinking problem, and we want you to go and get some help." My attitude was, Who are you trying to kid? I've got no problem. I may be overdrinking a little, but I can work it out myself.

Edna: One of them said to him, "Dad, if you don't have a problem would you be willing to go to the hospital right now, to the emergency ward, and have your blood alcohol level taken?" Bill sat here and looked around at his family. It was as if the whole situation had finally been placed in the balance. He said, "Okay, I'll go."

The doctor took the blood alcohol reading, found it high, and asked Bill when he'd had his last drink. Bill told him, and he said, "Mr. Gadsby, you're suffering from alcoholism."

We wanted to put him into treatment that night. I'd gone out and had bought special insurance coverage for exactly that purpose, and I thought it was for that hospital. But as it turned out we weren't covered there, so we had to turn around and go home. . . . It was a very long night, but Bill made it through without a drink.

Bill: The next day we drove thirty miles down to Riverview Centre on the Detroit River. I was there three weeks. It was great. They teach you what alcohol addiction is all about. It's a disease, you know, it takes an awful toll on you, both physically and mentally. And of course it's awfully hard on everybody around you. You can even affect complete strangers. I think about some of the nights I've come home drunk in the car and I shake my head. Edna used to say I had an angel on my shoulder. If you go back to booze after you've been in Riverview, you've got to be a fool.

Edna: We were very involved as a family at that point. We attended lectures at the centre, visited Bill, gained a whole new understanding of his condition. When Bill was at his worst I used to say to him, "Why can't you quit? You have so many good things going for you; we have a strong healthy marriage; we love each other deeply; we have four daughters who think the world begins and ends with their dad; we have nine wonderful grandchildren. *Why can't you stop drinking? Why are you doing this to us?"* ... Only when you understand the disease do you realize that an alcoholic can't stop drinking without help, without treatment.

Bill: Right now I go to AA meetings two or three nights a week – sit around and gab, tell the guys stories. The attitude is, I'm sober today, I'll take care of tomorrow when it comes. I get up in the mornings and I feel good. I stay up at night and watch the news. I used to go to bed at eight, dead tired from drinking.

My buddies here in Detroit, my hockey buddies, are just so happy for me. I came right out at a Red Wing Alumni meeting and announced that I wasn't drinking anymore.

Edna: Everybody's been supportive. Our minister, Mike Dunkleberger, wrote Bill several letters while he was in the treatment centre, phoned him, urged him not to get discouraged. *He* knew something had been wrong. Bill took him to lunch one day half in the bag. As I said to Colleen Howe a while back, I hope the news that Bill has taken treatment gets around as quickly as the news that he was drinking.

Bill: Right now, I'm working hard on expanding my hockey schools. This is my sixth year in operation, but all along I've just done one week a year, adults only. I've always had a feeling I could do well with an expanded program, for both kids *and* adults, but I could never commit enough time to it while I was working for someone else. When the adult school did well a couple of years ago, I really got the bug. I've advertised by going to various amateur hockey associations in the Detroit area, getting all the kids' names and addresses, and sending out applications and promotional material. At the moment I'm getting five, six calls a day from people wanting to participate. A woman just called from Grosse Point wanting four applications! There haven't been too many hockey schools in this area; and it looks like it's going to go well. I'm really excited about it. You might say I'm on a high – a natural high. . . . I'll tell you something – my ups and downs have strengthened my faith both in myself and in God. With the Lord on one side and AA on the other, I think I'm going to be all right.

Gordie Howe Right Wing

DETROIT RED WINGS

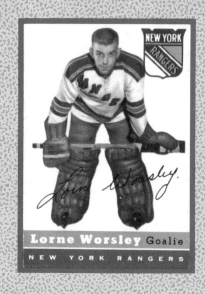

Lorne Worsley Goalie

NEW YORK RANGERS

5 Maurice Richard RIGHT WING

BLACK HAWKS

BILL HAY forward